AF661606

HISTORY OF CLASSICAL LITERATURE

HISTORY OF CLASSICAL LITERATURE

P. K. Sinha
Jagdish K. Ghosh

Commonwealth

History of Classical Literature

© Reserved

ISBN : 978-81-311-0322-7

Edition : 2021

Published by :
COMMONWEALTH PUBLISHERS (P) LTD.
4831/24, Prahlad Street,
Ansari Road, Darya Ganj,
New Delhi - 110002
Ph. : 23272541, 23242541
e-mail : commonwealthpublishers2016@gmail.com

Laser Typesetting by :
Dimple Computers
Delhi

Printed at :
Divine Digital Press
Delhi

Preface

The present book—*History of Classical Literature*—offers the general reader help of every kind in the understanding of classical literature. More than a book of authors and titles, this work illumines the faded images of mythological and historical figures, as well as providing information on general topics such as genre, theatre, politics, religion, the transmission of texts through the Renaissance, and such intimate mysteries as meter.

The main focus of this book remains the lives and works of the principal authors. Biographical entries offer the essential facts and sift the conjectural evidence, while entries on the major works include discussions of the philosophical dialogues and political speeches and plot summaries of the epic poems and plays. The various literary forms—epic, comedy, tragedy, rhetorical writing—are covered in depth.

This book is intended for advanced level students of literature, who are taking exams or modules in this field. It may also be suitable for teachers, researchers and the general reader who is interested in the history of literature. The breadth and accuracy of this volume will surely make it the standard reference book of its kind for years to come.

Authors

Contents

Preface *v*

1. Classical Greek Literature 1
2. Classical Latin Literature 44
3. Classical Sanskrit Literature 65
4. Classical Fables of Aesop 108
5. Classical Works of William Shakespeare 125
6. Classical Works of Mary Shelley 197
7. Milton's Paradise Lost 227
8. Classical Works of Leo Tolstoy 257

Bibliography 297

Index 299

1

Classical Greek Literature

In the classical period many of the genres of western literature became more prominent. Lyrical poetry, odes, pastorals, elegies, epigrams; dramatic presentations of comedy and tragedy; histories, rhetorical treatises, philosophical dialectics, and philosophical treatises all arose in this period. As the genres evolved, various expectations arose, such that a particular poetic genre came to require the Doric or Lesbos dialect.

The two major lyrical poets were Sappho and Pindar. The Classical era also saw the dawn of drama. Of the hundreds of tragedies written and performed during the classical age, only a limited number of plays by three authors have survived: Aeschylus, Sophocles, and Euripides.

Like tragedy, the comedy arose from a ritual in honor of Dionysus, but in this case the plays were full of frank obscenity, abuse, and insult. The surviving plays by Aristophanes are a treasure trove of comic presentation. Menander is considered the best of the writers of the New Comedy.

Two of the most influential historians who had yet lived flourished during Greece's classical age:

Herodotus and Thucydides. A third historian, Xenophon, began his "Hellenica" where Thucydides ended his work about 411 BC and carried his history to 362 BC.

The greatest prose achievement of the 4th century was in philosophy. Among the tide of Greek philosophy, three names tower above the rest: Socrates —even though he didn't write anything himself, Plato, and Aristotle.

The golden age of classical Greece lasted from the early fifth to the late fourth century BC, and was concentrated in Asia Minor and the Greek Isles. Although this era ended nearly 2,500 years ago, the influence of its civilization can still be felt in today's world. It is particularly apparent in the realm of literature, where modern Western literary traditions owe much to classical and ancient Greek myths and traditions.

Classical Greek literature developed out of an even older tradition of oral storytelling. For centuries, literacy was rare, and oral storytelling was the only way to transmit information to large groups of people. To aid the memory, wandering poets would set histories, legends, and religious stories into verse. Other poets would then memorize these epics, and the information could be passed on to the next generation. Such poems were generally set to music and sung, sometimes with the accompaniment of instruments or simple dances. These performances provided entertainment and education at the same time.

Around the eighth century BC, a poet who lived in Asia Minor began preserving these ballads and epic tales in writing. Although historical evidence is scanty, it is generally believed that this literary pioneer was named Homer. The famous heroic epic poems *The Iliad* and *The Odyssey* are both the work of this skilled poet. They are some of the earliest examples of Greek literature that have survived to this day, and are of interest to scholars not only for their historical value, but for the beauty of their language and imagery.

In the centuries after Homer, Greek literature continued to develop. Literacy became more common, but poetry remained the most popular way of spreading information to the people. The manner in which the poems were presented, however, became more sophisticated. While the early poems of the Homeric age were set to music and performed by the poet, sometimes with the aid of instruments or dance, the poems of the sixth century BC had developed into something more like plays. An actor would take turns reciting the lines of a poem with a chorus, or group of dancers. Often the actor and the members of the chorus would wear masks, and the chorus would complement the poetry with interpretive dances.

These new plays were generally performed at festivals honoring gods and goddesses, or celebrations of seasonal events, such as the first grain harvest or the summer rains. Formal competitions, where poets and playwrights would submit their work and vie for prizes, became popular. One of the most famous of these was the Great Dionysia, held during a springtime festival in Athens to honor the god Dionysus.

In the early years of the fifth century, Greek literature, theater, and culture began to blossom, and great advances were made in the sciences and the arts. The world of Greek literature was affected greatly, and several distinct varieties of dramatic poetry began to appear. The standard heroic epics of previous centuries were replaced by increasingly sophisticated tragic and comic plays with elaborate plots, character development, and production techniques.

Although these two types of plays were staged in very similar ways, they differed greatly in content. Tragic plays, despite the name, were not necessarily sad. They were earnestly dramatic, and dealt with a range of complex and serious topics such as psychology, philosophy, and morality. Comic plays, on the other hand, were filled with bawdy and raucous jokes, and were intended to provoke laughter and to entertain. Despite their light and humorous presentation, some of the better comic playwrights used these plays to express genuine and serious political and social commentary.

Both these types of plays benefited greatly from the innovations in technique introduced by the fifth-century tragic playwright Aeschylus. His contributions to tragic Greek theater were so great that he is still remembered as the Father of Tragedy. An incredibly popular and original playwright, he introduced the idea of having multiple actors on the stage at one time, and pioneered the idea of using costumes and visual effects such as paintings and scenery. His work changed forever the way Greeks would view poetry and theater.

Aeschylus was only the first of the great classic Greek dramatists. The generation that followed brought several other talented and powerful tragic playwrights. The most famous of these were Sophocles and Euripides. Both writers did much to expand the traditionally simple expectations of characters in plays. Sophocles' plays feature incredibly strong-willed, modern characters who struggle with serious moral concerns, and Euripides wrote some of the most chilling psychological dramas of classical Greece.

Comic theater also had its hero. A generation younger than Sophocles and Euripides, the comic playwright Aristophanes is today regarded as the best of the classic comic playwrights. His sometimes absurd, and sometimes elegant plays demonstrate a great skill in mixing comedy with honest and sincere ideas. Aristophanes' plays certainly contain many wild and vulgar jokes, yet they also discuss serious concerns of his time, such as politics, art, and education. His work provides modern readers with some of the clearest images of the life and daily affairs of fifth-century Greeks.

This literary revolution in the early part of the fifth century was not limited to the stage. The world of philosophy also experienced an awakening. Skills such as oration, logic, and rhetoric were polished, and the study of mathematics and the sciences was encouraged. Philosophers such as Socrates became famous for wandering about the city of Athens, engaging students and scholars in lively academic debates about morality and politics.

Socrates' most famous pupil, Plato, wrote a number of books and dialogs in which he explains the philosophy and thoughts of his teacher, and goes on to develop the ideas further. His work—which deals with a wide range of theoretical concerns, such as politics, ethics, and the importance of friendship—is invaluable for modern scholars who wish to understand the ancient Greek mindset.

Another very well-known philosopher of the time was Aristotle. Aristotle was, in his turn, a pupil of Plato's, and is best known for his numerous texts dealing with the natural sciences. Interested in almost every conceivable topic, Aristotle left behind texts detailing his thoughts and questions on physics and astronomy, as well as meteorology, sleep patterns, raising animals, and numerous other subjects.

The age of classical Greece drew to a close with the end of the fourth century BC. Yet through its literature, classical Greece still has an enormous effect on modern Western thought and traditions. Almost all Western literature, from histories to romance novels, from thrillers to poetry, is rooted in classical Greek traditions. Many of the themes present in those ancient plays and poems are in fact still popular in modern literature. And even those plays that deal with uniquely modern themes still owe much in the way of technique and style to the golden age of Greece.

Homer's Iliad

The Iliad is an epic poem in dactylic hexameters, traditionally attributed to Homer. Set in the Trojan War, the ten-year siege of Ilium by a coalition of Greek states, it tells of the battles and events during the weeks of a quarrel between King Agamemnon and the warrior Achilles. Although the story covers only a few weeks in the final year of the war, the Iliad mentions or alludes to many of the Greek legends about the siege.

Along with the Odyssey, also attributed to Homer, the Iliad is among the oldest extant works of Western literature, and its written version is usually dated to around the eighth century BC. The Iliad contains approximately 15,700 lines, and is written in a literary amalgam of several Greek dialects. The authorship of the poem is disputed.

First Verses of the Iliad

Muses, the story begins in media res towards the end of the Trojan war between the Trojans and the besieging Greeks. Chryses, a Trojan priest of Apollo, offers the Greeks wealth for the return of his daughter Chryseis, a captive of Agamemnon, Greek leader. Although most of the Greek army is in favour, Agamemnon refuses.

Chryses prays for Apollo's help, and Apollo causes a plague throughout the Greek army. After nine days of plague, Achilles, the leader of the Myrmidon contingent, calls an assembly to solve the plague problem. Under pressure, Agamemnon agrees to return Chryseis to her father, but also decides to take Achilles's captive, Briseis, as compensation. Angered, Achilles declares that he and his men will no longer fight for Agamemnon, but will go home. Odysseus takes a ship and brings Chryseis to her father, whereupon Apollo ends the plague. In the meantime, Agamemnon's messengers take Briseis away, and Achilles asks his mother, Thetis, to ask Zeus that the Greeks be fought to breaking point by the Trojans, so Agamemnon will realise how much the Greeks need him.

Thetis does so, Zeus agrees, and sends a dream to Agamemnon, urging him to attack the city. Agamemnon heeds the dream but decides to first test the morale of the Greek army by telling them to go home. The plan backfires, and only the intervention of Odysseus, inspired by Athena, stops the rout. Odysseus confronts and beats Thersites, a common soldier who voices discontent at fighting Agamemnon's war. After a meal, the Greeks deploy in companies upon the Trojan plain. The poet takes the opportunity to describe each Greek contingent. When news of the Greek deployment reaches king Priam, the Trojans too sortie upon the plain. In a similar list to that for the Greeks, the poet describes the Trojans and their allies. The armies approach each other on the plain, but before they met, Paris offers to end the war by fighting duel with Menelaus. While Helen tells Priam about the Greek commanders from the walls of Troy, both sides swear a truce and promise to abide by the outcome of the duel. Paris is beaten, but Aphrodite rescues him and leads him to bed with Helen before Menelaus could kill him. Pressured by Hera's hatred of Troy, Zeus arranges for the Trojan Pandaros to break the truce by wounding Menelaus with an arrow. Agamemnon rouses the Greeks, and battle is joined. In the fighting, Diomedes kills many Trojans and defeats Aeneas, whom again Aphrodite rescues, but Diomedes attacks and wounds the goddess. Apollo faces Diomedes, and warns him against warring with gods. Many heroes and commanders join in, including Hector, and the gods supporting each side try to influence the battle. Emboldened by Athena, Diomedes wounds Ares and puts him out of action.

Hector rallies the Trojans and stops a rout; Diomedes and Glaukos, Greek and Trojan, find common ground and exchange unequal gifts. Hector enters the city, urges prayers and sacrifices, incites Paris to battle, bids his wife Andromache and son Astyanax farewell on the city walls, and rejoins the battle. Hector duels with Ajax, but nightfall interrupts the fight and both sides retire. The Greeks agree to burn their dead and build a wall to protect their ships and camp, while the Trojans quarrel about returning Helen. Paris offers to return the treasure he took, and give further wealth as compensation, but without returning Helen, and the offer is refused. A day's truce is agreed for burning the dead, during which the Greeks also build their wall and trench. The next morning, Zeus forbids the gods from interfering, and fighting begins anew. The Trojans prevail and force the Greeks back to their wall while Hera and Athena are forbidden from helping. Night falls before the Trojans can assault the Greek wall. They camp in the field to assault at first light, and their watchfires light the plain like stars.

Meanwhile, the Greeks are desperate. Agamemnon admits his error, and sends an embassy composed of Odysseus, Ajax, Phoenix, and two heralds to offer Briseis and extensive gifts to Achilles, who has been camped next to his ships throughout, if only he would return to the fighting. Achilles and his companion Patroclus receive the embassy well, but Achilles angrily refuses Agamemnon's offer, and declares that he would only return to battle if the Trojans reach his ships and threaten them with fire. The embassy returns empty-handed. Later that night, Odysseus and Diomedes venture out to the Trojan lines, kill the Trojan Dolon, and wreak havoc in the camps of some Thracian allies of Troy. In the morning, the fighting is fierce and Agamemnon, Diomedes, and Odysseus are all wounded. Achilles sends Patroclus from his camp to enquire about the Greek casualties, and while there Patroclus is moved to pity by a speech of Nestor. The Trojans assault the Greek wall on foot. Hector, ignoring an omen, leads the terrible fighting. The Greeks are overwhelmed in rout, the wall's gate is broken, and Hector charges in. Many fall on both sides. The Trojan seer Polydamas urges Hector to fall back and warns him of Achilles, but is ignored. Hera seduces Zeus and lures him to sleep, allowing

Poseidon to help the Greeks, and the Trojans are driven back onto the plain. Zeus awakes and is enraged by Poseidon's intervention. Against the mounting discontent of the Greek-supporting gods, Zeus sends Apollo to aid the Trojans, who once again breach the wall, and the battle reaches the ships.

Patroclus could stand to watch no longer, and begs Achilles to be allowed to defend the ships. Achilles relents, and lends Patroclus his armour, but sends him off with a stern admonition to not pursue the Trojans, lest he take Achilles's glory. Patroclus leads the Myrmidons to battle and arrives as the Trojans set fire to the first ships. The Trojans are routed by the sudden onslaught. Patroclus, ignoring Achilles's command, pursues and reaches the gates of Troy, where Apollo himself stops him. Patroclus is set upon by Apollo and Euphorbos, and is finally killed by Hector. Hector takes Achilles's armour from the fallen Patroclus, but fighting develops around Patroclus's body. Achilles is mad with grief when he hears of Patroclus's death, and vows to take vengeance on Hector; his mother Thetis grieves, too, knowing that Achilles is fated to die if he kills Hector. Achilles is urged to help retrieve Patroclus's body, but has no armour. Made brilliant by Athena, Achilles stands next to the Greek wall and roars in rage. The Trojans are dismayed by his appearance and the Greeks manage to bear Patroclus's body away. Again Polydamas urges Hector to withdraw into the city, again Hector refuses, and the Trojans camp in the plain at nightfall. Patroclus is mourned, and meanwhile, by Thetis's request, Hephaistos fashions a new set of armour for Achilles, among which is an magnificently wrought shield. In the morning, Agamemnon gives Achilles all the promised gifts, including Briseis, but he is indifferent to them. Achilles fasts while the Greeks take their meal, and straps on his new armour, and heaves his great spear. His horse Xanthos prophesies to Achilles his death. Achilles drives his chariot into battle.

Zeus lifts the ban on the gods' interference, and the gods freely intervene on both sides. Burning with rage and grief, Achilles's onslaught is terrible, and slays many. Driving the Trojans before him, Achilles cuts off half in the river Skamandros and proceeds to slaughter them and fills the river with the dead. The river, angry at the killing, confronts Achilles, but is beaten back by Hephaistos's firestorm. The gods fight among themselves. The great gates of the city are opened to receive the fleeing Trojans, and Apollo leads Achilles away from the city by pretending to be a Trojan. When Apollo reveals himself to Achilles, the Trojans have retreated into the city, all except for Hector, who, having twice ignored the counsels of Polydamas, feels the shame of rout and resolves to face Achilles, in spite of the pleas of Priam and Hecuba, his parents. When Achilles approaches, Hector's will fails him, and he is chased around the city by Achilles. Finally, Athena tricks him to stop running, and he is caught and killed by Achilles. Achilles takes Hector's body and dishonours it. The ghost of Patroclus comes to Achilles in a dream and urges the burial of his body. The Greeks hold a day of funeral games, and Achilles gives out the prizes. Dismayed by Achilles's continued abuse of Hector's body, Zeus decides that it must be returned to Priam. Led by Hermes, Priam takes a wagon out of Troy, across the plains, and enters the Greek camp unnoticed. Zeus grasps Achilles by the knees and begs to have his son's body. Achilles is moved to tears, and the two lament their losses in the war. After a meal, Priam carries Hector's body back into Troy. Hector is buried, and the city mourns.

Characters

The many characters of the Iliad are catalogued; the latter-half of Book II, the "Catalogue of Ships", lists commanders and cohorts; battle scenes feature quickly-slain minor characters.

- The Achaeans—aka the Hellenes (Greeks), Danaans, and Argives.
  - Agamemnon—King of Mycenae; leader of the Greeks.
  - Achilles—Leader of the Myrmidons.
  - Odysseus—King of Ithaca; the wiliest Greek commander, and hero of the Odyssey.
  - Aias (Ajax the Greater)—son of Telamon, with Diomedes, he is second to Achilles in martial prowess.
  - Menelaus—King of Sparta; husband of Helen and brother of Agamemnon.
  - Diomedes—son of Tydeus, King of Argos.
  - Aias (Ajax the Lesser)—son of Oileus, often partner of Ajax the Greater.
  - Patroclus—Achilles' beloved comrade and friend.
- The Trojan men
  - Hector—son of King Priam; the foremost Trojan warrior.
  - Aeneas—son of Anchises and Aphrodite.
  - Deiphobus—brother cf Hector and Paris.

- Paris—Helen's lover-abductor.
- Priam—the aged King of Troy.
- Polydamas—a prudent commander whose advice is ignored; he is Hector's foil.
- Agenor—a Trojan warrior who attempts to fight Achilles (Book XXI).
- Dolon—a spy upon the Greek camp (Book X).
- Antenor—King Priam's advisor, who argues for returning Helen to end the war; Paris refuses.
- Polydorus—son of Priam and Laothoe.

- The Trojan women
  - Hecuba—Priam's wife; mother of Hector, Cassandra, Paris, and others.
  - Helen—Menelaus's wife; espoused first to Paris, then to Deiphobus.
  - Andromache—Hector's wife; mother of Astyanax
  - Cassandra- Priam's daughter; courted by Apollo, who bestows the gift of prophecy to her; upon her rejection, he curses her, and her warnings of Trojan doom go unheeded.
  - Briseis—a Trojan woman captured by the Greeks; she was Achilles' prize of the Trojan war.

These Olympic deities advise and manipulate the humans; except Zeus, they fight the Trojan War.

- The major deities:
  - Zeus
  - Hera

- Artemis
- Apollo
- Hades
- Aphrodite
- Ares
- Athena
- Hermes
- Poseidon
- Hephaestus

— The minor deities:

- Eris
- Iris
- Thetis
- Proteus
- Scamander

Themes: The substance of heroism

Nostos

Nostos occurs seven times in the poem; thematically, the concept of homecoming is much explored in Ancient Greek literature, especially in the post-war homeward fortunes experienced by Atreidae, Agamemnon, and Odysseus, thus, nostos is impossible without sacking Troy—King Agamemnon's motive for winning, at any cost.

Kleos

Kleos is the concept of glory earned in heroic battle; for most of the Greek invaders of Troy, notably Odysseus, kleos is earned in a victorious nostos (homecoming), yet not for Achilles, he must choose one reward, either nostos or kleos. In Book IX (IX.410-16), he poignantly tells Agamemnon's envoys—Odysseus, Phoenix, Ajax—begging his reinstatement to battle about having to choose between two fates.

In foregoing his nostos, he will earn the greater reward of kleos aphthiton. In the poem, aphthiton occurs five times, each occurrence denotes an object (i.e. Agamemnon's sceptre, the wheel of Hebe's chariot, the house of Poseidon, the throne of Zeus, the house of Hephaistos); translator Lattimore renders kleos aphthiton as forever immortal and as forever imperishable—connoting Achilles's mortality by underscoring his greater reward in returning to battle Troy.

The poem's initial word establishes the Iliad's principal theme: The Wrath of Achilles. His personal rage and wounded soldier's vanity propel the story—the Greeks' faltering in battle, the slayings of Patroclus and Hector, and the fall of Troy. In Book I, the Wrath of Achilles first emerges in the Achilles-convoked meeting, between the Greek kings and Calchas, the Seer. King Agamemnon dishonours Chryses, the Trojan Apollonian priest, by refusing with a threat the restitution of his daughter, Chryseis—despite the proffered ransom of "gifts beyond count"; the insulted priest prays his god's help—and a nine-day rain of arrows falls upon the Greeks. Moreover, in that meeting, Achilles accuses Agamemnon of being "greediest for gain of all men". To that, Agamemnon replies:

> But here is my threat to you.
> Even as Phoibos Apollo is taking away my Chryseis.
> I shall convey her back in my own ship, with my own

> followers; but I shall take the fair-cheeked Briseis,
> your prize, I myself going to your shelter, that you may learn well
> how much greater I am than you, and another man may shrink back
> from likening himself to me and contending against me.

After that, only Athena stays Achilles's wrath. Achilles vows to never again to obey orders from Agamemnon. Furious, Achilles cries to his mother, Thetis, who persuades Zeus's divine intervention—favouring the Trojans—until Achilles's rights are restored. Meanwhile, Hector leads the Trojans to almost pushing the Greeks back to the sea (Book XII); later, Agamemnon contemplates defeat and retreat to Greece (Book XIV). Again, the Wrath of Achilles turns the war's tide in seeking vengeance when Hector kills Patroclus. Aggrieved, Achilles tears his hair and dirties his face; Thetis comforts her mourning son, who tells her:

> So it was here that the lord of men Agamemnon angered me.
>
> Still, we will let all this be a thing of the past, and for all our
>
> sorrow beat down by force the anger deeply within us.
>
> Now I shall go, to overtake that killer of a dear life,
>
> Hektor; then I will accept my own death, at whatever
>
> time Zeus wishes to bring it about, and the other immortals.

Accepting prospective death as fair price for avenging Patroclus, returns to battle, dooming Hector and Troy, thrice chasing him 'round the Trojan walls, before slaying him, then dragging the corpse behind his chariot, back to camp.

Fate

Fate propels most of the events of the Iliad. Once set, gods and men abide it, neither truly able nor willing to contest it. How fate is set is unknown, but it is told by the Fates and Seers such as Calchas. Men and their gods continually speak of heroic acceptance and cowardly avoidance of one's slated fate. Yet, it does not determine every action, incident, and occurrence, but does determine the outcome of life—before killing him, Hector calls Patroclus a fool for cowardly avoidance of his fate, by attempting his defeat; Patroclus retorts:

> No, deadly destiny, with the son of Leto, has killed me, and of men it was Euphorbos; you are only my third slayer.
>
> And put away in your heart this other thing that I tell you.
>
> You yourself are not one who shall live long, but now already death and powerful destiny are standing beside you, to go down under the hands of Aiakos' great son, Achilleus.

Here, Achilles Patroclus alludes to fated death by Hector's hand, and Hector's fated death by Achilles's hand. Despite free will, each accepts the outcome of his life, yet, no-one knows if the gods can alter fate. The first instance of this doubt occurs in Book XVI; seeing Patroclus about to kill Sarpedon, his mortal son, Zeus says:

> Ah me, that it is destined that the dearest of men, Sarpedon, must go down under the hands of Menoitios' son Patroclus.
>
> About his dilemma, Hera asks Zeus:
>
> Majesty, son of Kronos, what sort of thing have you spoken?

> Do you wish to bring back a man who is mortal, one long since doomed by his destiny, from ill-sounding death and release him?
>
> Do it, then; but not all the rest of us gods shall approve you.

In deciding—between losing a son or abiding fate—Zeus, the King of the Gods, allows it. This motif recurs when he considers sparing Hector, whom he loves and respects. Again, Athena asks him:

> Father of the shining bold, dark misted, what is this you said?
>
> Do you wish to bring back a man who is mortal, one long since doomed by his destiny, from ill-sounding death and release him?
>
> Do it, then; but not all the rest of us gods shall approve you.

Again, Zeus appears capable of altering fate, but does not, deciding instead to abide set outcomes; yet, contrariwise, fate spares Aeneas, after Apollo convinces the over-matched Trojan to fight Achilles. Poseidon cautiously speaks:

> But come, let us ourselves get him away from death, for fear the son of Kronos may be angered if now Achilleus kills this man. It is destined that he shall be the survivor, that the generation of Dardanos shall not die....

Divinely-aided, Aeneas escapes the wrath of Achilles and survives the Trojan War. Whether or not the gods can alter fate, they do abide it, despite its countering their human allegiances, thus, the mysterious origin of fate is a power beyond the gods. Fate implies the primeval, tripartite division of the world that Zeus, Poseidon, and Hades effected in deposing their father, Cronus, for its dominion. Zeus took the Air and the

Sky, Poseidon the Waters, and Hades the Underworld, the land of the dead—yet, they share dominion of the Earth. Despite the earthly powers of the Olympic gods, only the Three Fates set the destiny of Man.

The Iliad as oral tradition

In antiquity, the Greeks applied the Iliad and the Odyssey as the bases of pedagogy; literature central to the educational-cultural function of the itinerant rhapsode, who composed consistent epic poems from memory and improvisation, and disseminated them, via song and chant, in his travels and at the Panathenaic Festival of athletics, music, poetics, and sacrifice, celebrating Athena's birthday.

Originally, Classical scholars treated the Iliad and the Odyssey as written poetry, and Homer as a writer, yet, by the 1920s, Milman Parry (1902-1935) demonstrated otherwise; his investigation of the oral Homeric style—stock epithets and reiteration (words, phrases, stanzas)—established those formulae as oral tradition artefacts easily applied to an hexametric line; a two-word stock epithet (e.g. "resourceful Odysseus") reiteration complements a character name by filling a half-line, thus, freeing the poet to compose a half-line of original formulaic text to complete his meaning. In Yugoslavia, Parry and his assistant, Albert Lord, studied the oral-formulaic composition of Bosniac oral poetry, yielding the Parry/Lord thesis that established Oral tradition studies, later developed by Eric Havelock, Marshall McLuhan, Walter Ong, et al.

In The Singer of Tales, Lord demonstrates likeness between the tragedies of the Greek Patroclus, in the Iliad, and of the Sumerian Enkidu, in the Epic of Gilgamesh, and refutes, with "careful analysis of the repetition of thematic patterns", that the Patroclus storyline upsets Homer's established compositional formulae of "wrath, bride-stealing, and rescue", thus, stock-phrase reiteration does not restrict his originality in fitting story to rhyme. Like-wise, in The Arming Motif, Prof. James Armstrong reports that the poem's formulae yield richer meaning because the "arming motif" diction—describing Achilles, Agamemnon, Paris, and Patroclus—serves to "heighten the importance of... an impressive moment", thus, reiteration "creates an atmosphere of smoothness", wherein, Homer distinguishes Patroclus from Achilles, and foreshadows the former's death with positive and negative turns of phrase.

In the Iliad, occasional syntactic inconsistency is an oral tradition effect—for example, Aphrodite is "laughter-loving", despite being painfully wounded by Diomedes; and the divine representations, mixing Mycenaean and Greek Dark Age mythologies, parallel the hereditary basilee nobles (lower social rank rulers) with minor Olympic gods, such as Scamander et al.

Rrelationship between Achilles and Patroclus

Classical-era, historical, and contemporary scholars have questioned the true nature of the relationship between Achilles and Patroclus, arguing that the evidence is equivocal for perceiving and defining it as either platonic or homosexual, although Aeschylus does portray them so in Fragment 134a. Necessarily, critics perceive and interpret that manly relationship with their own mores (social, cultural, sexual), thus, fifth-century BC Athenian scholars perceived it as pederastic (then an accepted male relationship), likewise the others perceived it as either a platonic warrior-bond or as a homosexual pairing of like-age men—despite Homer's description of Trojan women as war prizes, hence, the sexual-orientation speculation evinced by Achilles's outrage at King Agamemnon's confiscation of Bryseis, his war-prize concubine.

While the Homeric poems (the Iliad in particular) were not necessarily revered scripture of the ancient Greeks, they were most certainly seen as guides that were important to the intellectual understanding of any educated Greek citizen. This is evidenced by the fact that in the late fifth century BC, "it was the sign of a man of standing to be able to recite the Iliad and Odyssey by heart." Moreover, it can be argued that the warfare shown in the Iliad, and the way in which it was depicted, had a profound and very traceable effect on Greek warfare in general. In particular, the effect of epic literature can be broken down into three categories: tactics, ideology, and the mindset of commanders. In order to discern these effects, it is necessary to take a look at a few examples from each of these categories.

Much of the detailed fighting in the Iliad is done by the heroes in an orderly, one-on-one fashion. Much like the Odyssey, there is even a set ritual which must be observed in each of these conflicts. For example, a major hero may encounter a lesser hero from the opposing side, in which case the minor hero is introduced, threats may be exchanged, and then the minor hero is slain. The victor often strips the body of its armor and military accoutrements. Here is an excellent example of this ritual and this type of one-on- one combat in the Iliad:

There Telamonian Ajax struck down the son of Anthemion, Simoeisios in his stripling's beauty, whom once his mother descending from Ida bore beside the banks of Simoeis when she had followed her father and mother to tend the sheepflocks. Therefore they called him Simoeisios; but he could not render again the care of his dear parents; he was shortlived, beaten down beneath the spear of high- hearted Ajax, who struck him as he first came forward beside the nipple of the right breast, and the bronze spearhead drove clean through the shoulder

While there are discussions of soldiers arrayed in semblances of the phalanx throughout the Iliad, the focus of the poem on the heroic fighting, as mentioned above, would seem to contradict the tactics of the phalanx. However, the phalanx did have its heroic aspects. The masculine one- on- one fighting of epic is manifested in phalanx fighting on the emphasis of holding one's position in formation. This replaces the singular heroic competition found in the Iliad There is no better example of this than the Spartan tale of 300 picked men fighting against 300 picked Argives. In this battle of champions, only two men are left standing for the Argives and one for the Spartans. Othryades, the remaining Spartan, goes back to stand in his formation with mortal wounds while the remaining two Argives go back to Argos to report their victory. Thus, the Spartans claimed this as a victory, as their last man displayed the ultimate feat of bravery by maintaining his position in the phalanx. In terms of the ideology of commanders in later Greek history, the Iliad has an interesting effect. The Iliad expresses a definite disdain for tactical trickeration, when Hector says, before he challenges the great Ajax:

> However, despite examples of disdain for this tactical trickery, there is reason to believe that the

> Iliad, as well as later Greek warfare, endorsed tactical genius on the part of their commanders. For example, there are multiple passages in the Iliad with commanders such as Agamemnon or Nestor discussing the arraying of troops so as to gain an advantage. Indeed, the Trojan War is won by a notorious example of Greek guile in the Persian Horse. This is even later referred to by Homer in the Odyssey. The connection, in this case, between guileful tactics of the Greeks in the Iliad and those of the later Greeks is not a difficult one to find. Spartan commanders, often seen as the pinnacle of Greek military prowess, were known for their tactical trickery, and, for them, this was a feat to be desired in a commander. Indeed, this type of leadership was the standard advice of Greek tactical writers.

Ultimately, while Homeric (or epic) fighting is certainly not completely replicated in later Greek warfare, many of its ideals, tactics, and instruction are.

Mythologic characters

In the literary Trojan War of the Iliad, the Olympic gods, goddesses, and demigods fight and play great roles in human warfare. Unlike practical Greek religious observance, Homer's portrayals of them suited his narrative purpose, being very different from the polytheistic ideals Greek society used. To wit, the Classical-era historian Herodotus says that Homer, and his contemporary, the poet Hesiod, were the first artists to name and describe their appearance and characters.

In Greek Gods, Human Lives: What We Can Learn From Myths, Mary Lefkowitz discusses the relevance of divine action in the Iliad, attempting to answer the question of whether or not divine intervention is a discrete occurrence (for its own sake), or if such godly behaviours are mere human character metaphors. The intellectual interest of Classic-era authors, such as Thucydides and Plato, was limited to their utility as "a way of talking about human life rather than a description or a truth", because, if the gods remain religious figures, rather than human metaphors, their "existence"—without the foundation of either dogma or a bible of faiths—then allowed Greek culture the intellectual breadth and freedom to conjure gods fitting any religious function they required as a people.

The *Odyssey*

The *Odyssey* is one of two major ancient Greek epic poems attributed to Homer. It is, in part, a sequel to the *Iliad,* the other work traditionally ascribed to Homer. The poem is fundamental to the modern Western canon. Indeed it is the second--the *Iliad* being the first—extant work of Western literature. It was probably composed near the end of the eighth century BC, somewhere in Ionia, the Greek-speaking coastal region of what is now Turkey.

The poem mainly centers on the Greek hero Odysseus (or Ulysses, as he was known in Roman myths) and his long journey home following the fall of Troy. It takes Odysseus ten years to reach Ithaca after the ten-year Trojan War, twenty years in total. In his absence, it is assumed he has died, and his wife Penelope and son Telemachus must deal with a group of unruly suitors, the Mnesteres or Proci, competing for Penelope's hand in marriage.

It continues to be read in the Homeric Greek and translated into modern languages around the world. The original poem was composed in an oral tradition by an aoidos (epic poet/singer), perhaps a rhapsode (professional performer), and was intended more to be sung than read. The details of the ancient oral performance, and the story's conversion to a written work inspire continual debate among scholars. The *Odyssey* was written in a regionless poetic dialect of Greek and comprises 12,110 lines of dactylic hexameter. Among the most impressive elements of the text are its strikingly modern non-linear plot, and the fact that events are shown to depend as much on the choices made by women and serfs as on the actions of fighting men. In the English language as well as many others, the word *odyssey* has come to refer to an epic voyage.

Synopsis

Telemachus, Odysseus's son, is only a month old when Odysseus sets out for Troy to fight a war he wants no part of. At the point where the *Odyssey* begins, ten years after the end of the ten-year Trojan War, Telemachus is twenty and is sharing his absent father's house on the island of Ithaca with his mother Penelope and a crowd of 117 boisterous young men, "the Suitors", whose aim is to persuade Penelope that her husband is dead and that she should marry one of them.

Odysseus's protector, the goddess Athena, discusses his fate with Zeus, king of the gods, at a moment when Odysseus's enemy, the god of the sea Poseidon, is absent from Mount Olympus. Then, disguised as a Taphian chieftain named Mentes, she visits Telemachus to urge him to search for news of his father. He offers her hospitality; they observe the Suitors dining rowdily, and the bard Phemius performing a narrative poem for them. Penelope objects to Phemius's theme, the "Return from Troy" because it reminds her of her missing husband, but Telemachus rebuts her objections.

That night, Athena disguised as Telemachus finds a ship and crew for the true Telemachus. The next morning, Telemachus calls an assembly of citizens of Ithaca to discuss what should be done to the suitors. Accompanied by Athena (now disguised as his friend Mentor), he departs for the Greek mainland and the household of Nestor, most venerable of the Greek warriors at Troy, now at home in Pylos. From there, Telemachus rides overland, accompanied by Nestor's son, to Sparta, where he finds Menelaus and Helen, now reconciled. He is told that they returned to Greece after a long voyage by way of Egypt; there, on the magical island of Pharos, Menelaus encountered the old sea-god Proteus, who told him that Odysseus was a captive of the nymph Calypso. Incidentally, Telemachus learns the fate of Menelaus' brother Agamemnon, king of Mycenae and leader of the Greeks at Troy, murdered on his return home by his wife Clytemnestra and her lover Aegisthus.

Then the story of Odysseus is told. He has spent seven years in captivity on Calypso's island. She is persuaded to release him by the messenger god Hermes, who has been sent by Zeus in response to Athena's plea. Odysseus builds a raft and is given clothing, food and drink by Calypso. The raft is wrecked by Poseidon, but Odysseus swims ashore on the island of Scherie, where, naked and exhausted, he hides in a pile of leaves and falls asleep. The next morning, awakened by the laughter of girls, he sees the young Nausicaa, who has gone to the seashore with her maids to wash clothes. He appeals to her for help. She encourages him to seek the hospitality of her parents, Arete and Alcinous. Odysseus is welcomed and is not at first asked for his name. He remains for several days, takes part in a pentathlon, and hears the blind singer Demodocus perform two narrative poems. The first is an otherwise obscure incident of the Trojan War, the "Quarrel of Odysseus and Achilles"; the second is the amusing tale of a love affair between two Olympian gods, Ares and Aphrodite. Finally, Odysseus asks Demodocus to return to the Trojan War theme and tell of the Trojan Horse, a stratagem in which Odysseus had played a leading role. Unable to hide his emotion as he relives this episode, Odysseus at last reveals his identity. He then begins to tell the amazing story of his return from Troy.

After a piratical raid on Ismaros in the land of the Cicones, he and his twelve ships were driven off course by storms. They visited the lethargic Lotus-Eaters and were captured by the Cyclops Polyphemus, only escaping by blinding him with a wooden stake. They stayed with Aeolus, the master of the winds; he gave Odysseus a leather bag containing all the winds, except the west wind, a gift that should have ensured a safe return home. However, the sailors foolishly opened the bag while Odysseus slept, thinking that it contained gold. All of the winds flew out and the resulting storm drove the ships back the way they had come, just as Ithaca came into sight.

After pleading in vain with Aeolus to help them again, they re-embarked and encountered the cannibal Laestrygones. Odysseus's ship was the only one to escape. He sailed on and visited the witch-goddess Circe. She turned half of his men into swine after feeding them cheese and wine. Hermes warned Odysseus about Circe and gave Odysseus a drug called moly, a resistance to Circe's magic. Circe, being attracted to Odysseus' resistance, fell in love with him and released his men. Odysseus and his crew remained with her on the island for one year, while they feasted and drank. Finally, Odysseus' men convinced Odysseus that it was time to leave for Ithaca. Guided by Circe's instructions, Odysseus and his crew crossed the ocean and reached a harbor at the western edge of the world, where Odysseus sacrificed to the dead and summoned the spirit of the old prophet Tiresias to advise him. Next Odysseus met the spirit of his own mother, who had died of grief during his long absence; from her, he learned for the first time news of his own household, threatened by the greed of the suitors. Here, too, he met the spirits of famous women and famous men; notably he encountered the spirit of Agamemnon, of whose murder he now learned, who also warned him about the dangers of women.

Returning to Circe's island, they were advised by her on the remaining stages of the journey. They skirted the land of the Sirens, passed between the many-headed monster Scylla and the whirlpool Charybdis, and landed on the island of Thrinacia. There, Odysseus' men ignored the warnings of Tiresias and Circe, and hunted down the sacred cattle of the sun god Helios. This sacrilege was punished by a shipwreck in which all but Odysseus drowned. He was washed ashore on the island of Calypso, where she compelled him to remain as her lover for seven years before escaping.

Having listened with rapt attention to his story, the Phaeacians, who are skilled mariners, agree to help

Odysseus get home. They deliver him at night, while he is fast asleep, to a hidden harbor on Ithaca. He finds his way to the hut of one of his own former slaves, the swineherd Eumaeus. Athene disguises Odysseus as a wandering beggar in order to learn how things stand in his household. After dinner, he tells the farm laborers a fictitious tale of himself: he was born in Crete, had led a party of Cretans to fight alongside other Greeks in the Trojan War, and had then spent seven years at the court of the king of Egypt; finally he had been shipwrecked in Thesprotia and crossed from there to Ithaca.

Meanwhile, Telemachus sails home from Sparta, evading an ambush set by the suitors. He disembarks on the coast of Ithaca and makes for Eumaeus's hut. Father and son meet; Odysseus identifies himself to Telemachus (but still not to Eumaeus) and they determine that the suitors must be killed. Telemachus gets home first. Accompanied by Eumaeus, Odysseus now returns to his own house, still pretending to be a beggar. He experiences the suitors' rowdy behavior and plans their death. He meets Penelope and tests her intentions with an invented story of his birth in Crete, where, he says, he once met Odysseus. Closely questioned, he adds that he had recently been in Thesprotia and had learned something there of Odysseus's recent wanderings.

Odysseus's identity is discovered by the housekeeper, Eurycleia, as she is washing his feet and discovers an old scar Odysseus received during a boar hunt; he swears her to secrecy. The next day, at Athena's prompting, Penelope maneuvers the suitors into competing for her hand with an archery competition using Odysseus' bow. The man who can string the bow and shoot it through a dozen axe heads would win. Odysseus takes part in the competition himself; he alone is strong enough to string the bow and shoot it through the dozen axe heads, making him the winner. He turns his arrows on the suitors and with the help of Athena, Telemachus, Eumaeus and Philoteus the cowherd, all the suitors are killed. Odysseus and Telemachus hang twelve of their household maids, who betrayed Penelope and/or had sex with the suitors; they mutilate and kill the goatherd Melanthius, who had mocked and abused Odysseus. Now at last, Odysseus identifies himself to Penelope. She is hesitant, but accepts him when he mentions that their bed was made from an olive tree still rooted to the ground. Many modern and ancient scholars take this to be the original ending of the Odyssey, and the rest is an interpolation.

The next day he and Telemachus visit the country farm of his old father Laertes, who likewise accepts his identity only when Odysseus correctly describes the orchard that Laertes once gave him.

The citizens of Ithaca have followed Odysseus on the road, planning to avenge the killing of the Suitors, their sons. Their leader points out that Odysseus has now caused the deaths of two generations of the men of Ithaca—his sailors, not one of whom survived, and the suitors, whom he has now executed. The goddess Athena intervenes and persuades both sides to give up the vendetta. After this, Ithaca is at peace once more, concluding the *Odyssey*. Yet Odysseus' journey is not complete, as he is still fated to wander. The gods have decreed that Odysseus cannot rest until he wanders so far inland that he meets a people who have never heard of an oar or of the sea. He then must build a shrine and sacrifice before he can return home for good.

Character of Odysseus

Odysseus' heroic trait is his *mtis*, or "cunning intelligence"; he is often described as the "Peer of Zeus in Counsel." This intelligence is most often manifested by his use of disguise and deceptive speech. His disguises take forms both physical (altering his appearance) and verbal, such as telling the Cyclops Polyphemus that his name is, "Nobody", then escaping after blinding Polyphemus. When asked by other Cyclopes why he is screaming, Polyphemus replies that "Nobody" is hurting him, so the others assume that, "If alone as you are [Polyphemus] none uses violence on you, why, there is no avoiding the sickness sent by great Zeus; so you had better pray to your father, the lord Poseidon". The most evident flaw that Odysseus sports is that of his arrogance and his pride, or hubris. As he sails away from the island of the Cyclops, he shouts his name and boasts that no one can defeat the "Great Odysseus". The Cyclops then throws the top half of a mountain at him and prays to his father, Poseidon, saying that Odysseus has blinded him. This enrages Poseidon, causing the god to thwart Odysseus' homecoming for a very long time.

Structure

The *Odyssey* begins *in medias res* (in the middle of things), meaning that the plot begins in the middle of the overall story, and that prior events are described through flashbacks or storytelling. This device is imitated by later authors of literary epics, for example, Virgil in the *Aeneid*, as well as modern poets such as Alexander Pope in *The Rape of the Lock*.

In the first episodes, we trace Telemachus' efforts to assert control of the household, and then, at Athena's advice, to search for news of his long-lost father. Then the scene shifts: Odysseus has been a captive of the beautiful nymph Calypso, with whom he has spent seven of his ten lost years. Released by the intercession of his patroness Athena, through the aid of Hermes, he departs, but his raft is destroyed by his divine enemy Poseidon, who is angry because Odysseus blinded his son, Polyphemus. When Odysseus washes up on Scherie, home to the Phaeacians, he is assisted by the young Nausicaa and is treated hospitably. In return, he satisfies the Phaeacians' curiosity, telling them, and the reader, of all his adventures since departing from Troy. The shipbuilding Phaeacians then loan him a ship to return to Ithaca, where he is aided by the swineherd Eumaeus, meets Telemachus, regains his household, kills the suitors, and is reunited with his faithful wife, Penelope.

Nearly all modern editions and translations of the *Odyssey* are divided into 24 books. This division is convenient but not original; it was developed by Alexandrian editors of the 3rd century BC. In the Classical period, moreover, several of the books (individually and in groups) were given their own titles: the first four books, focusing on Telemachus, are commonly known as the *Telemachy*; Odysseus' narrative, Book 9, featuring his encounter with the cyclops Polyphemus, is traditionally called the *Cyclopeia*; and Book 11, the section describing his meeting with the spirits of the dead is known as the *Nekuia*. Books 9 through 12, wherein Odysseus recalls his adventures for his Phaeacian hosts, are collectively referred to as the *Apologoi*: Odysseus' "stories". Book

22, wherein Odysseus kills all the suitors, has been given the title *Mnesterophonia*: "slaughter of the suitors".

The last 548 lines of the *Odyssey*, corresponding to Book 24, are believed by many scholars to have been added by a slightly later poet. Several passages in earlier books seem to be setting up the events of Book 24, so if it were indeed a later addition, the offending editor would seem to have changed earlier text as well.

Events in the main sequence of the *Odyssey* (excluding the narrative of Odysseus) take place in the Peloponnese and in what are now called the Ionian Islands. There are difficulties in the identification of Ithaca, the homeland of Odysseus, which may or may not be the same island that is now called Ithake. The wanderings of Odysseus as told to the Phaeacians, and the location of the Phaeacians' own island of Scherie, pose more fundamental geographical problems: scholars both ancient and modern are divided as to whether or not any of the places visited by Odysseus (after Ismaros and before his return to Ithaca) are real.

Oedipus the King

Oedipus the King is an Athenian tragedy by Sophocles that was first performed c. 429 BC. It was the second of Sophocles's three Theban plays to be produced, but it comes first in the internal chronology, followed by Oedipus at Colonus and then Antigone. Over the centuries, it has come to be regarded by many as the Greek tragedy par excellence.

Background

Much of the myth of Oedipus takes place before the opening scene of the play. In his youth, Laius was a guest of King Pelops of Elis, and became the tutor of Chrysippus, youngest of the king's sons, in chariot racing then violated the sacred laws of hospitality by abducting and raping Chrysippus. This cast a doom over him and over his descendants.

The protagonist of the tragedy is the son of King Laius and Queen Jocasta of Thebes. After Laius learns from an oracle that "he is doomed/To perish by the hand of his own son," he binds tightly together with a pin the feet of the infant Oedipus and orders Jocasta to kill the infant. Hesitant to do so, she demands a servant to commit the act for her. Instead, the servant abandons the baby in the fields, leaving the baby's fate to the gods. A shepherd rescues the infant and names him Oedipus (or "swollen feet"). Intending to raise the baby himself, but not possessing of the means to do so, the shepherd gives it to a fellow shepherd from a distant land, who spends the summers sharing pastureland with his flocks. The second shepherd carries the baby with him to Corinth, where Oedipus is taken in and raised in the court of the childless King Polybus of Corinth as if he were his own.

As a young man in Corinth, Oedipus hears a rumour that he is not the biological son of Polybus and his wife Merope. When Oedipus calls them out on this, they deny it, but, still suspicious, he asks the Delphic Oracle who his parents really are. The Oracle seems to ignore this question, telling him instead that he is destined to "Mate with [his] own mother, and shed/ With [his] own hands the blood of [his] own sire." Desperate to avoid his foretold fate, Oedipus leaves Corinth in the belief that Polybus and Merope are indeed his true parents and that, once away from them, he will never harm them.

On the road to Thebes, he meets Laius, his true father. Unaware of each other's identities, they quarrel over whose chariot has right-of-way. King Laius moves to strike the insolent youth with his sceptre, but Oedipus throws him down from the chariot and kills him, thus fulfilling part of the oracle's prophecy. Shortly after, he solves the riddle of the Sphinx, which has baffled many a diviner: "What is the creature that walks on four legs in the morning, two legs at noon, and three in the evening?"

To this Oedipus replies, "Man" (who crawls on all fours as an infant, walks upright later, and needs a walking stick in old age), and the distraught Sphinx throws herself off the cliffside. Oedipus's reward for freeing the kingdom of Thebes from her curse is the kingship and the hand of Queen Dowager Jocasta, his biological mother. The prophecy is thus fulfilled, although none of the main characters know it.

The action of the play

A priest and the chorus of Thebans arrive at the palace to call upon their King, Oedipus, to aid them with the plague of Apollo ravaging the city. Oedipus had sent his brother-in-law Creon to ask help of the oracle at Delphi, and he returns at that moment. Creon says the plague is the result of religious pollution, caused because the murderer of their former King, Laius, had never been caught. Oedipus vows to find the murderer and curses him for the plague that he has caused.

Oedipus summons the blind prophet Tiresias for help. When Tiresias arrives he claims to know the answers to Oedipus's questions, but refuses to speak, instead telling Oedipus to abandon his search. Oedipus is enraged by Tiresias's refusal, and says the prophet must be complicit in the murder. Outraged, Tiresias tells the king that Oedipus himself is the murderer. Oedipus cannot see how this could be, and concludes that the prophet must have been paid off by Creon in an attempt to undermine him. The two argue vehemently and eventually Tiresias leaves, muttering darkly that when the murderer is discovered he shall be a native citizen of Thebes; brother and father to his own children; and son and husband to his own mother.

Creon arrives to face Oedipus's accusations. The King demands that Creon be executed, however the chorus convince him to let Creon live. Oedipus's wife Jocasta enters, and attempts to comfort Oedipus, telling him he should take no notice of prophets. Many years ago she and Laius received an oracle which never came true. It was said that Laius would be killed by his own son, but, as all Thebes knows, Laius was killed by bandits at a crossroads on the way to Delphi.

The mention of this crossroads causes Oedipus to pause and ask for more details. Oedipus asks Jocasta what Laius looked like, and suddenly becomes worried that Tiresias's accusations were true. Oedipus then sends for the one surviving witness of the attack to be brought to the palace from the fields where he now works as a shepherd. Jocasta, confused, asks Oedipus what is the matter, and he tells her.

Many years ago, at a banquet in Corinth, a man drunkenly accused Oedipus of not being his father's son. Bothered by the comment Oedipus went to Delphi and asked the oracle about his parentage. Instead of answers he was given a prophecy that he would one day murder his father and sleep with his mother. Upon hearing this he resolved to quit Corinth and never return. While travelling he came to the very crossroads where Laius was killed, and encountered a carriage which attempted to drive him off the road. An argument ensued and Oedipus killed the travellers, including a man who matches Jocasta's description of Laius.

Oedipus has hope, however, because the story is that Laius was murdered by several robbers. If the shepherd confirms that Laius was attacked by many men, then Oedipus is in the clear.

A man arrives from Corinth with the message that Oedipus's father has died. Oedipus, to the surprise of the messenger, is made ecstatic by this news, for it proves one half of the prophecy false, for now he can never kill his father. However he still fears that he may somehow commit incest with his mother. The messenger, eager to ease Oedipus's mind, tells him not to worry, because Merope the Queen of Corinth was not in fact his real mother.

It emerges that this messenger was formerly a shepherd on Mount Cithaeron, and that he was given a baby, which the childless Polybus then adopted. The baby, he says, was given to him by another shepherd from the Laius household, who had been told to get rid of the child. Oedipus asks the chorus if anyone knows who this man was, or where he might be now. They respond that he is the same shepherd who was witness to the murder of Laius, and whom Oedipus had already sent for. Jocasta, who has by now realised the truth, desperately begs Oedipus to stop asking questions, but he refuses and Jocasta runs into the palace.

When the shepherd arrives Oedipus questions him, but he begs to be allowed to leave without answering further. Oedipus presses him however, finally threatening him with torture or execution. It emerges that the child he gave away was Laius's own son, and that Jocasta had given the baby to the shepherd to secretly be exposed upon the mountainside. This was done in fear of the prophecy that Jocasta said had never come true: that the child would kill its father.

Everything is at last revealed, and Oedipus curses himself and fate before leaving the stage. The chorus laments how even a great man can be felled by fate, and shortly afterwards a servant exits the palace to speak of what has happened inside. When Jocasta entered the house she ran to the palace bedroom and hanged herself there. Shortly afterwards Oedipus enters in a fury, calling on his servants to bring him a sword so that might kill himself. Oedipus then rages through the house until Oedipus comes upon Jocasta's body. Giving a cry, Oedipus takes her down and removes the long gold pins that held her dress together, before plunging them into his own eyes in despair.

A blind Oedipus now exits the palace and begs to be exiled as soon as possible. Creon enters, saying that Oedipus shall be taken into the house until oracles can be consulted regarding what is best to be done. Oedipus's two daughters (and half-sisters), Antigone and Ismene, are sent out and Oedipus laments that they should be born to such a cursed family. He asks Creon to watch over them and Creon agrees, before sending Oedipus back into the palace.

On an empty stage the chorus repeat the common Greek maxim, that no man should be considered fortunate until he is dead.

Relationship with the Mythic Tradition

The two cities of Troy and Thebes were the major focus of Greek epic poetry. The events surrounding the Trojan War were chronicled in the Epic Cycle, of which much remains, and those about Thebes in the Theban Cycle, which have been lost. The Theban Cycle recounted the sequence of tragedies that befell the house of Laius, of which the story of Oedipus is a part.

In Homer's Odyssey we get our earliest account of the Oedipus myth when Odysseus encounters Jocasta (named Epicaste) in the underworld. Homer briefly summarises the story of Oedipus, including the incest, patricide, and Jocasta's subsequent suicide. However in the Homeric version Oedipus remains King of Thebes after the revelation and neither blinds himself, nor is sent into exile. In particular, it is said that the gods made the matter known, whilst in Oedipus the King Oedipus very much discovers the truth himself.

In 467 BC, Sophocles's fellow tragedian Aeschylus won first prize at the City Dionysia with a trilogy about the House of Laius, comprising Laius, Oedipus and Seven against Thebes (the only play which survives). Since he did not write connected trilogies as Aeschylus did, Oedipus the King focuses on the titular character while hinting at the larger myth obliquely.

Fate and Free Will

Fate is a theme that often occurs in Greek writing, tragedies in particular. The inevitability of oracular predictions is one such example: it is predicted that Oedipus shall "kill his father and mate with his mother"; thus his parents order a servant to kill him. When he then hears the prophecy for himself, Oedipus leaves Corinth but, in fact, runs away from the wrong people. In running away, he crosses paths with his biological family, something which otherwise would never have occurred.

Two oracles in particular dominate the plot of Oedipus the King. In lines 711 to 714, Jocasta relates the prophecy that was told to Laius before the birth of Oedipus. Namely:

> (The oracle) told him that it was his fate that he should die a victim at the hands of his own son, a son to be born of Laius and me.

The oracle told to Laius tells only of the patricide; the incest is missing. Prompted by Jocasta's recollection, Oedipus reveals the prophecy which caused him to leave Corinth that he was fated to lie with his mother, and show to daylight an accursed breed which men would not endure, and was doomed to be murderer of the father that begot him.

The implication of Laius's oracle is ambiguous. A prominent school of thought argues that the presentation of Laius's oracle in this play differs from that found in Aeschylus's Oedipus trilogy produced in 467 BC. Helaine Smith argues:

> Sophocles had the option of making the oracle to Laius conditional (if Laius has a son, that son will kill him) or unconditional (Laius will have a son who will kill him). Both Aeschylus and Euripides write plays in which the oracle is conditional; Sophocles... chooses to make Laius's oracle unconditional and thus removes culpability for his sins from Oedipus, for he could not have done other than what he did, no matter what action he took.

This interpretation has a long pedigree and several adherents. It finds support in Jocasta's repetition of the oracle at lines 854-55: "Loxias declared that the king should be killed by/ his own son." In the Greek, Jocasta uses the verb chrênai: "to be fated, necessary." This iteration of the oracle seems to suggest that it was unconditional and inevitable. Other scholars have nonetheless argued that Sophocles follows tradition in making Laius's oracle conditional, and thus avoidable. They point to Jocasta's initial disclosure of the oracle at lines 711-14. In the Greek, the oracle cautions: hôs auton hexoi moira pros paidos thanein/ hostis genoit' emou te kakeinou para. The two verbs in boldface indicate what is called a "future more vivid" condition: if a child is born to Laius, his fate to be killed by that child will overtake him.

Whatever the meaning of Laius's oracle, the one delivered to Oedipus is clearly unconditional. Given our modern conception of fate and fatalism, readers of the play have a tendency to view Oedipus as a mere puppet controlled by greater forces, a man crushed by the gods and fate for no good reason. This, however, is not an entirely accurate reading. While it is a mythological truism that oracles exist to be fulfilled, oracles do not cause the events that lead up to the outcome. In his landmark essay "On Misunderstanding the Oedipus Rex", E.R. Dodds draws a comparison with Jesus's prophecy at the Last Supper that Peter would deny him three times. Jesus knows that Peter will do this, but we as readers would in no way suggest that Peter was a puppet of fate being forced to deny Christ. Free will and predestination are by no means mutually exclusive, and such is the case with Oedipus.

The oracle delivered to Oedipus what is often called a "self-fulfilling prophecy", in that the prophecy itself sets in motion events that conclude with its own fulfilment. This, however, is not to say that Oedipus is a victim of fate and has no free will. The oracle inspires a series of specific choices, freely made by Oedipus, which lead him to kill his father and marry his mother. Oedipus chooses not to return to Corinth after hearing the oracle, just as he chooses to head toward Thebes, to kill Laius, to marry and to take Jocasta specifically as his bride; in response to the plague at Thebes, he chooses to send Creon to the Oracle for advice and then to follow that advice, initiating the investigation into Laius's murder. None of these choices is predetermined.

Another characteristic of oracles in myth is that they are almost always misunderstood by those who hear them; hence Oedipus's misunderstanding the significance of the Delphic Oracle. Oedipus visits Delphi to find out who his real parents are and assumes that the Oracle refuses to answer that question, offering instead an unrelated prophecy which forecasts patricide and incest. Oedipus's assumption is incorrect: the Oracle does answer his question. Stated less elliptically, the answer to his question reads thus:

Literal and metaphorical references to eyesight appear throughout Oedipus the King. Clear vision serves as a metaphor for insight and knowledge, but the clear-eyed Oedipus is blind to the truth about his origins and inadvertent crimes. The prophet Tiresias, on the other hand, although literally blind, "sees" the truth and relays what is revealed to him. Only after Oedipus has physically blinded himself does he gain a limited prophetic ability, as seen in Oedipus at Colonus.

Oedipus comes to the conclusion that he murdered his father and married his mother. While generally viewed as true, recent interpretation suggests this may not be the case. The argument hinges on Oedipus failing to clarify with the shepherd that he was in fact the murderer.

2

Classical Latin Literature

The period of Classical Latin, when Latin literature is widely considered to have reached its peak, is divided into the Golden Age, which covers approximately the period from the start of the 1st century BC up to the mid-1st century AD, and the Silver Age, which extends into the 2nd century AD. Literature written after the mid-2nd century has often been disparaged and ignored; in the Renaissance, for example, when many Classical authors were re-discovered and their style consciously imitated. Above all, Cicero was imitated, and his style praised as the pinnacle of Latin style. Medieval Latin was often dismissed as inferior; but in fact, many great works of Latin literature were produced throughout Late Antiquity and the Middle Ages, although they are no longer as widely known as those written in the Classical period. Three works survived to inspire architects and engineers in the Renaissance, the Naturalis Historia of Pliny the Elder, the books by Frontinus on the aqueducts of Rome and the De Architectura of Vitruvius.

Ancient Rome was a civilization that grew out of a small agricultural community founded on the Italian Peninsula as early as the 10th century BC. Located along the Mediterranean Sea, it became one of the largest empires in the ancient world. In its centuries of existence, Roman civilization shifted from a monarchy to an oligarchic republic to an increasingly autocratic empire.. It came to dominate South-Western Europe, South-Eastern Europe/Balkans and the Mediterranean region through conquest and assimilation.

Plagued by internal instability and attacked by various migrating peoples, the western part of the empire, including Italy, Hispania, Gaul, Britannia and Africa broke up into independent kingdoms in the 5th century AD.

The Eastern Roman Empire, which was governed from Constantinople, comprising Greece, the Balkans, Asia Minor, Syria and Egypt, survived this crisis. Despite the later loss of Syria and Egypt to the Arab Islamic Empire, the Eastern Roman Empire would live on for another millennium, until its last remains were finally annexed by the emerging Turkish Ottoman Empire. This eastern, Christian, medieval stage of the Empire is usually referred to as the Byzantine Empire by historians.

Roman civilization is often grouped into "classical antiquity" with ancient Greece, a civilization that inspired much of the culture of ancient Rome. Ancient Rome contributed greatly to the development of law, war, art, literature, architecture, technology, religion, and language in the Western world, and its history continues to have a major influence on the world today.

Life in ancient Rome revolved around the city of Rome, located on seven hills. The city had a vast number of monumental structures like the Colosseum, the Forum of Trajan and the Pantheon. It had fountains with fresh drinking-water supplied by hundreds of miles of aqueducts, theatres, gymnasiums, bath complexes complete with libraries and shops, marketplaces, and functional sewers. Throughout the territory under the control of ancient Rome, residential architecture ranged from very modest houses to country villas. In the capital city of Rome, there were imperial residences on the elegant Palatine Hill, from which the word *palace* is derived. The low Plebian and middle Equestrian classes lived in the city center, packed into apartments, or Insulae which were almost like modern ghettos. These areas, often built by upper class landlords for the rental incomes collected, were often centred upon collegia or taberna. These people, provided by a free supply of grain, and entertained by gladatorial games, were enrolled as clients of patrons amongst the upper class Patricians, whose assistance they sought and whose interests they upheld.

Language

The native language of the Romans was Latin, an Italic language the grammar of which relies little on word order, conveying meaning through a system of affixes attached to word stems. Its alphabet was based on the Etruscan alphabet, which was in turn based on the Greek alphabet. Although surviving Latin literature consists almost entirely of Classical Latin, an artificial and highly stylized and polished literary language from the 1st century BC, the actual spoken language of the Roman Empire was Vulgar Latin, which significantly differed from Classical Latin in grammar and vocabulary, and eventually in pronunciation.

While Latin remained the main written language of the Roman Empire, Greek came to be the language spoken by the well-educated elite, as most of the literature studied by Romans was written in Greek. In the eastern half of the Roman Empire, which later became the Byzantine Empire, Latin was never able to replace Greek, and after the death of Justinian, Greek became the official language of the Byzantine government. The expansion of the Roman Empire spread Latin throughout Europe, and over time Vulgar Latin evolved and dialectized in different locations, gradually shifting into a number of distinct Romance languages.

Culture

Roman painting styles show Greek influences, and surviving examples are primarily frescoes used to adorn the walls and ceilings of country villas, though Roman literature includes mentions of paintings on wood, ivory, and other materials. Several examples of Roman painting have been found at Pompeii, and from these art historians divide the history of Roman painting into four periods. The first style of Roman painting was practiced from the early 2nd century BC to the early- or mid-1st century BC. It was mainly composed of imitations of marble and masonry, though sometimes including depictions of mythological characters. The second style of Roman painting began during the early 1st century BC, and attempted to depict realistically three-dimensional architectural features and landscapes. The third style occurred during the reign of Augustus (27 BC – 14 AD), and rejected the realism of the second style in favor of simple ornamentation. A small architectural scene, landscape, or abstract design was placed in the center with a monochrome background. The fourth style, which began in the 1st century AD, depicted scenes from mythology, while retaining architectural details and abstract patterns.

Portrait sculpture during the period utilized youthful and classical proportions, evolving later into a mixture of realism and idealism. During the Antonine and Severan periods, more ornate hair and bearding became prevalent, created with deeper cutting and drilling. Advancements were also made in relief sculptures, usually depicting Roman victories.

Latin literature was from its very inception influenced heavily by Greek authors. Some of the earliest extant works are of historical epics telling the early military history of Rome. As the Republic expanded, authors began to produce poetry, comedy, history, and tragedy.

Roman music was largely based on Greek music, and played an important part in many aspects of Roman life. In the Roman military, musical instruments such as the *tuba* (a long trumpet) or the *cornu* (similar to a French horn) were used to give various commands, while the *bucina* (possibly a trumpet or horn) and the *lituus* (probably an elongated J-shaped instrument), were used in ceremonial capacities. Music was used in the amphitheaters between fights and in the *odea,* and in these settings is known to have featured the *cornu* and the *hydraulis* (a type of water organ). The majority of religious rituals featured musical performances, with *tibiae* (double pipes) at sacrifices, cymbals and Tambourines at orgiastic cults, and rattles and hymns across the spectrum. Some music historians believe that music was used at almost all public ceremonies. Music historians are not certain if Roman musicians made a significant contribution to the theory or practice of music.The graffiti, brothels, paintings, and sculptures found in Pompeii and Herculaneum suggest that the Romans had a very sex-saturated culture.

Interest in studying ancient Rome arose during the Age of Enlightenment in France. Charles Montesquieu wrote a work *Reflections on the Causes of the Grandeur and Declension of the Romans.* The first major work was *The History of the Decline and Fall of the Roman Empire* by Edward Gibbon, which encompassed the period from the end of 2nd century to the fall of the Byzantine Empire in 1453. Like Montesquieu, Gibbon paid high tribute to the virtue of Roman citizens. Barthold Georg Niebuhr was a founder of the examination of ancient Roman history and wrote *The Roman History,* tracing the period until the First Punic war. Niebuhr made an attempt to determine the way the Roman tradition evolved. According to him, Romans, like other people, had an historical ethos which was preserved mainly in the noble families.

Ovid's Metamorphoses

The Metamorphoses by the Roman poet Ovid is a narrative poem in fifteen books that describes the creation and history of the world. Completed in 8 AD, it has remained one of the most popular works of mythology, being the Classical work best known to medieval writers and thus having a great deal of influence on medieval poetry.

Ovid works his way through his subject matter, often in an apparently arbitrary fashion, by jumping from one transformation tale to another, sometimes retelling what had come to be seen as central events in the world of Greek myth and sometimes straying in odd directions. The poem is often called a mock-epic.

It is written in dactylic hexameter, the form of the great heroic and nationalistic epic poems, both those of the ancient tradition (the Iliad and Odyssey) and of Ovid's own day (the Aeneid). It begins with the ritual "invocation of the muse," and makes use of traditional epithets and circumlocutions. But instead of following and extolling the deeds of a human hero, it leaps from story to story with little connection.

The recurring theme, as with nearly all of Ovid's work, is that of love—be it personal love or love personified in the figure of Amor (Cupid). Indeed, the other Roman gods are repeatedly perplexed, humiliated, and made ridiculous by Amor, an otherwise relatively minor god of the pantheon who is the closest thing this mock-epic has to a hero. Apollo comes in for particular ridicule as Ovid shows how irrational love can confound the god of pure reason. The work as a whole inverts the accepted order, elevating humans and human passions while making the gods and their desires and conquests objects of low humor.

Main episodes

- Book I: Cosmogony, Ages of Man, Gigantes, Daphne, Io;
- Book II: Phaëton, Callisto, Jupiter and Europa;
- Book III: Cadmus, Actaeon, Echo and Pentheus;
- Book IV: Pyramus and Thisbe, Perseus and Andromeda.
- Book V: Phineas, the Rape of Proserpina;
- Book VI: Arachne, Niobe, Philomela and Procne;
- Book VII: Medea, Cephalus and Procris;
- Book VIII: Nisos and Scylla, Daedalus and Icarus, Baucis and Philemon;

- Book IX: Heracles, Byblis;
- Book X: Eurydice, Hyacinth, Pygmalion, Adonis, Atalanta, Cyparissus;
- Book XI: Orpheus, Midas, Alcyone and Ceyx;
- Book XII: Iphigeneia, Centaurs, Achilles; Aesacus
- Book XIII: the Sack of Troy, Aeneas;
- Book XIV: Scylla, Aeneas, Romulus;
- Book XV: Pythagoras, Hippolytus, Aesculapius, Caesar.

The story of Coronis and Phoebus Apollo was adapted by Geoffrey Chaucer in the Canterbury Tales, where it forms the basis for the Manciple's tale.

The Metamorphoses was a considerable influence on English playwright William Shakespeare. Shakespeare's Romeo and Juliet is influenced by the story of Pyramus and Thisbe (Metamorphoses Book 4), and, in A Midsummer Night's Dream, a band of amateur actors performs a play about Pyramus and Thisbe. In Titus Andronicus the story of Lavinia's rape is drawn from Tereus' rape of Philomela, and the text of Metamorphoses is used within the play to enable Titus to interpret his daughter's story. Yet, most tellingly, Shakespeare adapts, with minor changes, a passage from Book 7 of the Golding translation into an important speech in Act V of the Tempest.

Ovid's Metamorphoses was an immediate success (although Quintilian considered Ovid's tragedy Medea his best work), its popularity threatening that of Virgil's Aeneid. So definitive a work on mythology was it considered that Seneca joked in his Apocolocyntosis that the deification of Claudius should be added to the Metamorphoses. But the poem's immense popularity in antiquity and the Middle Ages belies the struggle for survival it faced in late antiquity. "A dangerously pagan work," the Metamorphoses was fortunate to survive Christianisation, and the vitriolic voices of Augustine and Jerome, who believed the only metamorphosis worth reading about was the transubstantiation. Indeed an extremely concise, "inoffensive" prose summary of the poem ("a metamorphosis-free Metamorphoses") manufactured in late antiquity for Christian readers threatened to eclipse the poem itself. Though the Metamorphoses did not suffer the ignominious fate of the Medea, and survived, no ancient scholia on the poem survive (although they did exist in antiquity), and the earliest manuscript is very late, dating from the 11th century.

The poem retained its popularity throughout Late Antiquity and the Middle Ages, and is represented by an extremely high number of surviving manuscripts (more than 400); the earliest of these are three fragmentary copies containing portions of Books 1-3, dating to the ninth century. Collaborative editorial effort has been investigating the various manuscripts of Metamorphoses, some forty-five complete texts or substantial fragments, all deriving from a Gallic archetype. The result of several centuries of critical reading is that the poet's meaning is firmly established on the basis of the manuscript tradition or restored by conjecture where the tradition is deficient. There are two modern critical editions: William S. Anderson's, first published in 1977 in the Teubner series, and R. J. Tarrant's, published in 2004 by the Oxford Clarendon Press.

Virgil's Aeneid

The Aeneid is a Latin epic poem written by Virgil in

the late 1st century BC (29-19 BC) that tells the legendary story of Aeneas, a Trojan who traveled to Italy, where he became the ancestor of the Romans. It is composed of roughly 12,000 lines in dactylic hexameter. The first six of the poem's twelve books tell the story of Aeneas' wanderings from Troy to Italy, and the poem's second half tells of the Trojans' ultimately victorious war upon the Latins, under whose name Aeneas and his Trojan followers are destined to be subsumed.

The hero Aeneas was already known to Greco-Roman legend and myth, having been a character in the Iliad; Virgil took the disconnected tales of Aeneas' wanderings, his vague association with the foundation of Rome and a personage of no fixed characteristics other than a scrupulous piety, and fashioned this into a compelling founding myth or nationalist epic that at once tied Rome to the legends of Troy, glorified traditional Roman virtues and legitimised the Julio-Claudian dynasty as descendants of the founders, heroes and gods of Rome and Troy.

Story

The Aeneid can be divided into two halves based on the disparate subject matter of Books 1-6 (Aeneas' journey to Italy) and Books 7-12 (the war in Italy). These two halves are commonly regarded as reflecting Virgil's ambition to rival Homer by treating both the Odyssey's wandering theme and the Iliad's warfare themes. This is, however, a rough correspondence the limitations of which should be borne in mind.

Journey to Italy (books 1-6)

Virgil begins his poem with a statement of his theme (Arma virumque cano..., "I sing of arms and of the man...") and an invocation to the Muse, falling some ten lines after the poem's inception: (Musa, mihi causas memora..., "O Muse, recount to me the causes..."). Virgil then explains the reason for the principal conflict in the story: the resentment held by the goddess Juno against the Trojan people. This is consistent with her role throughout the Homeric epics.

Also in the manner of Homer, the story proper begins in medias res, with the Trojan fleet in the eastern Mediterranean, heading in the direction of Italy. The fleet, led by Aeneas, is on a voyage to find a second home. It has been foretold that in Italy, he will give rise to a race both noble and courageous, a race which will become known to all nations. Juno is wrathful, because she had not been chosen in the judgment of Paris against Aeneas's mother Venus, and because her favorite city, Carthage, will be destroyed by Aeneas' descendants. Also, Ganymede, a Trojan prince, was chosen to be the god's cup bearer-replacing Juno's daughter Hebe. Juno proceeds to Aeolus, King of the Winds, and asks that he release the winds to stir up a storm in exchange for a bribe (Deiopea, the loveliest of all the sea nymphs, as a wife). Aeolus agrees, and the storm devastates the fleet. Neptune takes notice: although he himself is no friend of the Trojans, infuriated by Juno's intrusion into his domain, and stills the winds and calms the waters. The fleet takes shelter on the coast of Africa. There, Aeneas's mother, Venus, in the form of a hunting woman very similar to the goddess Diana, encourages him and tells him the history of the city. Eventually, Aeneas ventures in, and in the temple of Juno, seeks and gains the favor of Dido, Queen of Carthage, the city which has only recently been founded by refugees from Tyre and which will later become one of Rome's greatest enemies.

At a banquet given in the honour of the Trojans, Aeneas recounts sadly the events which occasioned the Trojans' fortuitous arrival. Aeneas begins the tale shortly after the events described in the Iliad. Crafty Ulysses devised a way for Greek warriors to gain entry into Troy by hiding in a large wooden horse. The Greeks pretended to sail away, leaving a man, Sinon, to tell the Trojans that the horse was an offering and that if it were taken into the city, the Trojans would be able to conquer Greece. The Trojan priest Laocoön, who had seen through the Greek plot and urged the horse's destruction, hurled his spear at the wooden horse. Just after, in what would be seen by the Trojans as punishment from the gods, Laocoön was suddenly grabbed and eaten, along with his two sons, by two giant sea snakes. So the Trojans brought the horse inside the fortified walls, and after nightfall the armed Greeks emerged and began to slaughter the city's inhabitants. Aeneas woke up and saw with horror what was happening to his beloved city. At first he tried to fight against the enemy, but soon he lost his comrades and was left alone to fend off tens of Greeks. Hector,the fallen Trojan prince,tells him to flee with his family. Aeneas tells of his escape with his son Ascanius and father Anchises, his wife Creusa having been separated from the others and subsequently killed in the general catastrophe. Aeneas tells how rallying the other survivors, Aeneas built a fleet of ships and made landfall at various locations in the Mediterranean, notably Aenea in Thrace, Pergamea in Crete, and Buthrotum in Epirus. This last had been built in an attempt to replicate Troy. In Buthrotum, Aeneas met Andromache, the widow of Hector. She still laments for the loss of her valiant husband and beloved child. There, too, Aeneas saw and met Helenus, one of Priam's sons, who had the gift of prophecy. Through him, Aeneas learned the destiny laid out for him: he was divinely advised to seek out the land of Italy (also known as Ausonia or Hesperia), where his descendants would not only prosper, but in time rule the entire known world. In addition, Helenus also bade him go to the Sibyl in Cumae. Heading out into the open sea, Aeneas left Buthrotum, first making landfall in Italy at Castrum Minervae, but continuing on towards the west coast of the peninsula. While in the open sea, Anchises, the father of Aeneas, peacefully died. The fleet had rounded Sicily and was making for the mainland, when Juno raised up the storm which drove it back across the sea to Carthage.

Meanwhile, Venus has her own plans. She goes to her son, Aeneas' half-brother Cupid, and tells him to imitate Ascanius. Disguised as such, he goes to Dido, and offers the gifts expected from a guest. With her motherly love revived in the sight of the boy, her heart is pierced and she falls in love with the boy and his father. During the banquet, Dido realises that she has fallen madly in love with Aeneas, although she had previously sworn fidelity to the soul of her late husband, Sychaeus, who had been murdered by her cupidinous brother Pygmalion. Juno seises upon this opportunity to make a deal with Venus, Aeneas' mother, with the intention of distracting him from his destiny of founding a city in Italy. Aeneas is inclined to return Dido's love, and during a hunting expedition, a storm drives them into a cave in which Aeneas and Dido presumably have sex, an event that Dido takes to indicate a marriage between them. But when Jupiter sends Mercury to remind Aeneas of his duty, he has no choice but to part. Her heart broken, Dido commits suicide by stabbing herself upon a pyre with Aeneas' sword. Before dying, she predicts eternal strife between Aeneas's people and hers; "rise up from my bones, avenging spirit" is an obvious invocation to Hannibal. However, destiny calls and the Trojan fleet sails on to Italy.

Aeneas's father Anchises having been hastily interred on Sicily during the fleet's previous landfall there, the Trojans returned to the island to hold funeral games in his honour. Eventually, the fleet lands on the mainland of Italy and the quest enters a new phase. Aeneas, with the guidance of the Cumaean Sibyl, descends into the underworld through an opening at Cumae; there he speaks with the spirit of his father and has a prophetic vision of the destiny of Rome. Upon returning to the land of the living, Aeneas leads the Trojans to settle in the land of Latium, where he courts Lavinia, the daughter of king Latinus.

War in Italy (books 7-12)

Although Aeneas would have wished to avoid it, war eventually breaks out. Juno is heavily involved in causing this war-she convinces the Queen of Latium to demand that Lavinia be married to Turnus, the king of a local people, the Rutuli. Juno continues to stir up trouble, even summoning the Fury Alecto to ensure that a war takes place.

Seeing the masses of Italians that Turnus has brought against him, Aeneas seeks help from the Tuscans, enemies of Turnus. Aeneas meets King Evander from Arcadia, whose son Pallas agrees to lead troops against the other Italians. Meanwhile, the Trojan camp is being attacked, and a midnight raid leads to the deaths of Nisus and his companion Euryalus, in one of the most emotional passages in the book. The gates, however, are defended until Aeneas returns with his Tuscan and Arcadian reinforcements.

In the battling that follows, many heroes are killed, notably Pallas, who is killed by Turnus, and Mezentius, Turnus' close associate who inadvertently allows his son to be killed while he himself flees; he reproaches himself and faces Aeneas in single combat-an honourable but essentially futile pursuit. Another notable hero, Camilla, a sort of Amason character, fights bravely but is eventually killed. Camilla had been a virgin devoted to Diana and to her nation; the man who killed her was struck dead by Diana's sentinel Opis after doing so, even though he tried to escape.

After this, single combat is proposed between Aeneas and Turnus, but Aeneas was so obviously superior that the Italians, urged on by Turnus' divine sister, Juturna, break the truce. Aeneas is injured, but returns to the battle shortly afterwards. Turnus and Aeneas dominate the battle on opposite wings, but when Aeneas makes a daring attack at the city of Latium itself, he forces Turnus into single combat once more. In a dramatic scene, Turnus' strength deserts him as he tries to hurl a rock, and he is struck by Aeneas' spear in the leg. As Turnus is begging on his knees for his life, the poem ends with Aeneas killing him in rage when he sees that Turnus is wearing the belt of his friend Pallas as a trophy.

History

The Aeneid was written in a time of major political and social change in Rome, with the fall of the

Republic and the Final War of the Roman Republic having torn through society and many Romans' faith in the "Greatness of Rome" severely faltering. However, the new emperor, Augustus Caesar, began to institute a new era of prosperity and peace, specifically through the re-introduction of traditional Roman moral values. In addition, the Aeneid attempted to legitimise the rule of Julius Caesar (and by extension, of his adopted son Augustus and his heirs) by renaming Aeneas' son, Ascanius (called Ilus from Ilium, meaning Troy), Iulus and offering him as an ancestor of the gens Julia, the family of Julius Caesar, and many other great imperial descendants as part of the prophecy given to him in the Underworld.

Despite the polished and complex nature of the Aeneid (legend stating that Virgil wrote only three lines of the poem each day), the number of half-complete lines and the abrupt ending are generally seen as evidence that Virgil died before he could finish the work. It is common, however, for epic poems to contain incomplete, disputed, or badly adulterated text,[dubious—discuss] and because this poem was composed and preserved in writing rather than orally, the Aeneid is more complete than most classical epics. Furthermore, it is possible to debate whether Virgil intended to rewrite and add to such lines. Some of them would be difficult to complete, and in some instances, the brevity of a line increases its dramatic impact (some arguing the violent ending as a typically Virgilian comment on the darker, vengeful side of humanity). However, these arguments may be anachronistic-half-finished lines might equally, to Roman readers, have been a clear indication of an unfinished poem and have added nothing whatsoever to the dramatic effect.

The perceived deficiency of any account of Aeneas' marriage to Lavinia or his founding of the Roman race led some writers, such as the fifteenth-century Italian poet Maffeo Vegio (through his Mapheus Vegius widely printed in the Renaissance), Pier Candido Decembrio (whose attempt was never completed), and Claudio Salvucci (in his 1994 epic poem The Laviniad) to compose their own supplements.

Some legends state that Virgil, fearing that he would die before he had properly revised the poem, gave instructions to friends (including the current emperor, Augustus) that the Aeneid should be burned upon his death, owing to its unfinished state and because he had come to dislike one of the sequences in Book VIII, in which Venus and Vulcan have sexual intercourse, for its nonconformity to Roman moral virtues. The friends did not comply with Virgil's wishes and Augustus himself ordered that they be disregarded. After minor modifications, the Aeneid was published.

The first full and faithful rendering of the poem in an Anglic language is the Scots translation by Gavin Douglas-his Eneados, completed in 1513, which also included Maffeo Vegio's supplement. Even in the twentieth century, Ezra Pound considered this still to be the best Aeneid translation, praising the "richness and fervour" of its language and its hallmark fidelity to the original. The English translation by the 17th-century poet John Dryden is another important version that can be said to retain the power and flow of the original, although Dryden took numerous, significant liberties with the text. Most classic translations, including both Douglas and Dryden, employed a rhyme scheme, a very non-Roman convention that is not usually followed in modern versions.

Recent English verse translations include those by British Poet Laureate C Day Lewis (1963) which strove to render Virgil's original hexameter line, Allen Mandelbaum (honoured by a 1973 National Book Award), Library of Congress Poet Laureate Robert Fitzgerald (1981), Stanley Lombardo (2005), and Robert Fagles (2006).

Style

The Aeneid, like other classical epics, is written in dactylic hexameter, meaning that each line has six feet made up of dactyls, or one long syllable and two shorts, and spondees, or two long syllables. As with other classical Latin poetry, the meter is based on the length of syllables rather than the stress, though the interplay of meter and stress is also important. Virgil also incorporated such poetic devices as alliteration, onomatopoeia, synecdoche, and assonance.

Time

The Aeneid makes several references to its timing. It is mentioned that following the destruction of Troy, Aeneas spent six years wandering the Mediterranean before meeting Dido, and it is later mentioned that on his arrival in Sicily from Carthage that seven years have now passed since the end of Troy. Unfortunately the age of Aeneas's son, Ascanius, cannot provide a clue to the sequence of events; in Book 4, for example, he is pictured both as participating in the hunt, and being impersonated by Cupid as a child in the arms of Dido, shooting arrows into her heart. During Book 4, however there is an indirect reference to a timeline. It is stated that Dido and Aeneas were together through the long winter, implying that Aeneas and his crew must have only stayed in Carthage for the winter, before they heeded Jupiter's message sent by Mercury to leave Carthage.

Pietas, possibly the key quality of any 'honorable' Roman, consisted of a series of duties: duty towards the gods (hence the English word piety), duty towards one's homeland, duty towards one's followers and duty to one's family-especially one's father. Therefore, a further theme of the poem explores the strong relationship between fathers and sons. The bonds between Aeneas and Ascanius, Aeneas and Anchises, Evander and Pallas, Mezentius and Lausus are all worthy of note. This theme reflects Augustan moral reforms and was perhaps intended to set an example for Roman youth.

The major moral of the Aeneid is acceptance of the workings of the gods as fate through the use of pietas or piety. In composing the character of Aeneas, Virgil alludes to Augustus, suggesting that the gods work their ways through humans, using Aeneas to found Rome and Augustus to lead it, and that one must accept one's fate.

Allegory

The most debated theories with regard to the Aeneid involve whether Virgil meant to convey a so-called "hidden message" or allegory within the poem. The first section in question is:

> There are two gates of Sleep, one said to be of horn, whereby the true shades pass with ease, the other all white ivory agleam without a flaw, and yet false

> dreams are sent through this one by the ghost to the upper world. Anchises now, his last instructions given, took son and Sibyl and let them go by the Ivory Gate.

Aeneas's exiting of the underworld through the gate of false dreams has been variously interpreted: One suggestion is that the passage simply refers to the time of day at which Aeneas returned to the world of the living; another is that it implies that all of Aeneas's actions in the remainder of the poem are somehow "false." In an extension of the latter interpretation, it has been suggested that Virgil is conveying that the history of the world since the foundation of Rome is but a lie. Other scholars claim that Virgil is establishing that the theological implications of the preceding scene (i.e. an apparent system of reincarnation) are not to be taken as literal.

The second section in question is:

> Then to his glance appeared the accurst swordbelt surmounting Turnus' shoulder, shining with its familiar studs-the strap Young Pallas wore when Turnus wounded him and left him dead upon the field; now Turnus bore that enemy token on his shoulder-enemy still. For when the sight came home to him, Aeneas raged at the relic of his anguish worn by this man as trophy. Blazing up and terrible in his anger, he called out: "You in your plunder, torn from one of mine, shall I be robbed of you? This wound will come from Pallas: Pallas makes this offering, and from your criminal blood exacts his due." He sank his blade in fury in Turnus' chest ...

It has been interpreted to mean that for the entire passage of the poem, Aeneas who symbolises pietas (reason) in a moment becomes furor (fury), thus destroying what is essentially the primary theme of the poem itself. Many have argued over these two sections. Some claim that Virgil meant to change them before he died, while others find that the location of the two passages, at the very end of the so-called Volume I (Books 1-6, the Odyssey), and Volume II (Books 7-12, the Iliad), and their short length, which contrasts with the lengthy nature of the poem, are evidence that Virgil placed them purposefully there.

Influence

The Aeneid has long been considered a fundamental member of the Western canon. As a result, many phrases from this poem entered the Latin language, much as passages from Shakespeare and Alexander Pope have entered the English language. One example is from Aeneas' reaction to a painting of the sack of Troy: Sunt lacrimae rerum et mentem mortalia tangunt-"These are the tears of things, and our mortality cuts to the heart.". The influence is also visible in very modern work: Brian Friel's Translations (a play written in the 1980s, set during the English colonisation of Ireland), makes references to the classics throughout and ends with a passage from the Aeneid:

> "Urbs antiqua fuit-there was an ancient city which, 'tis said, Juno loved above all the lands. And it was the goddess's aim and cherished hope that here should be the capital of all nations-should the fates perchance allow that. Yet in truth she discovered that a race was springing from Trojan blood to overthrow some day these Tyrian towers-a people late regem belloque superbum-kings of broad realms and proud in war who would come forth for Libya's downfall."

3

Classical Sanskrit Literature

Sanskrit literature came into being with the making of Vedas and left a rich legacy of literary knowledge for the times to come. However, the language of the Vedas differs from the language used in poetry and drama. Classical Sanskrit literature is found to be in vogue when it comes to writing poetry and dance dramas. This form of classic literature in Sanskrit is a huge contribution in the field of literary knowledge. Sanskrit poetry is different from Vedic poetry. Read on further about literature in classical Sanskrit and check our related sections on Sanskrit plays and Sanskrit poetry.

Sanskrit drama evolved as early as 2nd century B.C. Shudraka, the great Sanskrit writer wrote the earliest play in Sanskrit Mricchakatika around this time. The central theme of these dramas and plays used to be based on heroic tales of the protagonist. The Natya Shastra, which was written by Bharata, literally means the Science of Theater. It contained all the essential elements that go into making a successful dance drama. Other famous dramatists are Kalidasa, Bhasa, Asvaghosa, etc.

Classical Sanskrit poetry is a varied genre and has many forms of poetry in it. The most famous examples of epic poetry are Ramayana and Mahabharata, the two epics that are held in high reverence by Indians. Romantic poetry was given a boost during the time of Kalidasa, the great poet of India. The epics poems can be recited as well as sung. Thus, one can say that classical music also started from classical Sanskrit literature. Classic literature in Sanskrit is indeed a valuable treasure of Indian cultural heritage.

Plays

Mricchakatika

One of the earliest known Sanskrit plays, this play is thought to have been composed by Zhudraka in the 2nd century BC. Rife with romance, sex, royal intrigue and comedy, the juicy plot of the play has numerous twists and turns. The main story is about a young man named Charudatta, and his love for Vasantasena, a rich courtesan or nagarvadhu. The love affair is complicated by a royal courtier, who is also attracted to Vasantasena. The plot is further complicated by thieves and mistaken identities, and thus making it a greatly hilarious and entertaining play. It invited widespread admiration when staged in New York in 1924. The play was made into a 1984 Hindi movie *Utsav*, directed by Girish Karnad. The Indian play depicted in the film *Moulin Rouge!* may have been based on *The Little Clay Cart*.

Vikramorvasiyam

Vikramorvasiyam is a Sanskrit play by medieval Indian poet Kalidasa, on the Vedic love story of king Pururavas and celestial nymph Urvashi. The "Vikram" of the title is Chandragupta who adopted the title "Vikramaditya", meaning "valiant as the Sun" – the name is chosen here to allude to how Pururavas reflects the qualities of Chandragupta.

King Pururavas falls in love with a celestial nymph named Urvashi. After writing her mortal suitor a love letter on a birch leaf, Urvashi returns to the heavens to perform in a celestial play. However, she is so smitten that she misses her cue and pronounces her lover's name during the performance. As a punishment for ruining the play, Urvashi is banished from heaven, but cursed to return the moment her human lover lays eyes on the child that she will bear him. After a series of mishaps, including Urvashi's temporary transformation into a vine, the curse is eventually lifted, and the lovers are allowed to remain together on Earth.

Mlavikagnimitram

Mlavikagnimitram is a Sanskrit play by Klidsa. It is his first play.The play tells the story of the love of King Agnimitra, the Shunga king of Vidisha, for the beautiful hand-maiden of his chief queen. He falls in love with the picture of an exiled servant girl named Mlavik. When the queen discovers her husband's passion for this girl, she becomes infuriated and has Mlavik imprisoned, but as fate would have it, in the end she is discovered to be of royal birth and is accepted as one of his queens.

The play contains an account of the Rajasuya sacrifice performed by Pushyamitra, and an elaborate exposition of a theory on music and acting.

Abhijñnashakuntalam

Abhijñnashkuntala or Abhijñnashakuntalam is a well-known Sanskrit play by Klidsa. Its date is uncertain, but Kalidasa is often placed in the period between the 1st century BC and 4th century AD. The Sanskrit name means "pertaining to abhi-jñâna-Zakuntal", which means "token-recognized-Zakuntal", so a literal translation could be Of Zakuntal recognized by a token.

Although Kalidasa makes some minor changes to the plot, the play elaborates upon an episode mentioned in the *Mahabharata*. The protagonist is Shakuntala, daughter of the sage Vishwamitra and the apsaras Menaka. Abandoned at birth by her parents, Shakuntala is reared in the secluded, sylvan hermitage of the sage Kanva, and grows up a comely but innocent maiden.

While Kanva and the other elders of the heritage are away on a pilgrimage, Dushyanta, king of Hastinapura, comes hunting in the forest and chances upon the hermitage. He is captivated by Shakuntala, courts her in royal style, and marries her. He then has to leave to take care of affairs in the capital. She is given a ring by the king, to be presented to him when she appears in his court. She can then claim her place as queen.

The anger-prone sage Durvasa arrives when Shakuntala is lost in her fantasies, so that when she fails to attend to him, he curses her by bewitching Dushyanta into forgetting her existence. The only cure is for Shakuntala to show him the signet ring that he gave her.

She later travels to meet him, and has to cross a river. The ring is lost when it slips off her hand when she dips her hand in the water playfully. On arrival the king refuses to acknowledge her. Shakuntala is abandoned by her companions, who return to the hermitage. Fortunately, the ring is discovered by a fisherman in the belly of a fish, and Dushyanta realises his mistake - too late. The newly wise Dushyanta defeats an army of Titans, and is rewarded by Indra with a journey through the Hindu heaven. Returned to Earth years later, Dushyanta finds Shakuntala and their son by chance, and recognizes them.

Classical Fables

Panchatantra

The Panchatantra was originally a canonical collection of Sanskrit as well as Pali animal fables in verse and prose. The original Sanskrit text, now long lost, and which some scholars believe was composed in the 3rd century BCE, is attributed to Vishnu Sarma. However, based as it is on older oral traditions, its antecedents among storytellers probably hark back to the origins of language and the subcontinent's earliest social groupings of hunting and fishing folk gathered around campfires. It is "certainly the most frequently translated literary product of India" and there are over 200 versions in more than 50 languages.

Origins, content and function

The work is an ancient and vigorous multicultural hybrid that to this day continues an erratic process of cross-border mutation and adaptation as modern writers and publishers struggle to fathom, simplify and re-brand its complex origins.

One of the early Western scholars on the Panchatantra was Dr. Johannes Hertel who viewed the book as having a Machiavellian character. Other scholars dismiss this assessment as one-sided, and even view the stories as teaching dharma, or proper moral conduct. It illustrates, for the benefit of princes who may succeed to a throne, the central Hindu principles of *Raja niti* (political science) through an inter-woven series of colorful animal tales. These operate like a succession of Russian dolls, one narrative opening within another, sometimes three or four deep.

Each distinct part of the book contains (as Professor Edgerton noted in 1924) "at least one story, and usually more, which are 'emboxed' in the main story, called the 'frame-story'. Sometimes there is a double emboxment; another story is inserted in an 'emboxed' story. Moreover, the [whole] work begins with a brief introduction, which as in a frame all five... [parts] are regarded as 'emboxed'". Vishnu Sarma's idea was that humans can assimilate more about their own habitually unflattering behavior if it is disguised in terms of entertainingly configured stories about supposedly less illustrious beasts than themselves.

Another observation that Professor Edgerton makes challenges our persistent assumption that animal fables function mainly as adjuncts to religious dogma, acting as indoctrination devices to condition the moral behaviour of small children and obedient adults. Not the Machiavellian Panchatantra: "Vishnu Sarma undertakes," Edgerton notes, "to instruct three dull and ignorant princes in the principles of polity, by means of stories....[This is] a textbook of *artha*, 'worldly wisdom', or *niti*, polity, which the Hindus regard as one of the three objects of human desire, the other being *dharma*, 'religion or morally proper conduct' and *kama* 'love'.... The so-called 'morals' of the stories have no bearing on morality; they are unmoral, and often immoral. They glorify shrewdness, practical wisdom, in the affairs of life, and especially of politics, of government."

This realistic practicality explains why the original Sanskrit villain jackal, the decidedly jealous, sneaky and evil vizier-like Damanaka ('Victor') is his frame-story's winner, and not his goody-goody brother Karataka who is presumably left 'Horribly Howling' at the vile injustice of Part One's final murderous events. In fact, in its steady migration westward the persistent theme of evil-triumphant in *Kalila and Dimna*, Part One frequently outraged Jewish, Christian and Muslim religious leaders — so much so, indeed, that Ibn al-Muqaffa carefully inserts (no doubt hoping to pacify the powerful religious zealots of his own turbulent times) an entire extra chapter at the end of Part One of his Arabic masterpiece, putting Dimna in jail, on trial and eventually to death.

Needless to say there is no vestige of such dogmatic moralising in the collations that remain to us of the pre-Islamic original — *The Panchatantra*. Technically, from the perspective of a more subtle and flexible functionality, Joseph Jacobs in 1888 offers a less coercive interpretation of how the *Panchatantra/Kalila and Dimna* stories might work more effectively to modify human behaviour:... *if one thinks of it, the very* raison d'être *of the Fable is to imply its moral without mentioning it.*

In short the learning opportunity is interactive, voluntary, dynamic, reflective, open, frustrating and risky — compared to the simplified, fixed and often terrifyingly authoritative lessons delivered from priestly heights that briefly excite and amuse, then are soon forgotten, like electric shocks. In such circumstance (which is the norm) the human animal is conditioned to respond to the approved socialising, tagline 'message' of a local time-and-culture-bound 'moral', and prevented from glimpsing anything objective beyond it at an individual pace.

Basic plot of each chapter

Throughout its history, the book has been translated into many languages and several new chapters were added. Here, all chapters included in the subsequent translations from the Arabic version are listed. It must be also noted that the Arabic titles were included, and where appropriate, the Sanskrit ones too between brackets.

Chapter 1: The Lion and the Bull (Mitra Bhedha)

The first chapter deals with the jackal Dimna gaining favor with the lion (pictured as the king of all animals) and climbing the ranks rapidly, and the subsequent plot by the jackal to bring down the bull who also grew very close to the king, out of pure jealousy. The plot succeeds and the bull is murdered by the lion unjustly.

Moral: One must not accuse others falsely, and strive to preserve friendships.

Chapter 2: Investigating Dimna

This chapter, which was later included by Ibn El-Mougafa', tells of the trial of Dimna the jackal after he is suspected of intentionally leading to the death of the bull "shanzabeh" who is mentioned in the first chapter. The trial lasts for 2 days to no avail, until the tiger and the leopard come forward and accuse Dimna. He is subsequently put to rest.

Moral: Truth is bound to be revealed, sooner or later.

Chapter 3: The Captured Pigeon

One of the original chapters, it is the second chapter in the original book. It tells of the story of the crow who upon seeing the favour the rat performed to free the pigeon and her companions, decides to befriend the rat despite the latter's initial objections. The storyline evolves as this friendship grows to include the turtle and the fawn. They collaborate to save the fawn when he is trapped, and later they work together to save the turtle, who herself, falls in the trap. *Moral*: Friends are an integral part of life.

Chapter 4: The Owl and the Crows

The third chapter in the original book, and not unlike chapter 1 deals with deceit and glorifies it to a certain extent as it deals with the crow who pretends to be an outcast from his own group to gain entry into the rival owl group, and by doing so gains access to their secrets and learns of their vulnerabilities. He later summons his group of crows to set fire on all entrances to the cave where the owls live and suffocate them to death.

Moral: Mental strength and deceit are stronger than brute force.

Chapter 5: The Monkey and Alghlim

It deals with the artificially-constructed symbiotic relationship between the monkey and the Alghlim. Alghlim risked the relationship by conspiring to acquire the heart of the monkey to heal his wife, the monkey finds out about this and avoids this grim fate.

Moral: One must never betray friends, and should stay vigilant at all times.

Chapter 6: The hermit and the weasel

Originally the last chapter of the book, it deals with hermit who leaves his child with a weasel friend of his, and upon returning and finding blood on the weasel's mouth, he kills it. He later finds out that the weasel actually defended his son, and killed a snake that attempted to kill the boy.

Moral: One must never rush in making judgments.

Early cross-cultural migrations

The *Panchatantra* approximated its current literary form within the 4th – 6th centuries CE. No Sanskrit texts before 1000 CE have survived. According to Indian tradition, it was written around 200 BCE by Pandit Vishnu Sarma, a sage. One of the most influential Sanskrit contributions to world literature, it was exported (probably both in oral and literary formats) north to Tibet and China and east to South East Asia by Buddhist monks on pilgrimage.

According to the *Shahnameh* (*The Book of the Kings,* Persia's late 10th century national epic by Ferdowsi) the *Panchatantra* also migrated westwards, during the Sassanid reign of Khosru I Anushiravan around 570 CE when his famous physician Borzuy translated it from Sanskrit into the Middle Persian language, transliterated for Europeans as *Karirak ud Damanak* or *Kalile va Demne.*

How Two Jackals (in Part One) Branded This (five-part) Book

Karataka ('Horribly Howling') and Damanaka ('Victor') are the Sanskrit names of two jackals in the first section of the *Panchatantra*. They are retainers to a lion king and their lively adventures as well as the stories they and other characters tell one another make up roughly 45% of the book's length. By the time the Sanskrit version has migrated several hundred years through Pahlavi into Arabic, the two jackals' names have transmogrified into Kalila and Dimna, and – probably because of a combination of first-mover advantage, Dimna's charming villainy and that dominant 45% bulk – their single part/section/chapter has become the generic, classical name for the whole book. It is possible, too, that the Sanskrit word 'Panchatantra' as a Hindu concept could find no easy equivalent in Zoroastrian Pahlavi.

How Borzuy brought the Kalila from Hindustan

Initially Borzuy sought his king's permission to make a trip to Hindustan in search of a mountain herb he had read about that is "mingled into a compound and, when sprinkled over a corpse, it is immediately restored to life." The Shah gave his permission, equipped Borzuy fully for the journey and handed over to him a number of gifts, together with a letter for the Rāy of India, whom he requested to assist the physician in his search. On his arrival in Hindustan he was received with high honor and granted all facility for his task, including a retinue of local physicians to guide him on his way.

But when Borzuy locates and prepares the miraculous mountain herb and sprinkles it over various corpses provided for his experiments, alas – the magic potion does not work. He is distressed at his failure and angry at the false information that has led him so far astray, not to mention afraid of the shame which will descend upon him if he returns empty-handed to Persia and faces his king's displeasure. In desperation he asks the Indian physicians accompanying him what to do. Do they know anyone who can help him?

"With one voice they replied: 'There is an ancient sage here who surpasses us in years and wisdom and who in his science is superior to any of the great.'

"They guided Borzuy to this man, whose mind was filled with contemplation and whose lips were ever ready for speech. Borzuy laid all his trials before him, speaking of the book which he had discovered and the words which he had heard from men expert in knowledge. When the ancient sage began to speak he discoursed on every branch of science.

Modern adaptions

Recently Ibn al-Muqaffa's historical milieu itself, when composing his masterpiece in Baghdad during the bloody Abbasid overthrow of the Umayyad dynasty, has become the subject (and rather confusingly, also the title) of a gritty Shakespearean drama by the multicultural Kuwaiti playwright Sulayman Al-Bassam. Ibn al-Muqqafa's biographical background serves as an illustrative metaphor for today's escalating bloodthirstiness in Iraq — once again a historical vortex for clashing civilizations on a multiplicity of levels, including the obvious tribal, religious and political parallels.

Al-Bassam's imaginative modern work entitled *Kalila wa Dimna,* while provocative and educational, is technically a misnomer. There is only one brief play-within-a-play tableau that genuflects towards the actual telling any of the animal fables found in the Arabic original. Understandably this contradictory nuance (where are al-Muqaffa's classic fables?), obvious and even irritatingly puzzling to any literate Middle Easterner, appears to have been intellectualized away by some Eurocentric commentators. The English literary equivalent would be attending a play called *Hard Times* expecting to see something of the characters Grandgrind and Bounderby only to find yourself immersed in an imaginary biography of Charles Dickens and the social turmoil of his day, with only a three minute confrontational drawing-room scene alluding to a certain Mr Grandgrind and his part in the horrors of Victorian factory conditions and child labor.

Yet in the prevailing belief system of the Western post-modernist world, anything goes. Every expression achieves legitimacy. This tolerant climate is ideally suited to the book's *sui generis* flexibility. Any attempt to re-brand the *Panchatantra* or *Kalila and Dimna* or *The Fables of Bidpai* for the utilitarian Western consciousness, while at the same time avoiding cultural chauvinism, proves elusive and fanciful.

The persistent trend, for more than a hundred years and often encouraged by scholars defending their fields of literary expertise, is to select and promote a single ancient 'source text' as the 'true classic material', whether it be in Sanskrit, Syriac, Arabic or Persian, and ignore, even denigrate, the other three sources. Such behaviour can reach the extreme of one expert within a single language seemingly dismissing the contribution of another, as occurred in the 1990s when two English versions of the *Panchatantra* translated from separate Sanskrit manuscripts were published independently as 'classics' of Indian Wisdom by (a) Penguin and (b) Oxford

University Press. To literate outsiders such prejudicing of texts can appear absurd, even deliberately confusing. "So which translated Sanskrit manuscript," one might ask, "offers the true *Panchatantra* classic?" And the answer, entering the purest realm of literary quantum reality, must be "Both!". And if we include the many Arabic, Syriac and Persian versions known under the various guises of *Kalila and Dimna* or *Fables of Bidpai* and the derivatives thereof, then we can immediately add a couple hundred more versions, all of them also 'classics', yet each with an individual treatment and arrangement in the voice of a different "singer of the song", delivering the goods somewhere in the last 2000 years.

The regional difficulty, as the novelist Doris Lessing says at the start of her introduction to Ramsay Wood's 1980 "retelling" of only the first two (*Mitra Bhedha*—The Loss of Friends & *Mitra Laabha*—Gaining Friends) of the five Panchatantra principles, is that ".... it is safe to say that most people in the West these days will not have heard of it, while they will certainly at the very least have heard of the *Upanishads* and the *Vedas*. Until comparatively recently, it was the other way around. Anyone with any claim to a literary education knew that the *Fables of Bidpai* or the *Tales of Kalila and Dimna* — these being the most commonly used titles with us — was a great Eastern classic. There were at least twenty English translations in the hundred years before 1888. Pondering on these facts leads to reflection on the fate of books, as chancy and unpredictable as that of people or nations."

Hitopadesha

Hitopadesha is a collection of Sanskrit fables in prose

and verse written in the 12 century C.E. It is an independent treatment of the *Panchatantra.*

The only clue to the identity of the author of *Hitopadesha* is found in the concluding verses of the work, which gives us the name Narayana and which mention the patronage of a king called Dhavalachandra. As no other work by this author is known, and since the ruler mentioned has not been traced in other sources, we know almost nothing of either of them. It seems likely that Narayana was a pandit and preceptor employed in Dhavalachandra's court. Since the invocatory and final verses evoke the god Shiva, he was most probably a Shaivite. Originally written in Sanskrit, the stories of his book have traveled to several parts of the world.

The book has many stories in common with the Panchatantra; it is believed that the author Narayana loved the Pachatantra so much that he rewrote it, improving the flow and adding stories of his own.

The work has been translated into most of the major languages of the world. After Sir William Jones, who had encountered it in 1786, announced his "discovery", it was translated into English by Charles Wilkins, who had made the earliest English translation of the Bhagavad Gita. An English translation by Sir Edwin Arnold, then Principal of Puna College, Pune, India, was published in London in 1861.

One of the most widely read Sanskrit books in India, *Hitopadesha* tales are short stories that have the priceless treasure of morality and knowledge. After Bhagavad Gita, *Hitopadesha* is considered to be the most sold religious text in India. The tales from *Hitopadesha* are written in a very logical and clear way and one does not have to make much effort to figure out what moral a particular story is implying. The stories feature animals and birds as main characters.

Hitopadesha basically means to counsel or advice with benevolence. The author of *Hitopadesha,* Narayana says that the main purpose of creating the *Hitopadesha* is to instruct young minds in a way that they learn the philosophy of life and are able to grow into responsible adults. The stories are very interesting and youngsters not only find it interesting, but also accept it easily.

The *Hitopadesha* although similar in content and structure to the Panchatantra is more copious. It has been translated into many languages and has been circulated all around the world. It is very popular in many countries and is one of the most widely read children's book. Even in today's world, it continues to amaze people with its simple but meaningful stories and many people are still inspired by the tales of *Hitopadesha.* Its simplicity and logic is what makes it a favorite among children and their parents.

The *Hitopadesa* may thus be fairly styled "The Father of all Fables"; for from its numerous translations have come Esop and Pilpay, and in later days Reineke Fuchs. Originally compiled in Sanskrit, it was rendered, by order of Nushiraván, in the sixth century, A.D., into Persic. From the Persic it passed, A.D. 850, into the Arabic, and thence into Hebrew and Greek. In its own land it obtained as wide a circulation. The Emperor Akbar, impressed with the wisdom of its maxims and the ingenuity of its apologues, commended the work of translating it to his own minister Abdul Fazel. He accordingly put the book into a familiar style, and published it with explanations, under the title of the *Criterion of Wisdom.*

He followed the Emperor's suggestion that the incantions which often interrupt the narrative be abridged. To this day, in India, the *Hitopadesa*, under other names (as the Anvári Suhaili/1/, retains the delighted attention of young and old, and has some representative in all the Indian vernaculars.

Epical Poetry

The period between approximately the 6th to 1st centuries BC saw the composition and redaction of the two great epics, the *Mahabharata* and the *Ramayana*, with subsequent redaction progressing down to the 4th century AD. They are known as itihasa, or *"that which occurred"*.

Ramayana

The Ramayana is an ancient Sanskrit epic. It is attributed to the Hindu sage Valmiki and forms an important part of the Hindu canon. The Ramayana is one of the two great epics of India, the other being the *Mahabharata*. It depicts the duties of relationships, portraying ideal characters like the ideal servant, the ideal brother, the ideal wife and the ideal king.

The name *Ramayana* is a tatpurusha compound of *Rma* and *ayana* ("going, advancing"), translating to *"Rama's Journey"*. The Ramayana consists of 24,000 verses in seven books and 500 cantos (*sargas*), and tells the story of Rama (an incarnation of the Hindu preserver-god Vishnu), whose wife Sita is abducted by the demon king of Lanka, Ravana. Thematically, the epic explores the tenets of human existence and the concept of dharma.

Verses in the Ramayana are written in a 32-syllable meter called *anustubh*. The epic was an important influence on later Sanskrit poetry and Indian life and culture, particularly through its establishment of the shloka meter. Like its epic cousin the *Mahbhrata,* the Ramayana is not just an ordinary story: it contains the teachings of ancient Hindu sages and presents them in narrative allegory with philosophical and the devotional elements interspersed. The characters Rama, Sita, Lakshmana, Bharata, Hanuman and Ravana are all fundamental to the cultural consciousness of India.

There are other versions of the Ramayana, notably Buddhist (Dasaratha Jataka No. 461) and Jain in India, and also Thai, Laos, Burmese and Malaysian versions of the tale.

Textuality

Traditionally, the Ramayana is ascribed to Valmiki, regarded as India's first poet. The Indian tradition is unanimous in its agreement that the poem is the work of a single poet, the sage Valmiki, a contemporary of Rama and a peripheral actor in the epic drama. The story's original version in Sanskrit is known as *Valmiki Ramayana,* dating to approximately the 4th century B.C. According to Hindu tradition, the Ramayana takes place during a period of time known as Treta Yuga.

In its extant form, Valmiki's Ramayana is an epic poem of some 50,000 lines. The text survives in several thousand partial and complete manuscripts, the oldest of which appears to date from the 11th century A.D. The text has several regional renderings, recensions and subrecensions. Textual scholar Robert P. Goldman differentiates two major regional recensions: the northern (N) and the southern (S). Famous recensions include the *Ramayanam* of Kamban in Tamil (ca. 11th-

12th century), *Shri Rama Panchali* or *Krittivasi Ramayan* by Krittibas Ojha in Bengali, and *Ramacharitamanas* by Tulasidas in Awadhi which is a dialect of Hindi. Scholar Romesh Chunder Dutt writes that "the Ramayana, like the Mahabharata, is a growth of centuries, but the main story is more distinctly the creation of one mind."

There has been speculation as to whether the first and the last chapters of Valmiki's Ramayana were written by the original author. Raghunathan writes that many experts believe they are integral parts of the book in spite of some style differences and narrative contradictions between these two chapters and the rest of the book.

Period

According to literary scholarship, the main body of the Ramayana first appeared as an oral composition somewhere between 750 and 500 BCE. Cultural evidence (the presence of sati in the Mahabharata but not in the main body of the Ramayana) suggests that the Ramayana predates the Mahabharata. By tradition, the epic belongs to the Treta Yuga, one of the four eons (yuga) of Hindu chronology; thus, it is held to date back 880,000 years.

The core events of the epic may be of even greater age, as the names of the characters (Rama, Sita, Dasaratha, Janaka, Vasishta, Vishwamitra) are all known in Vedic literature such as the *Brahmanas* which are older than the Valmiki Ramayana. However, nowhere in the surviving Vedic poetry is a story similar to the Ramayana of Valmiki. According to the modern academic view, Brahma, one of the main characters of *Ramayana,* and Vishnu, who according to

Bala Kanda was incarnated as Rama, are not Vedic deities, and come first into prominence with the epics themselves and further during the 'Puranic' period of the later 1st millennium CE. There is also a version of Ramayana, known as Ramopakhyana, found in the epic *Mahabharata*. This version, depicted as a narration to Yudhishtra, does not accord divine characteristics to Rama.

There is general consensus that books two to six form the oldest portion of the epic while the first book *Bala Kanda* and the last the *Uttara Kanda* are later additions. The author or authors of *Bala Kanda* and *Ayodhya Kanda* appear to be familiar with the eastern Gangetic basin region of northern India and the Kosala and Magadha region during the period of the sixteen *janapadas* as the geographical and geopolitical data is in keeping with what is known about the region. However, when the story moves to the *Aranya Kanda* and beyond, it seems to turn abruptly into fantasy with its demon-slaying hero and fantastic creatures. The geography of central and South India is increasingly vaguely described. The knowledge of the location of the island of Sri Lanka also lacks detail. Basing his assumption on these features, the historian H.D. Sankalia has proposed a date of the 4th century BC for the composition of the text. A. L. Basham, however, is of the opinion that Rama may have been a minor chief who lived in the 8th or the 7th century BC.

Characters

Rama is the hero of the tale. Portrayed as the seventh incarnation of the god Vishnu, he is the eldest and favorite son of the King of Ayodhya, Dasharatha, and his wife Kousalya. He is portrayed as the epitome of virtue. Dasharatha is forced by Kaikeyi, one of his wives, to command Rama to relinquish his right to the throne for fourteen years and go into exile.

Sita is the beloved wife of Rama and the daughter of king Janaka. Sita is also known as Janaki. She is the incarnation of goddess Lakshmi, the consort of Vishnu. Sita is portrayed as the epitome of female purity and virtue. She follows her husband into exile and is abducted by Ravana. She is imprisoned on the island of Lanka until Rama rescues her by defeating the demon king Ravana. Later, she gives birth to Lava and Kusha, the heirs of Rama.

Hanuman is a vanara belonging to the kingdom of Kishkindha. He is portrayed as an incarnation of the god Shiva (the Eleventh Rudra) and an ideal *bhakta* of Rama. He is born as the son of Kesari, a vanara king, and the goddess Anjana. He plays an important part in locating Sita and in the ensuing battle.

Lakshmana, the younger brother of Rama, who chose to go into exile with him. He is portrayed as an incarnation of the Shesha, the nga associated with the god Vishnu. He spends his time protecting Sita and Rama. He is forced to leave Sita, who was deceived by the demon Maricha into believing that Rama was in trouble. Sita is abducted by Ravana upon him leaving her.

Ravana, a rakshasa, is the king of Lanka. After performing severe penance for ten thousand years he received a boon from the creator-god Brahma that he could not be killed by gods, demons or spirits. He is portrayed as a powerful demon king, who disturbs the penances of *Rishis.* Vishnu incarnates as the human Rama to defeat him, thus circumventing the boon given by Brahma.

Dasharatha is the king of Ayodhya and the father of Rama. He has three queens, Kousalya, Sumitra and Kaikeyi, and three other sons: Bharata, Lakshmana and Shatrughna. Kaikeyi, Dasharatha's favourite queen, forces him to make his son Bharata crown prince and send Rama into exile. Dasharatha dies heartbroken after Rama goes into exile.

Bharata is the son of Dasharatha. When he learns that his mother Kaikeyi had forced Rama into exile and caused Dasharatha to die brokenhearted, he storms out of the palace and goes in search of Rama in the forest. When Rama refuses to return from his exile to assume the throne, Bharata obtains Rama's sandals and places them on the throne as a gesture that Rama is the true king. Bharata then rules Ayodhya as the regent of Rama for the next fourteen years.

Shatrughna is the son of Dasharatha and his third wife Queen Sumitra. He is the youngest brother of Rama and also the twin brother of Lakshmana.

Synopsis

The poem is traditionally divided into several major *kandas* or books, that deal chronologically with the major events in the life of Rama—*Bala kanda, Ayodhya Kanda, Aranya Kanda, Kishkinda Kanda, Sundara Kanda, Yuddha Kanda,* and *Uttara Kanda*. The *Bala Kanda* describes the birth of Rama, his childhood and marriage to Sita. The *Ayodhya Kanda* describes the preparations for Rama's coronation and his exile into the forest. The third part, *Aranya Kanda,* describes the forest life of Rama and the kidnapping of Sita by the demon king Ravana. The fourth book, *Kishkinda Kanda,* describes the meeting of Hanuman with Rama, the destruction of the vanara king Vali and the coronation of his younger brother Sugriva to the throne of the kingdom of Kishkindha. The fifth book is *Sundara Kanda,* which narrates the heroism of Hanuman, his flight to Lanka and meeting with Sita. The sixth book, *Yuddha Kanda,* describes the battle between Rama's and Ravana's armies. The last book, *Uttara Kanda,* describes the birth of Lava and Kusha to Sita, their coronation to the throne of Ayodhya, and Rama's final departure from the world.

One of the most important literary works of ancient India, the Ramayana has had a profound impact on art and culture in the Indian subcontinent and Southeast Asia. The story ushered in the tradition of the next thousand years of massive-scale works in the rich diction of regal courts and Brahminical temples. It has also inspired much secondary literature in various languages, notably the Kambaramayanam by the Tamil poet Kambar of the 13th century, the Telugu-language Molla Ramayana, 14th century Kannada poet Narahari Kavi's Torave Ramayan, and 15th century Bengali poet Krittibas Ojha's Krittivasi Ramayan, as well as the 16th century Awadhi version, Ramacharitamanas, written by Tulsidas.

The Ramayana became popular in Southeast Asia during the 8th century and was represented in literature, temple architecture, dance and theatre. Today, dramatic enactments of the story of Ramayana, known as Ramlila, take place all across India and in many places across the globe within the Indian diaspora.

As in many oral epics, multiple versions of the Ramayana survive. In particular, the Ramayana related in North India differs in important respects from that preserved in South India and the rest of South-East

Asia. There is an extensive tradition of oral storytelling based on the Ramayana in Thailand, Cambodia, Malaysia, Laos, Vietnam, Indonesia and Maldives.Father Kamil Bulke, author of *Ramakatha*, has identified over 300 variants of Ramayana.

Mahabharata

The *Mahabhrata* is one of the two major Sanskrit epics of ancient India, the other being the *Rmyana*. The epic is part of the Hindu *itihsa* (or "history"). A major text of Hinduism and a cornerstone of Hindu mythology, it is of immense importance to the culture of the Indian subcontinent. Its consideration of human goals (*dharma* or duty, *artha* or purpose, *kma*, pleasure or desire and *moksha* or liberation) is part of a long-standing tradition which seeks to explain the relationship of the individual to society and the world (the nature of the 'Self') and the workings of karma.

Traditionally, the authorship of the *Mahabharata* is attributed to Vyasa. There have been many attempts to unravel its historical growth and compositional layers. The origins of the text's core narrative may be a struggle for control of the upper Ganges and Yamuna as part of the eastern migration of the Aryans, in the late Vedic period (ca. 8th c. BCE). The earliest parts of the extant text, on the other hand, are not appreciably older than around 400 BCE. The text probably reached its final form by the early Gupta period (ca. 4th c. CE). The title may be translated as "the great tale of the Bhrata dynasty". According to the *Mahabharata* itself, the tale is extended from a shorter version of 24,000 verses, called simply *Bharata'*.

With about one hundred thousand verses, long prose passages, and about 1.8 million words in total, the *Mahabharata* is the longest epic poem in the world. It is roughly ten times the length of the *Iliad* and *Odyssey* combined, roughly five times longer than Dante's *Divine Comedy,* and about four times the length of the *Ramayana.*

Besides its epic narrative of the Kurukshetra War and the fates of the Kauravas and the Pandavas, the *Mahabharata* contains much philosophical and devotional material, such as the Shrimad Bhagavad Gita (6.25-42) which has a very high level of philosophical and religious content, or a discussion of the four "goals of life" or *purusharthas* (12.161). The latter are enumerated as *dharma* (right action), *artha* (purpose), *kama* (pleasure), and *moksha* (liberation). Among the principal works and stories that are a part of the *Mahabharata* are the following:

- the Bhagavad Gita in book 6 (Bhishmaparva): Krishna advises and teaches Arjuna when he is ridden with doubt.
- the story of Damayanti, sometimes called (Nala and Damayanti) in book 3 (Aranyakaparva), a love story.
- An abbreviated version of the Ramayana, in book 3 (Aranyakaparva)
- Rishyasringa, the horned boy and rishi, in book 3 (Aranyakaparva)

Arshia Sattar states that the central theme of the Mahabharata, as well as the Ramayana, is respectively Krishna's and Ram's hidden divinity and its progressive revelation.

Textual History and Structure

The epic is traditionally ascribed to Vyasa, who is also

a major character in the epic. The first section of the *Mahabharata* states that it was Ganesha who, at the request of Vyasa, wrote down the text to Vyasa's dictation. Ganesha is said to have agreed to write it only on condition that Vyasa never pause in his recitation. Vyasa agreed, provided Ganesha took the time to understand what was said before writing it down.

The epic employs the story within a story structure, otherwise known as frametales, popular in many Indian religious and secular works. It is recited to the King Janamejaya who is the great-grandson of Arjuna, by Vaisampayana, a disciple of Vyasa. The recitation of Vaisampayana to Janamejaya is then recited again by a professional storyteller named Ugrasrava Sauti, many years later, to an assemblage of sages.

It is usually thought that the full length of the *Mahabharata* has accreted over a long period. Research on the *Mahabharata* has put an enormous effort into recognizing and dating various layers within the text. The *Mahabharata* itself distinguishes a core portion of 24,000 verses, the *Bharata* proper, as opposed to additional secondary material, while the *Ashvalayana Grhyasutra* makes a similar distinction. According to the *Adi-parva* of the *Mahabharata* (shlokas 81, 101-102), the text was originally 8,800 verses when it was composed by Vyasa and was known as the *Jaya* (Victory), which later became 24,000 verses in the *Bharata* recited by Vaisampayana, and finally over 90,000 verses in the *Mahabharata* recited by Ugrasrava Sauti.

The state of the text has been described by some early 20th century Indologists as unstructured and chaotic. Hermann Oldenberg (1922) supposed that the original poem must once have carried an immense "tragic force", but dismissed the full text as a "horrible chaos."

The earliest known references to the *Mahabharata* and its core *Bharata* date back to the *Ashtadhyayi* (sutra 6.2.38) of Panini, and in the *Ashvalayana Grhyasutra* (3.4.4). This may suggest that the core 24,000 verses, known as the *Bharata,* as well as an early version of the extended *Mahabharata,* were composed by the 4th century BCE.

The Mahabharata is presumed to predate the Greek epic Iliad, and some episodes of the Mahabharata are syncretistically said to identify with the story of the Iliad. Christian Lassen, in his *Indische Alterthumskunde,* supposed that the reference is ultimately to Dhritarashtra's sorrows, the laments of Gandhari and Draupadi, and the valor of Arjuna and Duryodhana or Karna. This interpretation, endorsed in such standard references as Albrecht Weber's *History of Indian Literature,* has often been repeated.

Later, the copper-plate inscription of the Maharaja Sharvanatha (533-534) from Khoh (Satna District, Madhya Pradesh) describes the *Mahabharata* as a "collection of 100,000 verses" (*shatasahasri samhita*). The redaction of this large body of text was carried out after formal principles, emphasizing the numbers 18 and 12. The addition of the latest parts may be dated by the absence of the *Anushasana-parva* from *MS Spitzer,* the oldest surviving Sanskrit philosophical manuscript dated to the first century, that contains among other things a list of the books in the *Mahabharata.* From this evidence, it is likely that the redaction into 18 books took place in the first century.

An alternative division into 20 parvas appears to have co-existed for some time. The division into 100 sub-parvas (mentioned in Mbh. 1.2.70) is older, and most parvas are named after one of their constituent sub-parvas. The *Harivamsa* consists of the final two of the 100 sub-parvas, and was considered an appendix (*khila*) to the *Mahabharata* proper by the redactors of the 18 parvas

The Adi-parva includes the snake sacrifice (*sarpasattra*) of Janamejaya, explaining its motivation, detailing why all snakes in existence were intended to be destroyed, and why in spite of this, there are still snakes in existence. This *sarpasattra* material was often considered an independent tale added to a version of the *Mahabharata* by "thematic attraction" (Minkowski 1991), and considered to have particularly close connection to Vedic (Brahmana) literature, in particular the Panchavimsha Brahmana which describes the *sarpasattra* as originally performed by snakes, among which are snakes named Dhrtarashtra and Janamejaya, two main characters of the *Mahabharata's sarpasattra,* and Takshaka, the name of a snake also in the *Mahabharata*. The Shatapatha Brahmana gives an account of an Ashvamedha performed by Janamejaya Parikshit.

According to what one character says at Mbh. 1.1.50, there were three versions of the epic, beginning with *Manu* (1.1.27), *Astika* (1.3, sub-parva 5) or *Vasu* (1.57), respectively. These versions would correspond to the addition of one and then another 'frame' settings of dialogues. The *Vasu* version would omit the frame settings and begin with the account of the birth of Vyasa. The *astika* version would add the *sarpasattra* and *ashvamedha* material from Brahmanical **literature**, introduce the name *Mahabharata,* and identify Vyasa as the work's author. The redactors of these additions were probably Pancharatrin scholars who according to Oberlies (1998) likely retained control over the text until its final redaction. Mention of the Huna in the *Bhishma-parva* however appears to imply that this parva may have been edited around the 4th century.

Synopsis

The core story of the work is that of a dynastic struggle for the throne of Hastinapura, the kingdom ruled by the Kuru clan. The two collateral branches of the family that participate in the struggle are the Kaurava and the Pandava. Although the Kaurava is the senior branch of the family, Duryodhana, the eldest Kaurava, is younger than Yudhisthira, the eldest Pandava. Both Duryodhana and Yudhisthira claim to be first in line to inherit the throne.

The struggle culminates in the great battle of Kurukshetra, in which the Pandavas are ultimately victorious. The battle produces complex conflicts of kinship and friendship, instances of family loyalty and duty taking precedence over what is right, as well as the converse. The *Mahabharata* itself ends with the death of Krishna, and the subsequent end of his dynasty and ascent of the Pandava brothers to heaven. It also marks the beginning of the Hindu age of Kali (Kali Yuga), the fourth and final age of mankind, in which great values and noble ideas have crumbled, and man is heading toward the complete dissolution of right action, morality and virtue

The older generations

Janamejaya's ancestor Shantanu, the king of Hastinapura, has a short-lived marriage with the goddess Ganga and has a son, Devavrata (later to be called Bhishma), who becomes the heir apparent. Many years later, when King Shantanu goes hunting, he sees Satyavati, the daughter of a fisherman, and asks her father for her hand. Her father refuses to consent to the marriage unless Shantanu promises to make any future son of Satyavati the king upon his death. To resolve his father's dilemma, Devavrata agrees to relinquish his right to the throne. As the fisherman is not sure about the prince's children honouring the promise, Devavrata also takes a vow of lifelong celibacy to guarantee his father's promise.

Shantanu has two sons by Satyavati, Chitrangada and Vichitravirya. Upon Shantanu's death, Chitrangada becomes king. He lives a very short uneventful life and dies. Vichitravirya, the younger son, rules Hastinapura. Meanwhile, the King arranges a swayamvara for his three daughters, neglecting to invite the royal family of Hastinapur. In order to arrange the marriage of young Vichitravirya, Bhishma attends the swayamvara of the three princesses Amba, Ambika and Ambalika, uninvited, and proceeds to abduct them. Ambika and Ambalika consent to be married to Vichtravirya.

The oldest princess Amba, however, informs Bhishma that she wishes to marry Shalvaraj (king of Shalva) whom Bhishma defeated at their swayamvar. Bhishma lets her leave to marry Shalvaraj, but Shalvaraj refuses to marry her, still smarting at his humiliation at the hands of Bhishma. Amba then returns to marry Bhishma but he refuses due to his vow of celibacy. Amba becomes enraged and becomes Bhishma's bitter enemy, holding him responsible for her plight. Later she is reborn to King Drupada as

Shikhandi (or Shikhandini) and causes Bhishma's fall, with the help of Arjuna, in the battle of Kurukshetra.

The Pandava and Kaurava princes

When Vichitravirya dies young without any heirs, Satyavati asks her first son Vyasa to father children with the widows. The eldest, Ambika, shuts her eyes when she sees him, and so her son Dhritarashtra is born blind. Ambalika turns pale and bloodless upon seeing him, and thus her son Pandu is born pale and unhealthy (the term Pandu may also mean 'jaundiced'). Due to the physical challenges of the first two children, Satyavati asks Vyasa to try once again. However, Ambika and Ambalika send their maid instead, to Vyasa's room. Vyasa fathers a third son, Vidura, by the maid. He is born healthy and grows up to be one of the wisest characters in the *Mahabharata*. He serves as Prime Minister (Mahamantri or Mahatma) to King Pandu and King Dhritarashtra.

When the princes grow up, Dhritarashtra is about to be crowned king by Bhishma when Vidura intervenes and uses his knowledge of politics to assert that a blind person cannot be king. This is because a blind man cannot control and protect his subjects. The throne is then given to Pandu because of Dhritarashtra's blindness. Pandu marries twice, to Kunti and Madri. Dhritarashtra marries Gandhari, a princess from Gandhara, who blindfolds herself so that she may feel the pain that her husband feels. Her brother Shakuni is enraged by this and vows to take revenge on the Kuru family. One day, when Pandu is relaxing in the forest, he hears the sound of a wild animal. He shoots an arrow in the direction of the sound. However the arrow hits the sage Kindama, who curses him that if he engages in a sexual act, he will die. Pandu then retires to the forest along with his two wives, and his brother Dhritarashtra rules thereafter, despite his blindness.

Pandu's older queen Kunti, however, had been given a boon by Sage Durvasa that she could invoke any god using a special mantra. Kunti uses this boon to ask Dharma the god of justice, Vayu the god of the wind, and Indra the lord of the heavens for sons. She gives birth to three sons, Yudhisthira, Bhima, and Arjuna, through these gods. Kunti shares her mantra with the younger queen Madri, who bears the twins Nakula and Sahadeva through the Ashwini twins. However, Pandu and Madri indulge in sex, and Pandu dies. Madri dies on his funeral pyre out of remorse. Kunti raises the five brothers, who are from then on usually referred to as the Pandava brothers.

Dhritarashtra has a hundred sons through Gandhari, all born after the birth of Yudhishtira. These are the Kaurava brothers, the eldest being Duryodhana, and the second Dushasana. Other Kaurava brothers were Vikarna and Sukarna. The rivalry and enmity between them and the Pandava brothers, from their youth and into manhood, leads to the Kurukshetra war.

The House of Lac

After the deaths of their mother (Madri) and father (Pandu), the Pandavas and their mother Kunti return to the palace of Hastinapur. Yudhisthira is made Crown Prince by Dhritarashtra, under considerable pressure from his kingdom. Dhritarashtra wanted his own son Duryodhana to become king and lets his ambition get in the way of preserving justice.

Shakuni, Duryodhana and Dusasana plot to get rid of the Pandavas. Shakuni calls the architect Purvanchan to build a palace out of flammable materials like lac and ghee. He then arranges for the Pandavas and the Queen Mother Kunti to stay there, with the intention of setting it alight. However, the Pandavas are warned by their wise uncle, Vidura, who sends them a miner to dig a tunnel. They are able to escape to safety and go into hiding. Back at Hastinapur, the Pandavas and Kunti are presumed dead.

Marriage to Draupadi

During the course of their hiding the Pandavas learn of a swayamvara which is taking place for the hand of the Pñcla princess Draupadi. The Pandavas enter the competition in disguise as Brahmins. The task is to string a mighty steel bow and shoot a target on the ceiling, which is the eye of a moving artificial fish, while looking at its reflection in oil below. Most of the princes fail, many being unable to lift the bow. Arjuna succeeds however. The Pandavas return home and inform their mother that Arjuna has won a competition and to look at what they have brought back. Without looking, Kunti asks them to share whatever it is Arjuna has won among themselves. Thus Draupadi ends up being the wife of all five brothers.

Indraprastha

After the wedding, the Pandava brothers are invited back to Hastinapura. The Kuru family elders and relatives negotiate and broker a split of the kingdom, with the Pandavas obtaining a new territory. Yudhishtira has a new capital built for this territory at Indraprastha which is now Delhi. Neither the Pandava nor Kaurava sides are happy with the arrangement however.

Shortly after this, Arjuna elopes with and then marries Krishna's sister, Subhadra. Yudhishtira wishes to establish his position as king; he seeks Krishna's advice. Krishna advises him, and after due preparation and the elimination of some opposition, Yudhishthira carries out the *rjaskya yagna* ceremony; he is thus recognised as pre-eminent among kings.

The Pandavas have a new palace built for them, by Maya the Danava. They invite their Kaurava cousins to Indraprastha. Duryodhana walks round the palace, and mistakes a glossy floor for water, and will not step in. After being told of his error, he then sees a pond, and assumes it is not water and falls in. Draupadi laughs at him and ridicules him by saying that this is because of his blind father Dhritrashtra. He then decides to avenge his humiliation.

The dice game

Shakuni, Duryodhana's uncle, now arranges a dice game, playing against Yudhishtira with loaded dice. Yudhishtira loses all his wealth, then his kingdom. He then even gambles his brothers, himself, and finally his wife into servitude. The jubilant Kauravas insult the Pandavas in their helpless state and even try to disrobe Draupadi in front of the entire court, but her honour is saved by Krishna who miraculously creates lengths of cloth to replace the ones being removed.

Dhritarashtra, Bhishma, and the other elders are aghast at the situation, but Duryodhana is adamant that there is no place for two crown princes in Hastinapura. Against his wishes Dhritarashtra orders for another dice game. The Pandavas are required to go into exile for 12 years, and in the 13th year must remain hidden. If discovered by the Kauravas, they will be forced into exile for another 12 years.

Exile and return

The Pandavas spend thirteen years in exile; many adventures occur during this time. They also prepare alliances for a possible future conflict. They spend their final year in disguise in the court of Virata, and are discovered just after the end of the year. At the end of their exile, they try to negotiate a return to Indraprastha. However, this fails, as Duryodhana objects that they were discovered while in hiding, and that no return of their kingdom was agreed. War becomes inevitable.

The battle at Kurukshetra

The two sides summon vast armies to their help, and line up at Kurukshetra for a war. The Kingdoms of Panchala, Dwaraka, Kasi, Kekaya, Magadha, Matsya, Chedi, Pandya, Telinga, and the Yadus of Mathura and some other clans like the Parama Kambojas were allied with the Pandavas. The allies of the Kauravas included the kings of Pragjyotisha, Anga, Kekaya, Sindhudesa (including Sindhus, Sauviras and Sivis), Mahishmati, Avanti in Madhyadesa, Madra, Gandhara, Bahlikas, Kambojas and many others. Prior to war being declared, Balarama, had expressed his unhappiness at the developing conflict, and left to go on pilgrimage, thus he does not take part in the battle itself. Krishna takes part in a non-combatant role, as charioteer for Arjuna.

Before the battle, Arjuna, seeing himself facing his great grandfather Bhishma and his teacher Drona on the other side, has doubts about the battle and he fails to lift his Gndeeva bow. Krishna wakes him up to his call of duty in the famous Bhagavad Gita section of the epic. Though initially sticking to chivalrous notions of warfare, both sides soon adopt dishonourable tactics. At the end of the 18-day battle, only the Pandavas, Satyaki, Kripa, Ashwathama, Kritavarma, Yuyutsu and Krishna survive.

The end of the Pandavas

After "seeing" the carnage, Gandhari who had lost all her sons, curses Krishna to be a witness to a similar annihilation of his family, for though divine and capable of stopping the war, he had not done so. Krishna accepts the curse, which bears fruit 36 years later.

The Pandavas who had ruled their kingdom meanwhile, decide to renounce everything. Clad in skins and rags they retire to the Himalaya and climb towards heaven in their bodily form. A stray dog travels with them. One by one the brothers and Draupadi fall on their way. As each one stumbles, Yudhishitra gives the rest the reason for their fall (Draupadi was partial to Arjuna, Nakula and Sahadeva were vain and proud of their looks, Bhima and Arjuna were proud of their strength and archery skills, respectively). Only the virtuous Yudhisthira, who had tried everything to prevent the carnage, and the dog remain. The dog reveals himself to be the god Yama (also known as Yama Dharmaraja), and then takes him to the underworld where he sees his siblings and wife. After explaining the nature of the test, Yama takes Yudhishtira back to heaven and explains that it was necessary to expose him to the underworld because (Rajyante narakam dhruvam) any ruler has to visit the underworld at least once. Yama then assures him that his siblings and wife would join him in heaven after they had been exposed to the underworld for measures of time according to their vices.

Arjuna's grandson Parikshit rules after them and dies bitten by a snake. His furious son, Janamejaya, decides to perform a snake sacrifice (*sarpasattra*) in order to destroy the snakes. It is at this sacrifice that the tale of his ancestors is narrated to him.

Versions, translations, and derivative works

Many regional versions of the work developed over time, mostly differing only in minor details, or with verses or subsidiary stories being added. These include some versions from outside the Indian subcontinent, such as the Kakawin Bharatayuddha from Java. The plays of the Tamil street theatre, terukkuttu, use themes from the Tamil language versions of Mahabharata, focusing on Draupadi.

The Five *Mahkavyas*

This refers to the poetry produced from the approximately the 3rd to 8th centuries. Klidsa is the foremost example of a classical poet.

But a striking characteristic of Indian literary tradition is that sometimes poets show off their technical dexterity with highly Oulipian word-games, like stanzas that read the same backwards and forwards, words that can be split in different ways to produce different meanings, sophisticated metaphors, and so on. This style is referred to as Kavya. A classic example is the poet Bharavi and his magnum opus, the Kiratarjuniya (6th-7th century). Magh is noted for his epic poem (mahAkAvya) Shishupala Vadha, the 20 cantos of which are based on the Mahabharata episode where the defiant king Shishupala is beheaded by Krishna's chakra (disc)

The greatest works of poetry in this period are the five *Mahkavyas*, or great compositions:

— *Kumrasambhava* by Klidsa
— *Raghuvamsha* by Klidsa
— *Kiratarjuniya* by Bharavi
— *Shishupala Vadha* by Mgha
— *Naishadha-Charita* by Sriharsha

Some scholars include the Bhattikavya as a sixth Mahkavya.

Other major literary works from this period are *Kadambari* by Banabhatta, the first Sanskrit novelist (6th-7th centuries), the Kama Sutra by Vatsyayana, and the three *shatakas* of Bharthari.

Raghuvamsa

Kalidasa's Raghuvamsha tells the story of the family of Dileepa and his descendants, including the conqueror Raghu. The warrior Raghu leads a military expedition to Transoxiana. He defeats and subjugates local peoples along the way (presumably on his march through Central Asia) until he reaches the Vankshu, as the ancient Indians called the Oxus River. There, Raghu's army battles the Hepthalites, or White Huns, whom the Indians called Hunas and Mlecchas (barbarians). The Hepthalites are defeated, and the Raghuvamsha boasts of "The exploits of Raghu, whose valor expressed itself amongst the husbands of the Huna women, became manifest in the scarlet color of their cheeks."

The 6th century Gothic (or Alanic) historian Jordanes wrote that the Western Huns, upon the death of Attila, "disfigured their faces horribly, with deep wounds, so that the gallant warrior should be mourned not with the lamentations and tears of women, but with the blood of men." A similar custom was observed among the Kutrigurs, Turks, Magyars, and Tajiks.

After crossing the Oxus, Raghu and his army encountered the Kambojas, an ancient Indo-Scythian people often mentioned in Indian texts. The Kambojas submitted to Raghu and offered him gifts and treasures. Evidently, the Kambojas dwelt in the vicinity of the Pamirs. Kalidasa describes the preponderance of walnut trees in the Oxus country, this particular region is still known for the cultivation of walnuts.

Kumrasambhava

Kumrasambhava is an Sanskrit epic poem written by the illustrious poet Klidsa. It is one of the most important examples of Kavya poetry.

Kumrasambhava literally means "Birth of Kumara", i.e. Kartikeya. This epic of seventeen cantos entails Shringara Rasa, the rasa of love, romance, and eroticism, more than Vira rasa (the rasa of heroism). Tarakasur, a rakshasha (or demon) was blessed that he could be killed by none other than Lord Shiva's son, however, Shiva had won over Kama-deva (the god of love). Parvati performed great tapasya (or spiritual penance) to win the love of Lord Shiva. Consequently, Shiva and Parvati's son Kartikeya is born and kills Tarakasur to restore the glory of Indra, the king of Gods.

Klidsa had left his home in pursuit of knowledge and to become worthy of his intellectual wife Vidyottama (lit. "epitome of erudition"). When he returned from this conquest, his wife asked, "Asti Kashchit Wagvisheshah" ("Have you attained any evident erudition which should prompt me to extend a special welcome to you?") Klidsa impressed his wife with the answer she expected and over the next few years created three great epics based on the three letters uttered by his wife: 'Asti' - Kumarasambhava, 'Kashchit' - Meghaduta, and 'Wagvisheshah' - Raghuvamsha. It is said that Klidsa was cursed with leprosy when he completed the eighth canto describing the act of love between Lord Shiva and Parvati. Some also believe that the rest of the epic was completed by an eponymous writer.

Meghaduta

Meghaduta is a lyric poem written by Klidsa, considered to be one of the greatest Sanskrit poets. A short poem of only 111 stanzas, it is one of Klidsa's most famous works. It recounts how a yakca, a subject of King Kubera (the god of wealth) after being exiled for a year to Central India for some unknown transgression, convinces a passing cloud to take a message to his wife on Mount Kailsa in the Himlaya mountains. The yakca accomplishes this by describing the many beautiful sights the cloud will see on its northward course to the city of Alak, where his wife awaits his return. In 1813, the poem was first translated into English by Horace Hayman Wilson. An excerpt is quoted in Canadian director Deepa Mehta's film, Water. The poem was also the inspiration for Gustav Holst's 'The Cloud Messenger Op. 30' (1909-10).Kirtrjuniya

Kiratarjuniya

Kiratarjuniya is a Sanskrit *kavya* by Bhravi, written in the 6th century or earlier. It is an epic poem in eighteen cantos describing the combat between Arjuna and lord Shiva in the guise of a *kirta* or mountain-dwelling hunter. Along with the *Naicadhacarita* and the *Ziuplavadha,* it is considered to be one of the three best among the six Sanskrit *mahakavyas,* or great epics.

The *Kiratarjuniya* predominantly features the *Vaia rasa,* or the mood of valour., and expands upon a minor episode in the *Vana Parva* ("Forest book") in the *Mahabharata.* While the Pandavas are exiled in the forest, Draupadi and Bhima incite Yudhisthira to declare war with the Kauravas, while he does not relent. Finally, Arjuna, at the instruction of Indra, propitiates Lord Shiva with penance (*tapasya*) in the forest. Pleased by his austerities, Lord Shiva decides to reward him. When a demon named Muka, in the form of a wild boar, charges toward Arjuna, Shiva appears in the form of a Kirta, a wild mountaineer. Arjuna and the Kirta simultaneously shoot an arrow at the boar, and kill it. They argue over who shot first, and a battle ensues. They fight for a long time, and Arjuna is shocked that he cannot conquer this Kirta. Finally, he recognises the god, and surrenders to him. Shiva, pleased with his bravery, gives him the powerful weapon, the Pashupatastra, which later in the *Mahabharata* aids him against Karna and the Kauravas during the Kurukshetra war.

Over a tenth of the verses from this work are quoted in various anthologies and works on poetics. The most popular verse is the 37th from the eighth canto, which describes nymphs bathing in a river, and is noted for its beauty. Another verse from the fifth canto (*utphulla sthalanalini...*) is noted for its imagery, and has given Bharavi the sobriquet of "Chhatra Bharavi", as he describes the pollen of the lotus flowers being blown by the wind into a golden umbrella (*Chhatra*) in the sky. Thus, for having verses that are pleasing to lay people as well as clever verses appreciated by scholars, the work is considered to have 'harmony' or 'appropriateness' at all levels, and has been said to possess *samastalokarañjakatva,* the quality of delighting all the people.

The *Kirtrjuniya* is the only known work of Bharavi. It "is regarded to be the most powerful poem in the Sanskrit language". A. K. Warder considers it the "most perfect epic available to us", over Avaghoca's *Buddhacarita,* noting its greater force of expression, with more concentration and polish in every detail. Despite using extremely difficult language and rejoicing in the finer points of Sanskrit grammar, Bharavi achieves conciseness and directness. His alliteration, "crisp texture of sound", and choice of metre closely correspond to the narrative.

Shishupala Vadha

The Shishupala Vadha (the slaying of Shishupala") is a work of classical Sanskrit poetry, one of the six *Mahakavya* or "epic poems". It was composed in ca. 8th century by Magha, and why it is called *Magha-kavya.*

The tale is that of Shishupala, king of the Chedis in central India, probably the same as Bundelkhand. Shishupala challenged Krishna to fight, upon which the latter struck his head off with his discus.

The poem is noted for its intricate wordplay, and textual complexity. The 19th canto contains the following stanza which is an example of what has been called "the most complex and exquisite type of palindrome ever invented". It was devised by the Sanskrit aestheticians, who termed it *sarvatobhadra,* that is, "perfect in every direction" - it yields the same text if read forwards, backwards, down, or up:

Puranas

The corpus of the Hindu Puranas likewise falls into the classical period of Sanskrit literature, dating to between the 5th and 10th centuries, and marks the emergence of the Vaishna and Shaiva denominations of classical Hinduism. The Puranas are classified into a Mah- ("great") and a Upa- ("lower, additional") corpus. A Purana usually gives prominence to a certain deity (Shiva, Vishnu or Krishna, Durga) and depicts the other gods as subservient.

4

Classical Fables of Aesop

The Life and History of Aesop is involved, like that of Homer, the most famous of Greek poets, in much obscurity. Sardis, the capital of Lydia; Samos, a Greek island; Mesembria, an ancient colony in Thrace; and Cotiaeum, the chief city of a province of Phrygia, contend for the distinction of being the birthplace of Aesop. Although the honor thus claimed cannot be definitely assigned to any one of these places, yet there are a few incidents now generally accepted by scholars as established facts, relating to the birth, life, and death of Aesop. He is, by an almost universal consent, allowed to have been born about the year 620 B.C., and to have been by birth a slave.

He was owned by two masters in succession, both inhabitants of Samos, Xanthus and Jadmon, the latter of whom gave him his liberty as a reward for his learning and wit. One of the privileges of a freedman in the ancient republics of Greece, was the permission to take an active interest in public affairs; and Aesop, like the philosophers Phaedo, Menippus, and Epictetus, in later times, raised himself from the indignity of a servile condition to a position of high renown. In his desire alike to instruct and to be instructed, he travelled through many countries, and among others came to Sardis, the capital of the famous king of Lydia, the great patron, in that day, of learning and of learned men. He met at the court of Croesus with Solon, Thales, and other sages, and is related so to have pleased his royal master, by the part he took in the conversations held with these philosophers, that he applied to him an expression which has since passed into a proverb, "The Phrygian has spoken better than all."

On the invitation of Croesus he fixed his residence at Sardis, and was employed by that monarch in various difficult and delicate affairs of State. In his discharge of these commissions he visited the different petty republics of Greece. At one time he is found in Corinth, and at another in Athens, endeavouring, by the narration of some of his wise fables, to reconcile the inhabitants of those cities to the administration of their respective rulers Periander and Pisistratus.

One of these ambassadorial missions, undertaken at the command of Croesus, was the occasion of his death. Having been sent to Delphi with a large sum of gold for distribution among the citizens, he was so provoked at their covetousness that he refused to divide the money, and sent it back to his master. The Delphians, enraged at this treatment, accused him of impiety, and, in spite of his sacred character as ambassador, executed him as a public criminal. This cruel death of Aesop was not unavenged. The citizens of Delphi were visited with a series of calamities, until they made a public reparation of their crime; and, "The blood of Aesop" became a well- known adage, bearing witness to the truth that deeds of wrong would not pass unpunished. Neither did the great fabulist lack posthumous honors; for a statue was erected to his memory at Athens, the work of Lysippus, one of the most famous of Greek sculptors. Phaedrus thus immortalizes the event:*

> Aesopo ingentem statuam posuere Attici,
> Servumque collocarunt aeterna in basi:
> Patere honoris scirent ut cuncti viam;
> Nec generi tribui sed virtuti gloriam.

These few facts are all that can be relied on with any degree of certainty, in reference to the birth, life, and death of Aesop. They were first brought to light, after a patient search and diligent perusal of ancient authors, by a Frenchman, M. Claude Gaspard Bachet de Mezeriac, who declined the honor of being tutor to Louis XIII of France, from his desire to devote himself exclusively to literature. He published his Life of Aesop, Anno Domini 1632. The later investigations of a host of English and German scholars have added very little to the facts given by M. Mezeriac. The substantial truth of his statements has been confirmed by later criticism and inquiry. It remains to state, that prior to this publication of M. Mezeriac, the life of Aesop was from the pen of Maximus Planudes, a monk of Constantinople, who was sent on an embassy to Venice by the Byzantine Emperor Andronicus the elder, and who wrote in the early part of the fourteenth century. His life was prefixed to all the early editions of these fables, and was republished as late as 1727 by Archdeacon Croxall as the introduction to his edition of Aesop. This life by Planudes contains, however, so small an amount of truth, and is so full of absurd pictures of the grotesque deformity of Aesop, of wondrous apocryphal stories, of lying legends, and gross anachronisms, that it is now universally condemned as false, puerile, and unauthentic. 1 It is given up in the present day, by general consent, as unworthy of the slightest credit. G.F.T.

The Aesop Romance

Along with the scattered references in the ancient sources regarding the life and death of Aesop, there is a highly fictional biography now commonly called *The Aesop Romance* (also known as the *Vita* or *The Life of Aesop* or *The Book of Xanthus the Philosopher and Aesop His Slave*). Multiple, sometimes contradictory, versions of this work exist, and while parts appear to originate beginning in the 4th century A.D., some elements may date from as early as the 4th century B.C. "Like *The Alexander Romance, The Aesop Romance* became a folkbook, a work that belonged to no one, and the occasional writer felt free to modify as it might suit him." Scholars long dismissed any historical or biographical validity in *The Aesop Romance*; serious study of the work began only toward the end of the 20th century. A full assessment of its value has yet to be presented.

In *The Aesop Romance,* Aesop is a slave of Phrygian orgin on the island of Samos, and extremely ugly. At first he lacks the power of speech, but after showing kindness to a priestess of Isis, is granted by the goddess not only speech but a gift for clever storytelling, which he uses alternately to assist and confound his master, Xanthus, embarrassing the philosopher in front of his students and even sleeping with his wife. After interpreting a portent for the people of Samos, Aesop is given his freedom and acts as an emissary between the Samians and King Croesus. Later he travels to the courts of (the imaginary) Lycurgus of Babylon and Nectanabo of Egypt in a section that appears to borrow heavily from the romance of Ahiqar. The story ends with Aesop's journey to Delphi and his death there.

Aesop the Fabulist

Though Aesop became famous across the ancient world as the preeminent teller of fables, he did not create the genre; the earliest known story with talking animals in ancient Greek is the fable of the hawk and the nightingale from Hesiod, who lived at least three centuries before Aesop. Aesop may or may not have written his fables—*The Aesop Romance* claims that he wrote them down and deposited them in the library of Croesus; Herodotus calls Aesop a "writer of fables" and Aristophanes speaks of "reading" Aesop—but no writings by Aesop have survived.

Socrates while in prison turned some of the fables into verse, working from memory (which may indicate that he knew them by oral tradition); a small fragment is extant. The early Roman playwright and poet Ennius also rendered at least one fable in Latin verse, of which the last two lines still exist.

The body of work identified as Aesop's Fables was transmitted by a series of later authors writing in both Greek and Latin. Demetrius of Phalerum (ca. 350-ca. 280 BC) made a collection in ten books, probably in prose (*Lopson Aisopeion sunagogai*) for the use of orators, which has been lost. Next appeared an edition in elegiac verse, cited by the Suda, but the author's name is unknown. Phaedrus, a freedman of Augustus, rendered the fables into Latin. Babrius turned the fables into Greek choliambics in the earlier part of the 3rd century A.D. Avianus (of uncertain date, perhaps the 4th century) translated 42 of the fables into Latin elegiacs.Aesop's Fables continued to be revised and translated through the ensuing centuries, with the addition of material from other cultures, so that the fables known today in some cases bear little relation to the original fables of Aesop. With a surge in scholarly interest in Aesop and Aesopic fable beginning toward the end of the 20th century, some attempt has been made to determine the nature and content of the very earliest fables which may be most closely linked to the historic Aesop.

Origins

According to the Greek historian Herodotus, the fables were written by a slave named Aesop, who lived in Ancient Greece during the 5th century BC. Aesop is also mentioned in several other Ancient Greek works – Aristophanes, in his comedy *The Wasps*, represented the protagonist Philocleon as having learnt the "absurdities" of Aesop from conversation at banquets; Plato wrote in *Phaedo* that Socrates whiled away his jail time turning some of Aesop's fables "which he knew" into verses; Demetrius of Phalerum compiled the fables into a set of eleven books (*Lopson Aisopeion sunagogai*), which have been lost, for the use of orators. There was also an edition in elegiac verse by an anonymous author, which was often cited in the *Suda*. Two fables of Aesop are similar to those found in Panchtantra, an Indian story book of older origin.

Nonetheless, for two main reasons, because numerous morals within Aesop's attributed fables contradict each other, and ancient accounts of Aesop's life contradict each other, the modern view is that Aesop probably did not solely compose all those fables attributed to him, if he even existed at all. Modern scholarship reveals fables and proverbs of "Aesopic" form existing in both ancient Sumer and Akkad, as early as the third millennium BCE. Therefore, at their most ancient roots, the fables of Aesop are composed in a literary format which appears first not in Ancient Greece or Ancient India or Ancient Egypt, but instead in ancient Sumer and Akkad.

From circa 2000 BCE, in Mesopotamia, then, storytelling in this format finally reached ancient Greece at least by circa 600 BCE during the time of Aesop. How it eventually reached ancient Greece however remains another mystery. Nevertheless it is known that fables existed long before Aesop's time in Ancient Egypt, Assyria, Babylonia, and Sumer. It is also known that some fables reaching us today and which had traditionally been attributed to Aesop actually have their most ancient origins resting in Ancient India. Some other fables cannot be dated any earlier than Babrius and Phaedrus, several centuries after Aesop, and yet others even later, to Gian Francesco Poggio Bracciolini and Jean de La Fontaine slightly before and after the end of the Middle Ages respectively.

There was an edition of Aesop's fables in elegiac verse by an anonymous author, which was often cited in the *Suda*. Two fables of Aesop are similar to those found in Panchtantra, an Indian story book of older origin.

Translation and Transmission

The first extensive translation of Aesop into Latin was done by Phaedrus, a freedman of Caesar Augustus in the 1st century AD, although at least one fable had already been translated by the poet Ennius. Avianus also translated forty two of the fables into Latin elegiacs, probably in the 4th century AD.

The collection under the name of Aesop's Fables evolved from the late Greek version of Babrius, who turned them into choliambic verses, at an uncertain time between 3rd century BC and 3rd century AD. In about 100 BC, Indian philosopher Syntipas translated Babrius into Syriac, from where Andreopulos translated back to Greek, since original Greek scripts had all been lost. Aesop's fables and the *Panchatantra* share about a dozen tales, leading to discussions whether the Greeks learned these fables from Indian storytellers or the other way, or if the influences were mutual. Ben E. Perry, one of the foremost authorities on Aesopic fable, argued for the second possibility in his book *Babrius and Phaedrus*. In his introduction he wrote:

> *""In the entire Greek tradition there is not, so far as I can see, a single fable that can be said to come either directly or indirectly from an Indian source; but many fables or fable-motifs which make their first appearance in Greek or Near Eastern literature are found later in the Panchatantra and other Indian story-books, including the Buddhist Jatakas." "*

In the 9th century, Ignatius Diaconus created a version of fifty-five fables in choliambic tetrameters, into which stories from Oriental sources were added, ultimately mutated from the Sanskrit *Panchatantra*. From these collections the 14th-century monk Maximus Planudes compiled the collection which has come down under the name of Aesop.

The first printed version of Aesop's Fables in English was published on March 26, 1484 by William Caxton. Around the same time, the Scottish poet Robert Henryson was composing his poem, *The Morall*

Fabillis of Esope the Phrygian, a sophisticated interconnected sequence of fable adaptations which made a work of high art out of the genre. At the heart of his version, Aesop himself enters in the unusual guise of a Roman. Henryson's Scots fable version is not known to have occurred in print form until the 16th century. Caxton's version was updated by Sir Roger L'Estrange in 1692.

Some Classical Fables

The Wolf and the Lamb

Wolf, meeting with a Lamb astray from the fold, resolved not to lay violent hands on him, but to find some plea to justify to the Lamb the Wolf's right to eat him. He thus addressed him: "Sirrah, last year you grossly insulted me." "Indeed," bleated the Lamb in a mournful tone of voice, "I was not then born." Then said the Wolf, "You feed in my pasture." "No, good sir," replied the Lamb, "I have not yet tasted grass." Again said the Wolf, "You drink of my well." "No," exclaimed the Lamb, "I never yet drank water, for as yet my mother's milk is both food and drink to me." Upon which the Wolf seized him and ate him up, saying, "Well! I won't remain supperless, even though you refute every one of my imputations." The tyrant will always find a pretext for his tyranny.

The Bat and the Weasels

A Bat who fell upon the ground and was caught by a Weasel pleaded to be spared his life. The Weasel refused, saying that he was by nature the enemy of all birds. The Bat assured him that he was not a bird, but a mouse, and thus was set free. Shortly afterwards the Bat again fell to the ground and was caught by another

Weasel, whom he likewise entreated not to eat him. The Weasel said that he had a special hostility to mice. The Bat assured him that he was not a mouse, but a bat, and thus a second time escaped. It is wise to turn circumstances to good account.

The Ass and the Grasshopper

An Ass having heard some Grasshoppers chirping, was highly enchanted; and, desiring to possess the same charms of melody, demanded what sort of food they lived on to give them such beautiful voices. They replied, "The dew." The Ass resolved that he would live only upon dew, and in a short time died of hunger.

The Lion and the Mouse

A Lion was awakened from sleep by a Mouse running over his face. Rising up angrily, he caught him and was about to kill him, when the Mouse piteously entreated, saying: "If you would only spare my life, I would be sure to repay your kindness." The Lion laughed and let him go. It happened shortly after this that the Lion was caught by some hunters, who bound him by st ropes to the ground. The Mouse, recognizing his roar, came gnawed the rope with his teeth, and set him free, exclaim "You ridiculed the idea of my ever being able to help you, expecting to receive from me any repayment of your favor; I now you know that it is possible for even a Mouse to con benefits on a Lion."

The Charcoal-Burner and the Fuller

A Charcoal-Burner carried on his trade in his own house. One day he met a friend, a Fuller, and entreated him to come and live with him, saying that they should be far better neighbors and that their housekeeping expenses would be lessened. The Fuller replied, "The arrangement is impossible as far as I am concerned, for whatever I should whiten, you would immediately blacken again with your charcoal." Like will draw like.The Father And His Sons

The Father and his Sons

A Father had a family of sons who were perpetually quarreling among themselves. When he failed to heal their disputes by his exhortations, he determined to give them a practical illustration of the evils of disunion; and for this purpose he one day told them to bring him a bundle of sticks. When they had done so, he placed the faggot into the hands of each of them in succession, and ordered them to break it in pieces. They tried with all their strength, and were not able to do it. He next opened the faggot, took the sticks separately, one by one, and again put them into his sons' hands, upon which they broke them easily. He then addressed them in these words: "My sons, if you are of one mind, and unite to assist each other, you will be as this faggot, uninjured by all the attempts of your enemies; but if you are divided among yourselves, you will be broken as easily as these sticks."

The Boy Hunting Locusts

A Boy was hunting for locusts. He had caught a goodly number, when he saw a Scorpion, and mistaking him for a locust, reached out his hand to take him. The Scorpion, showing his sting, said: If you had but touched me, my friend, you would have lost me, and all your locusts too!"

The Cock and the Jewel

A Cock, scratching for food for himself and his hens, found a precious stone and exclaimed: "If your owner had found thee, and not I, he would have taken thee up, and have set thee in thy first estate; but I have found thee for no purpose. I would rather have one barleycorn than all the jewels in the world."

The Kingdom of the Lion

Teh beasts of the field and forest had a Lion as their king. He was neither wrathful, cruel, nor tyrannical, but just and gentle as a king could be. During his reign he made a royal proclamation for a general assembly of all the birds and beasts, and drew up conditions for a universal league, in which the Wolf and the Lamb, the Panther and the Kid, the Tiger and the Stag, the Dog and the Hare, should live together in perfect peace and amity. The Hare said, "Oh, how I have longed to see this day, in which the weak shall take their place with impunity by the side of the strong." And after the Hare said this, he ran for his life.

The Wolf and the Crane

A Wolf who had a bone stuck in his throat hired a Crane, for a large sum, to put her head into his mouth and draw out the bone. When the Crane had extracted the bone and demanded the promised payment, the Wolf, grinning and grinding his teeth, exclaimed: "Why, you have surely already had a sufficient recompense, in having been permitted to draw out your head in safety from the mouth and jaws of a wolf." In serving the wicked, expect no reward, and be thankful if you escape injury for your pains.

The Fisherman Piping

A Fisherman skilled in music took his flute and his nets to the seashore. Standing on a projecting rock, he played several tunes in the hope that the fish, attracted by his melody, would of their own accord dance into his net, which he had placed below. At last, having long waited in vain, he laid aside his flute, and casting his net into the sea, made an excellent haul of fish. When he saw them leaping about in the net upon the rock he said: "O you most perverse creatures, when I piped you would not dance, but now that I have ceased you do so merrily."

Hercules and the Wagoner

A Carter was driving a wagon along a country lane, when the wheels sank down deep into a rut. The rustic driver, stupefied and aghast, stood looking at the wagon, and did nothing but utter loud cries to Hercules to come and help him. Hercules, it is said, appeared and thus addressed him: "Put your shoulders to the wheels, my man. Goad on your bullocks, and never more pray to me for help, until you have done your best to help yourself, or depend upon it you will henceforth pray in vain." Self-help is the best help.

The Ants and the Grasshopper

The Ants were spending a fine winter's day drying grain collected in the summertime. A Grasshopper, perishing with famine, passed by and earnestly begged for a little food. The Ants inquired of him, "Why did you not treasure up food during the summer?' He replied, "I had not leisure enough. I passed the days in singing." They then said in derision: "If you were foolish enough to sing all the summer, you must dance supperless to bed in the winter."

The Dog and the Shadow

A Dog, crossing a bridge over a stream with a piece of flesh in his mouth, saw his own shadow in the water and took it for that of another Dog, with a piece of meat double his own in size. He immediately let go of his own, and fiercely attacked the other Dog to get his larger piece from him. He thus lost both: that which he grasped at in the water, because it was a shadow; and his own, because the stream swept it away.

The Mole and his Mother

A Mole, a creature blind from birth, once said to his Mother: "I am sure than I can see, Mother!" In the desire to prove to him his mistake, his Mother placed before him a few grains of frankincense, and asked, "What is it?' The young Mole said, "It is a pebble." His Mother exclaimed: "My son, I am afraid that you are not only blind, but that you have lost your sense of smell.

The Herdsman and the Lost Bull

A Herdsman tending his flock in a forest lost a Bull-calf from the fold. After a long and fruitless search, he made a vow that, if he could only discover the thief who had stolen the Calf, he would offer a lamb in sacrifice to Hermes, Pan, and the Guardian Deities of the forest. Not long afterwards, as he ascended a small hillock, he saw at its foot a Lion feeding on the Calf. Terrified at the sight, he lifted his eyes and his hands to heaven, and said: "Just now I vowed to offer a lamb to the Guardian Deities of the forest if I could only find out who had robbed me; but now that I have discovered the thief, I would willingly add a full-grown Bull to the Calf I have lost, if I may only secure my own escape from him in safety."

The Hare and the Tortoise

A Hare one day ridiculed the short feet and slow pace of the Tortoise, who replied, laughing: "Though you be swift as the wind, I will beat you in a race." The Hare, believing her assertion to be simply impossible, assented to the proposal; and they agreed that the Fox should choose the course and fix the goal. On the day appointed for the race the two started together. The Tortoise never for a moment stopped, but went on with a slow but steady pace straight to the end of the course. The Hare, lying down by the wayside, fell fast asleep. At last waking up, and moving as fast as he could, he saw the Tortoise had reached the goal, and was comfortably dozing after her fatigue. Slow but steady wins the race.

The Pomegranate, Apple-Tree, and Bramble

The Pomegranate and Apple-Tree disputed as to which was the most beautiful. When their strife was at its height, a Bramble from the neighboring hedge lifted up its voice, and said in a boastful tone: "Pray, my dear friends, in my presence at least cease from such vain disputings."

The Farmer and the Stork

A Farmer placed nets on his newly-sown plowlands and caught a number of Cranes, which came to pick up his seed. With them he trapped a Stork that had fractured his leg in the net and was earnestly beseeching the Farmer to spare his life. "Pray save me,

Master," he said, "and let me go free this once. My broken limb should excite your pity. Besides, I am no Crane, I am a Stork, a bird of excellent character; and see how I love and slave for my father and mother. Look too, at my feathers— they are not the least like those of a Crane." The Farmer laughed aloud and said, "It may be all as you say, I only know this: I have taken you with these robbers, the Cranes, and you must die in their company." Birds of a feather flock together.

The Farmer and the Snake

One winter a Farmer found a Snake stiff and frozen with cold. He had compassion on it, and taking it up, placed it in his bosom. The Snake was quickly revived by the warmth, and resuming its natural instincts, bit its benefactor, inflicting on him a mortal wound. "Oh," cried the Farmer with his last breath, "I am rightly served for pitying a scoundrel." The greatest kindness will not bind the ungrateful.

The Fawn and his Mother

A Fawn once said to his Mother, "You are larger than a dog, and swifter, and more used to running, and you have your horns as a defense; why, then, O Mother! do the hounds frighten you so?" She smiled, and said: "I know full well, my son, that all you say is true. I have the advantages you mention, but when I hear even the bark of a single dog I feel ready to faint, and fly away as fast as I can." No arguments will give courage to the coward.

The Bear and the Fox

A Bear boasted very much of his philanthropy, saying

that of all animals he was the most tender in his regard for man, for he had such respect for him that he would not even touch his dead body. A Fox hearing these words said with a smile to the Bear, "Oh! that you would eat the dead and not the living."

The Swallow and the Crow

The Swallow and the Crow had a contention about their plumage. The Crow put an end to the dispute by saying, "Your feathers are all very well in the spring, but mine protect me against the winter." Fair weather friends are not worth much.

The Mountain in Labor

A Mountain was once greatly agitated. Loud groans and noises were heard, and crowds of people came from all parts to see what was the matter. While they were assembled in anxious expectation of some terrible calamity, out came a Mouse. Don't make much ado about nothing.

The Ass, The Fox, and The Lion

The Ass and the Fox, having entered into partnership together for their mutual protection, went out into the forest to hunt. They had not proceeded far when they met a Lion. The Fox, seeing imminent danger, approached the Lion and promised to contrive for him the capture of the Ass if the Lion would pledge his word not to harm the Fox. Then, upon assuring the Ass that he would not be injured, the Fox led him to a deep pit and arranged that he should fall into it. The Lion, seeing that the Ass was secured, immediately clutched the Fox, and attacked the Ass at his leisure.

5

Classical Works of William Shakespeare

William Shakespeare (1564–1616), 'The Bard of Avon', English poet and playwright wrote the famous 154 *Sonnets* and numerous highly successful oft quoted dramatic works including the tragedy of the Prince of Denmark, *Hamlet*;

> *"Neither a borrower nor a lender be;*
> *For loan oft loses both itself and friend,*
> *And borrowing dulls the edge of husbandry.*
> *This above all: to thine ownself be true,*
> *And it must follow, as the night the day,*
> *Thou canst not then be false to any man.*
> *Farewell: my blessing season this in thee!"*
>
> —Lord Polonius, *Hamlet* Act I, Scene 3

While Shakespeare caused much controversy, he also earned lavish praise and has profoundly impacted the world over in areas of literature, culture, art, theatre, and film and is considered one of the best English language writers ever. From the Preface of the *First Folio* (1623) "To the memory of my beloved, The Author, Mr. William Shakespeare: and what he hath left us"—Ben Jonson;

> *"Thou art a Moniment, without a tombe*
> *And art alive still, while thy Booke doth live,*
> *And we have wits to read, and praise to give."*

Over the centuries there has been much speculation surrounding various aspects of Shakespeare's life including his religious affiliation, sexual orientation, sources for collaborations, authorship of and chronology of the plays and sonnets. Many of the dates of play performances, when they were written, adapted or revised and printed are imprecise. This biography attempts only to give an overview of his life, while leaving the more learned perspectives to the countless scholars and historians who have devoted their lives to the study and demystification of the man and his works.

England's celebration of their patron Saint George is on 23 April, which is also the day claimed to be the birth date of Shakespeare. Although birth and death dates were not recorded in Shakespeare's time, churches did record baptisms and burials, usually a few days after the actual event. The infant William was baptised on 26 April 1564 in the parish church Holy Trinity of Stratford upon Avon. He lived with his fairly well-to-do parents on Henley Street, the first of the four sons born to John Shakespeare (c1530-1601) and Mary Arden (c1540-1608), who also had four daughters. John Shakespeare was a local businessman and also involved in municipal affairs as Alderman and Bailiff, but a decline in his fortunes in his later years surely had an effect on William.

In his younger years Shakespeare attended the Christian Holy Trinity church, the now famous elegant limestone cross shaped cathedral on the banks of the Avon river, studying the Book of Common Prayer and the English Bible. In 1605 he became lay rector when he paid £440 towards its upkeep, hence why he is buried in the chancel. Early on Shakespeare likely attended the Elizabethan theatrical productions of travelling theatre troups, come to Stratford to entertain the local official townsmen, including the Queen's Men, Worcester's Men, Leicester's Men, and Lord Strange's Men. There is also the time when Queen Elizabeth herself visited nearby Kenilworth Castle and Shakespeare, said to have been duly impressed by the procession, recreated it in some of his later plays.

Although enrolment registers did not survive, around the age of eleven Shakespeare probably entered the grammar school of Stratford, King's New School, where he would have studied theatre and acting, as well as Latin literature and history. When he finished school he might have apprenticed for a time with his father, but there is also mention of his being a school teacher. The next record of his life is in 1582, when still a minor at the age of eighteen and requiring his father's consent, Shakespeare and Anne Hathaway (1556–1623) married in the village of Temple Grafton. Baptisms of three children were recorded; Susanna (1583-1649), who went on to marry noted physician John Hall, and twins Judith (1585-1662) who married Richard Quiney, and Hamnet (1585-1596) his only son and heir who died at the age of eleven.

It is not exactly clear what Shakespeare was doing in the first few years after the marriage, but he did go to London and worked at The Globe theatre, possibly as one of the Queen's Men whose works were harshly anti Catholic in a time of rising Protestantism.

By 1593 the plague was haunting London and many who were able fled the teeming city for the cleansing airs of open country. While it was a time for many upstart theatres, the popular public entertainment of the day, they were often shut down and forbidden to open for stretches of time. Shakespeare probably spent these dark days travelling between London, Stratford, and the provinces, which gave him time to pen many more plays and sonnets. Among the first of his known printed works is the comedic and erotically charged Ovidian narrative poem *Venus and Adonis* (1593). It was wildly popular, dedicated with great esteem to his patron Henry Wriothesly, third earl of Southampton, the young man that some say Shakespeare may have had more than platonic affection for. It was followed by the much darker *The Rape of Lucrece* in 1594, *The Passionate Pilgrim* in 1599 and the allegorical *The Phoenix and the Turtle* (1601).

At this time of prolific writing, Shakespeare began his association until his death with The Lord Chamberlain's Men. With the accession of James I they became the King's Men, who bought and performed most of Shakespeare's plays. The troupe included his friend and actor Richard Burbage. They performed frequently at court, and in the theatres that Shakespeare was co-owner of including the Blackfriars, The Theatre, and The Globe in London until it burnt down during a performance of *King Henry VIII*. It is said that Shakespeare himself acted in a number of roles including the ghost in *Hamlet* and Old Adam in *As You Like It*. In the late 1590s he bought 'New Place' on Chapel Street in Stratford, one of his many real estate investments.

Shakespeare wrote most of his plays as 'quarto texts', that being on a sheet of paper folded four ways. A few of his plays were printed in his lifetime, though they appeared more voluminously after his death, sometimes plagiarised and often changed at the whim of the printer. *First Folio* would be the first collection of his dramatic works, a massive undertaking to compile thirty-six plays from the quarto texts, playbooks, transcriptions, and the memories of actors. The approximately nine hundred page manuscript took about two years to complete and was printed in 1623 as *Mr. William Shakespeares Comedies, Histories, & Tragedies.* It also featured on the frontispiece the famous engraved portrait of Shakespeare said to be by Martin Droeshout (1601-c1651).

Under the favour of the court The Kings' Men became the eminent company of the day. Most likely Anne and the children lived in Stratford while Shakespeare spent his time travelling between Stratford and London, dealing with business affairs and writing and acting. In 1616 his daughter Judith married Quiney who subsequently admitted to fornication with Margaret Wheeler, and Shakespeare took steps to bequeath a sum to Judith in her own name. William Shakespeare died on 23 April 1616, according to his monument, and lies buried in the chancel of the Holy Trinity Church in Stratford upon Avon. While there is little known of her life, Anne Hathaway outlived her husband by seven years, dying in 1623 and is buried beside him. It is not clear as to how or why Shakespeare died, but in 1664 the reverend John Ward, vicar of Stratford recorded that *"Shakespeare, Drayton and Ben Johnson had a merie meeting, and itt seems drank too hard, for Shakespeare died of a feavour there contracted."* His tombstone is inscribed with the following epitaph;

> Good friend for Jesus sake forbeare
> To digg the dust encloased heare
> Blessed by many spares hes stones
> *And curst be he y moves my bones*

Shakespearean Classical Poetry

It is generally agreed that most of the Shakespearean Sonnets were written in the 1590s, some printed at this time as well. Others were written or revised right before being printed. 154 sonnets and "A Lover's Complaint" were published by Thomas Thorpe as *Shake-speares Sonnets* in 1609. The order, dates, and authorship of the Sonnets have been much debated with no conclusive findings. Many have claimed autobiographical details from them, including sonnet number 145 in reference to Anne. The dedication to "Mr. W.H." is said to possibly represent the initials of the third earl of Pembroke William Herbert, or perhaps being a reversal of Henry Wriothesly's initials. Regardless, there have been some unfortunate projections and interpretations of modern concepts onto centuries old works that, while a grasp of contextual historical information can certainly lend to their depth and meaning, can also be enjoyed as valuable poetical works that have transcended time and been surpassed by no other.

Evoking Petrarch's style and lyrically writing of beauty, mortality, and love with its moral anguish and worshipful adoration of a usually unattainable love, the first 126 sonnets are addressed to a young man, sonnets 127-152 to a dark lady. Ever the dramatist Shakespeare created a profound intrigue to scholars and novices alike as to the identities of these people.

In 1593 and 1594, when the theatres were closed because of plague, Shakespeare published two narrative poems on erotic themes, *Venus and Adonis* and *The Rape of Lucrece*. He dedicated them to Henry Wriothesley, Earl of Southampton. In *Venus and Adonis*, an innocent Adonis rejects the sexual advances of

Venus; while in *The Rape of Lucrece*, the virtuous wife Lucrece is raped by the lustful Tarquin. Influenced by Ovid's *Metamorphoses*, the poems show the guilt and moral confusion that result from uncontrolled lust. Both proved popular and were often reprinted during Shakespeare's lifetime. A third narrative poem, *A Lover's Complaint*, in which a young woman laments her seduction by a persuasive suitor, was printed in the first edition of the *Sonnets* in 1609. Most scholars now accept that Shakespeare wrote *A Lover's Complaint*. Critics consider that its fine qualities are marred by leaden effects. *The Phoenix and the Turtle*, printed in Robert Chester's 1601 *Love's Martyr*, mourns the deaths of the legendary phoenix and his lover, the faithful turtle dove. In 1599, two early drafts of sonnets 138 and 144 appeared in *The Passionate Pilgrim*, published under Shakespeare's name but without his permission.

Shakespeare's Sonnets

Shakespeare's sonnets, or simply The Sonnets, is a collection of poems in sonnet form written by William Shakespeare that deal with such themes as time, love, beauty and mutability. They were probably written over a period of several years. All 154 poems appeared in a 1609 collection, entitled *SHAKE-SPEARES SONNETS*, comprising 152 previously unpublished sonnets and two (numbers 138 and 144) that had previously been published in a 1599 miscellany entitled *The Passionate Pilgrim*.

The first 17 sonnets are written to a young man, urging him to marry and have children, thereby passing down his beauty to the next generation. These are called the procreation sonnets. Most of them, however, 18-126, are addressed to a young man expressing the poet's love for him. Sonnets 127-152 are written to the poet's mistress expressing his strong love for her. The final two sonnets, 153-154, are allegorical. The final thirty or so sonnets are written about a number of issues, such as the young man's infidelity with the poet's mistress, self-resolution to control his own lust, beleaguered criticism of the world, etc.

The Sonnets were published under conditions that have become unclear to history. Although the works were written by Shakespeare, it is not known if the publisher, believed to be Thomas Thorpe, used an authorized manuscript from him, or an unauthorized copy. Also, there is a mysterious dedication at the beginning of the text wherein a certain "Mr. W.H." is described by the publisher as "the onlie begetter" of the poems, but it is not known who this man was. In addition, several aspects of The Sonnets have been noted in the ongoing Shakespeare authorship question.

The sonnets are almost all constructed from three four-line stanzas (called quatrains) and a final couplet composed in iambic pentameter (a meter used extensively in Shakespeare's plays) with the rhyme scheme *abab cdcd efef gg* (this form is now known as the Shakespearean sonnet). The only exceptions are Sonnets 99, 126, and 145. Number 99 has fifteen lines. Number 126 consists of six couplets, and two blank lines marked with italic brackets; 145 is in iambic tetrameters, not pentameters. Often, the beginning of the third quatrain marks the volta ("turn"), or the line in which the mood of the poem shifts, and the poet expresses a revelation or epiphany.

There is another variation on the standard English structure, found for example in sonnet 29. The normal rhyme scheme is changed by repeating the b of quatrain one in quatrain three where the f should be. This leaves the sonnet distinct between both English and Spenserian styles.

Characters

Readers of the sonnets today commonly refer to these characters as the Fair Youth, the Rival Poet, and the Dark Lady. The narrator expresses admiration for the Fair Youth's beauty, and later has an affair with the Dark Lady. It is not known whether the poems and their characters are fiction or autobiographical. If they are autobiographical, the identities of the characters are open to debate. Various scholars, most notably A. L. Rowse, have attempted to identify the characters with historical individuals.

Fair Youth. The 'Fair Youth' is an unnamed young man to whom sonnets 1-126 are addressed. The poet writes of the young man in romantic and loving language, a fact which has led several commentators to suggest a homosexual relationship between them, while others read it as platonic love, or even as the love of a father for his son.

The earliest poems in the collection do not imply a close personal relationship; instead, they recommend the benefits of marriage and children. With the famous sonnet 18 ("Shall I compare thee to a summer's day") the tone changes dramatically towards romantic intimacy. Sonnet 20 explicitly laments that the young man is not a woman. Most of the subsequent sonnets describe the ups and downs of the relationship, culminating with an affair between the poet and the

Dark Lady. The relationship seems to end when the Fair Youth succumbs to the Lady's charms.

There have been many attempts to identify the Friend. Shakespeare's one-time patron, the Henry Wriothesley, 3rd Earl of Southampton is the most commonly suggested candidate, although Shakespeare's later patron, William Herbert, 3rd Earl of Pembroke, has recently become popular. Both claims have much to do with the dedication of the sonnets to 'Mr. W.H.', "the only begetter of these ensuing sonnets": the initials could apply to either Earl. However, while Shakespeare's language often seems to imply that the 'friend' is of higher social status than himself, this may not be the case. The apparent references to the poet's inferiority may simply be part of the rhetoric of romantic submission. An alternative theory, most famously espoused by Oscar Wilde's short story 'The Portrait of Mr. W.H.' notes a series of puns that may suggest the sonnets are written to a boy actor called William Hughes; however, Wilde's story acknowledges that there is no evidence for such a person's existence. Samuel Butler believed that the friend was a seaman, and recently Joseph Pequigney ('Such Is My love') an unknown commoner.

The Dark Lady. Sonnets 127-152 are addressed to a woman commonly known as the 'Dark Lady' because her hair is said to be black and her skin "dun". These sonnets are explicitly sexual in character, in contrast to those written to the "Fair Youth". It is implied that the speaker of the sonnets and the Lady had a passionate affair, but that she was unfaithful, perhaps with the "Fair Youth". The poet self-deprecatingly describes himself as balding and middle-aged at the time of writing.

Many attempts have been made to identify the "Dark Lady" with historical personalities, such as Mary Fitton or the poet Emilia Lanier, who was Rowse's favoured candidate, though neither lady fits the author's descriptions. She has also been identified with Elizabeth Wriothesley, Countess of Southampton.

Some readers have suggested that the reference to her "dun" (a dull, grayish, brown color) skin and "black wires...on her head" in Sonnet 130 suggests that she was of African descent (as imagined in Anthony Burgess's novel about Shakespeare, *Nothing Like the Sun*). Others, however, maintain that the Dark Lady is merely a fictional character who never really existed in real life; they suggest that the "darkness" of the lady is not intended literally, but rather represents the "dark" forces of physical lust as opposed to the ideal Platonic love associated with the "Fair Youth". Some have identified her with Hermia in A Midsummer Night's Dream, who is also described as dark-haired.

William Wordsworth was unimpressed by these sonnets. He wrote that

These sonnets, beginning at 127, to his Mistress, are worse than a puzzle-peg. They are abominably harsh, obscure & worthless. The others are for the most part much better, have many fine lines, very fine lines & passages. They are also in many places warm with passion. Their chief faults, and heavy ones they are, are sameness, tediousness, quaintness, & elaborate obscurity.

The Rival Poet. The Rival Poet's identity has always remained a mystery, though there is a general consensus that there are two likely candidates named Christopher Marlowe and George Chapman. However, there is no hard evidence that the character had a real-life counterpart. The Poet sees the Rival as competition for fame and patronage. The sonnets most commonly identified as The Rival Poet group exist within the Fair Youth series in sonnets 78–86.

Themes

One interpretation is that Shakespeare's Sonnets are in part a pastiche or parody of the three centuries-long tradition of Petrarchan love sonnets; in them, Shakespeare consciously inverts conventional gender roles as delineated in Petrarchan sonnets to create a more complex and potentially troubling depiction of human love. Shakespeare also violated many sonnet rules which had been strictly obeyed by his fellow poets: he speaks on human evils that do not have to do with love, he comments on political events, he makes fun of love, he parodies beauty, he plays with gender roles, he speaks openly about sex and even introduces witty pornography.

Legacy

Coming as they do at the end of conventional Petrarchan sonneteering, Shakespeare's sonnets can also be seen as a prototype, or even the beginning, of a new kind of 'modern' love poetry. During the eighteenth century, their reputation in England was relatively low; as late as 1805, The Critical Review could still credit Milton with the perfection of the English sonnet. As part of the renewed interest in Shakespeare's original work that accompanied Romanticism, the sonnets rose steadily in reputation during the nineteenth century.

The outstanding cross-cultural importance and influence of the sonnets is demonstrated by the large number of translations that have been made of them. To date in the German-speaking countries alone, there have been 70 complete translations since 1784. There is no major written language into which the sonnets have not been translated, including Latin, Turkish, Japanese, Esperanto, and even Klingon.

The sonnets are often referenced in popular culture. For example in a 2007 episode of Doctor Who, entitled The Shakespeare Code, Shakespeare began a good-bye to Martha Jones in the form of Sonnet 18, referring to her as his dark lady. This is intended to indicate that Martha is the famed Dark Lady from these sonnets.

Plays

Most playwrights of the period typically collaborated with others at some point, and critics agree that Shakespeare did the same, mostly early and late in his career. Some attributions, such as *Titus Andronicus* and the early history plays, remain controversial, while *The Two Noble Kinsmen* and the lost *Cardenio* have well-attested contemporary documentation. Textual evidence also supports the view that several of the plays were revised by other writers after their original composition.

The first recorded works of Shakespeare are *Richard III* and the three parts of *Henry VI*, written in the early 1590s during a vogue for historical drama. Shakespeare's plays are difficult to date, however, and studies of the texts suggest that *Titus Andronicus, The Comedy of Errors, The Taming of the Shrew* and *The Two Gentlemen of Verona* may also belong to Shakespeare's earliest period. His first histories, which draw heavily on the 1587 edition of Raphael Holinshed's *Chronicles of England, Scotland, and Ireland,* dramatise the destructive results of weak or corrupt rule and have been interpreted as a justification for the origins of the Tudor dynasty. The early plays were influenced by the works of other Elizabethan dramatists, especially Thomas Kyd and Christopher Marlowe, by the traditions of medieval drama, and by the plays of Seneca. *The Comedy of Errors* was also based on classical models, but no source for the *The Taming of the Shrew* has been found, though it is related to a separate play of the same name and may have derived from a folk story. Like *The Two Gentlemen of Verona,* in which two friends appear to approve of rape, the *Shrew's* story of the taming of a woman's independent spirit by a man sometimes troubles modern critics and directors.

Shakespeare's early classical and Italianate comedies, containing tight double plots and precise comic sequences, give way in the mid-1590s to the romantic atmosphere of his greatest comedies. *A Midsummer Night's Dream* is a witty mixture of romance, fairy magic, and comic lowlife scenes. Shakespeare's next comedy, the equally romantic *Merchant of Venice,* contains a portrayal of the vengeful Jewish moneylender Shylock, which reflects Elizabethan views but may appear derogatory to modern audiences. The wit and wordplay of *Much Ado About Nothing,* the charming rural setting of *As You Like It,* and the lively merrymaking of *Twelfth Night* complete Shakespeare's sequence of great comedies. After the lyrical *Richard II,* written almost entirely in verse, Shakespeare introduced prose comedy into the histories of the late 1590s, *Henry IV, parts 1* and 2, and *Henry V.* His characters become more complex and tender as he switches deftly between comic and serious scenes, prose and poetry, and achieves the narrative variety of his mature work. This period begins and ends with two tragedies: *Romeo and Juliet,* the famous romantic tragedy of sexually charged adolescence, love, and death; and *Julius Caesar*—based on Sir Thomas North's 1579 translation of Plutarch's *Parallel Lives*—which introduced a new kind of drama. According to Shakespearean scholar James Shapiro, in *Julius Caesar* "the various strands of politics, character, inwardness, contemporary events, even Shakespeare's own reflections on the act of writing, began to infuse each other".

In the early 1600s, Shakespeare wrote the so-called "problem plays" *Measure for Measure, Troilus and Cressida,* and *All's Well That Ends Well* and a number of his best known tragedies. Many critics believe that Shakespeare's greatest tragedies represent the peak of his art. The titular hero of one of Shakespeare's most famous tragedies, *Hamlet,* has probably been discussed more than any other Shakespearean character, especially for his famous soliloquy "To be or not to be; that is the question." Unlike the introverted Hamlet, whose fatal flaw is hesitation, the heroes of the tragedies that followed, Othello and King Lear, are undone by hasty errors of judgement. The plots of Shakespeare's tragedies often hinge on such fatal errors or flaws, which overturn order and destroy the hero and those he loves. In *Othello,* the villain Iago stokes Othello's sexual jealousy to the point where he murders the innocent wife who loves him. In *King Lear,* the old king commits the tragic error of giving up his powers, initiating the events which lead to the murder of his daughter and the torture and blinding of the Earl of Gloucester. According to the critic Frank Kermode, "the play offers neither its good characters nor its audience any relief from its cruelty". In *Macbeth,* the shortest and most compressed of Shakespeare's tragedies, uncontrollable ambition incites Macbeth and his wife, Lady Macbeth, to murder the rightful king and usurp the throne, until their own guilt destroys them in turn. In this play, Shakespeare adds a supernatural element to the tragic structure. His last major tragedies, *Antony and Cleopatra* and *Coriolanus,* contain some of Shakespeare's finest poetry and were considered his most successful tragedies by the poet and critic T. S. Eliot.

In his final period, Shakespeare turned to romance or tragicomedy and completed three more major plays: *Cymbeline, The Winter's Tale* and *The Tempest,* as well as the collaboration, *Pericles, Prince of Tyre.* Less bleak than the tragedies, these four plays are graver in tone than the comedies of the 1590s, but they end with reconciliation and the forgiveness of potentially tragic errors. Some commentators have seen this change in mood as evidence of a more serene view of life on Shakespeare's part, but it may merely reflect the theatrical fashion of the day. Shakespeare collaborated on two further surviving plays, *Henry VIII* and *The Two Noble Kinsmen,* probably with John Fletcher.

The Merchant of Venice

The Merchant of Venice is a play by William Shakespeare, believed to have been written between 1596 and 1598. Classified as a comedy in the First Folio, and while it shares certain aspects with Shakespeare's other romantic comedies, the play is perhaps more remembered for its dramatic scenes, and is best known for the character of Shylock. A deeply racist tale with strong anti-Jewish stance, **this play** bends logic to a great extent, serving as a pretext for holocaust. Through Shylock, progenitor stereotype of a Jew as a brutal, hateful, monstrous tormentor motivated by zealous animalistic vindictiveness uncapable of Christian mercifulness and grace, Shakespeare influenced many pogroms, providing a powerful jusification and inspiration for anti-semitic propaganda.

Synopsis

Bassanio, a young Venetian, of noble rank but having squandered his estate, wishes to travel to Belmont to woo the beautiful and wealthy heiress Portia. He approaches his friend Antonio, a wealthy and generous merchant, who has previously and repeatedly bailed him out, for three thousand ducats needed to subsidize his traveling expenditures as a suitor for three months. Antonio agrees, but he is cash-poor; his ships and merchandise are busy at sea. He promises to cover a bond if Bassanio can find a lender, so Bassanio turns to the Jewish moneylender Shylock and names Antonio as the loan's guarantor.

Shylock hates Antonio, both because he is a Christian and because he insulted and spat on Shylock for being a Jew. Also, Antonio undermines Shylock's moneylending business by lending money at zero interest. Shylock proposes a condition for the loan: if Antonio is unable to repay it at the specified date, he may take a pound of Antonio's flesh. Bassanio does not want Antonio to accept such a risky condition; Antonio is surprised by what he sees as the moneylender's generosity (no "usance" — interest — is asked for), and he signs the contract. With money at hand, Bassanio leaves for Belmont with his friend Gratiano, who has asked to accompany him. Gratiano is a likeable young man, but is often flippant, overly talkative, and tactless. Bassanio warns his companion to exercise self-control, and the two leave for Belmont and Portia.

Meanwhile in Belmont, Portia is awash with suitors. Her father has left a will stipulating each of her suitors must choose correctly from one of three caskets – one each of gold, silver, and lead – before he could win Portia's hand. In order to be granted an opportunity to marry Portia, each suitor must agree in advance to live out his life as a bachelor if he loses the contest. The suitor who correctly looks past the outward appearance of the caskets will find Portia's portrait inside and win her hand.

The first suitor, the luxury and money-obsessed Prince Of Morocco, reasons to choose the gold casket, because lead proclaims "Choose me and risk hazard", and he has no wish to risk everything for lead, and the silver's "Choose me and get what you deserve" sounds like an invitation to be tortured, but "Choose me and get what all men desire" all but spells it out that he that chooses gold will get Portia, as what all men desire is Portia. Inside the casket are a few gold coins and a skull with a scroll containing the famous verse *All that glisters is not gold / Often have you heard that told / Many a man his life hath sold But my outside to behold / Gilded tombs do worms enfold / Had you been as wise as bold, Young in limbs, in judgment old / Your answer had not been inscroll'd: /Fare you well; your suit is cold.* His judgment captured by outward appearances, he is an unfit suitor for Portia and his bachelor life begins.

The second suitor is the conceited Prince Of Aragon. He decides not to choose lead, because it is so common, and will not choose gold because he will then get what many men desire and wants to be distinguished from the barbarous multitudes. He decides to choose silver, because the silver casket proclaims "Choose Me And Get What You Deserve", which he imagines must be something great, because he egotistically imagines himself as great. Inside the casket, however, is the picture of a court jester's head on a baton and remarks "What? A grinning idiot? Did deserve no more than this?" The scroll reads: *Some there be that shadows kiss/Some have but a shadow's Bliss/ Take what wife you will to bed/I will ever be your Head*— meaning that he was foolish to imagine that a pompous man like him could ever be a fit husband for Portia, and that he was always a fool, he always will be a fool, and the fact that he chose the silver casket is mere proof that he is a fool.

The last suitor is Bassanio. He realizes that the line about "Choose me and risk everything you've got." could be a reference to the fact that marriage is a tremendous gamble and could mean a drastic turning point in one's life, and chooses lead. He gets it right.

At Venice, Antonio's ships are reported lost at sea. This leaves him unable to satisfy the bond (in financial language, insolvent). Shylock is even more determined to exact revenge from Christians after his daughter Jessica flees his home to convert to Christianity and elope with Lorenzo, taking a substantial amount of Shylock's wealth with her, as well as a turquoise ring which was a gift to Shylock from his late wife, Leah. Shylock has Antonio arrested and brought before court. At Belmont, Portia and Bassanio have just been married, as have Gratiano and Portia's handmaid Nerissa. Bassanio receives a letter telling him that Antonio has defaulted on his loan from Shylock.

Shocked, Bassanio and Gratiano leave for Venice immediately, with money from Portia, to save Antonio's life by offering the money to Shylock. Unknown to Bassanio and Gratiano, Portia has sent her servant, Balthazar, to seek the counsel of Portia's cousin, Bellario, a lawyer, at Padua.

Date and text

The date of composition for *The Merchant of Venice* is believed to be between 1596 and 1598. The play was mentioned by Francis Meres in 1598, so it must have been familiar on the stage by that date, and the title page of the first edition in 1600 states that it had been performed "divers times" by that date. Salarino's reference to his ship the "Andrew" is thought to be an allusion to the Spanish ship *St. Andrew* captured by the English at Cadiz in 1596. A date of 1596–97 is considered consistent with the play's style.

The play was entered in the Register of the Stationers Company, the method at that time of obtaining copyright for a new play, by James Roberts on July 22, 1598 under the title *The Merchant of Venice,* otherwise called *The Jew of Venice.* On October 28, 1600 Roberts transferred his right to the play to the stationer Thomas Hayes; Hayes published the first quarto before the end of the year. It was printed again in a pirated edition in 1619, as part of William Jaggard's so-called False Folio. (Afterward, Thomas Hayes' son and heir Laurence Hayes asked for and was granted a confirmation of his right to the play, on July 8, 1619.) The 1600 edition is generally regarded as being accurate and reliable, and is the basis of the text published in the 1623 in the First Folio, which adds a number of stage directions, mainly musical cues.

As You Like It

As You Like It is a pastoral comedy by William Shakespeare believed to have been written in 1599 or early 1600 and first published in the folio of 1623. The work was based upon the early prose romance *Rosalynde* by Thomas Lodge. The play's first performance is uncertain, though a performance at Wilton House in 1603 has been suggested as a possibility. *As You Like It* follows its heroine Rosalind as she flees persecution in her uncle's court, accompanied by her cousin Celia and Touchstone the court jester, to find safety and eventually love in the Forest of Arden. Historically, critical response has varied, with some critics finding the work of lesser quality than other Shakespearean works and some finding the play a work of great merit.

The play features one of Shakespeare's most famous and oft-quoted speeches, "All the world's a stage," and is the origin of the phrase "too much of a good thing." The play remains a favorite among audiences and has been adapted for radio, film, and musical theatre.

Synopsis

The play is set in a duchy in France, but most of the action takes place in a location called the 'Forest of Arden.' Frederick has usurped the Duchy and exiled his older brother, Duke Senior. The Duke's daughter Rosalind has been permitted to remain at court because she is the closest friend and cousin of Frederick's only child, Celia. Orlando, a young gentleman of the kingdom who has fallen in love at first sight of Rosalind, is forced to flee his home after being persecuted by his older brother, Oliver.

Frederick becomes angry and banishes Rosalind from court. Celia and Rosalind decide to flee together accompanied by the jester Touchstone, with Rosalind disguised as a young man.

Rosalind, now disguised as Ganymede ("Jove's own page"), and Celia, now disguised as Aliena (Latin for "stranger"), arrive in the Arcadian Forest of Arden, where the exiled Duke now lives with some supporters, including "the melancholy Jaques," who is introduced to us weeping over the slaughter of a deer. "Ganymede" and "Aliena" do not immediately encounter the Duke and his companions, as they meet up with Corin, an impoverished tenant, and offer to buy his master's rude cottage.

Orlando and his servant Adam (a role possibly played by Shakespeare himself, though this story is apocryphal), meanwhile, find the Duke and his men and are soon living with them and posting simplistic love poems for Rosalind on the trees. Rosalind, also in love with Orlando, meets him as Ganymede and pretends to counsel him to cure him of being in love. Ganymede says "he" will take Rosalind's place and "he" and Orlando can act out their relationship.

Meanwhile, the shepherdess Phebe, with whom Silvius is in love, has fallen in love with Ganymede (actually Rosalind), though "Ganymede" continually shows that "he" is not interested in Phebe. The cynical Touchstone has also made amorous advances towards the dull-witted goat-herd girl Audrey, and attempts to marry her before his plans are thwarted by the intrusive Jaques.

Finally, Silvius, Phebe, Ganymede, and Orlando are brought together in an argument with each other over who will get whom. Ganymede says he will solve the problem, having Orlando promise to marry Rosalind, and Phebe promise to marry Silvius if she cannot marry Ganymede. The next day, Ganymede reveals himself to be Rosalind, and since Phebe has found her love to be false, she ends up with Silvius.

Orlando sees Oliver in the forest and rescues him from a lioness, causing Oliver to repent for mistreating Orlando (some directors treat this as a tale, rather than reality). Oliver meets Aliena (Celia's false identity) and falls in love with her, and they agree to marry. Orlando and Rosalind, Oliver and Celia, Silvius and Phebe, and Touchstone and Audrey all are married in the final scene, after which they discover that Frederick has also repented his faults, deciding to restore his legitimate brother to the dukedom and adopt a religious life. Jaques, ever melancholy, declines their invitation to stay in the forest with them and also decides to adopt a religious life.

Twelfth Night

Twelfth Night, or What You Will is a comedy by William Shakespeare, believed to have been written around 1601-02 as a Twelfth Night's entertainment for the close of the Christmas season. The play expanded on the musical interludes and riotous disorder expected of such an occasion, with plot elements drawn from the short story "Of Apollonius and Silla" by Barnabe Rich based on a story by Matteo Bandello. The first recorded performance was on 2 February 1602, at Candlemas, the formal end of Christmastide in the year's calendar. The play was not published until its inclusion in the 1623 *First Folio.*

The subtitle is believed to be an afterthought, created after John Marston premièred a play titled

What You Will during the course of the writing. The title *Twelfth Night, or What You Will,* prepares the audience for its jovial feel of festivities consisting of drink, dance, and giving in to general self-indulgence. The subtitle *What You Will,* implies that the audience is also involved in the merry spirit found in the play. The subtitle also refers to the wealthier characters who do little work and possess the liberty to do as they please, focuses on the aristocrats of society who are entitled to their pleasures while the only hard work being done is by their servants.

Synopsis

Illyria, the setting of *Twelfth Night,* is important to the play's romantic atmosphere. The actual Illyria is an ancient region on the eastern coast of the Adriatic Sea covering parts of modern Albania, Croatia, and Montenegro and the city state of Ragusa has been proposed as the setting. Alternatively, Illyria may have been suggested by the Roman comedy *Menæchmi,* the plot of which also involves a pair of twins who are mistaken for each other. Shakespeare himself mentioned it previously, in *Henry VI, Part II,* noting its reputation for pirates. It has been noted that the play's setting also has English characteristics such as Viola's use of "Westward ho!", a typical cry of 16th century London boatmen, and also Antonio's recommendation to Sebastian of "the Elephant" as where it is "best to lodge" in Illyria; the Elephant was a pub not far from the Globe theatre.

Like many of Shakespeare's comedies, this one centres on mistaken identity. The leading character, Viola, is shipwrecked on the shores of Illyria during the opening scenes. She loses contact with her twin brother, Sebastian, whom she believes is dead.

Masquerading as a young page under the name Cesario, she enters the service of Duke Orsino. Orsino is in love with the bereaved Lady Olivia, whose father and brother have recently died, and who will have nothing to do with any suitors, the Duke included. Orsino decides to use "Cesario" as an intermediary. Olivia, believing Viola to be a man, falls in love with this handsome and eloquent messenger. Viola, in turn, has fallen in love with the Duke, who also believes Viola is a man, and who regards her as his confidant.

Much of the play is taken up with the comic subplot, in which several characters conspire to make Olivia's pompous head steward, Malvolio, believe that his lady Olivia wishes to marry him. It involves Olivia's uncle, Sir Toby Belch; another would-be suitor, a silly squire named Sir Andrew Aguecheek; her servants Maria and Fabian; and her father's favorite fool, Feste. Sir Toby and Sir Andrew disturb the peace of their lady's house by keeping late hours and perpetually singing catches at the very top of their drunken voices, prompting Malvolio to chastise them. This is the basis for Sir Toby's, Sir Andrew's, and Maria's revenge on Malvolio.

The riotous company convince Malvolio that Olivia is secretly in love with him, and write a letter in Olivia's hand, asking Malvolio to wear yellow stockings cross-gartered, to be rude to the rest of the servants, and to smile in all circumstances. Olivia, saddened by Viola's attitude to her, asks for her chief steward, and is shocked by a Malvolio who has seemingly lost his mind. She leaves him to the contrivances of his tormentors.

Pretending that Malvolio is insane, they lock him up in a dark cellar (a common "treatment" for the mentally ill), with a slit for light. Feste visits him to mock his "insanity", once disguised as a priest, and again as himself. At the end of the play Malvolio learns of their conspiracy and storms off promising revenge, but the Duke sends Fabian to pacify him.

Meanwhile Sebastian, Viola's brother, believed deceased, arrives on the scene, sowing confusion. Mistaking him for Viola, Olivia asks him to marry her, and they are secretly united. Finally, when the twins appear in the presence of both Olivia and the Duke, there is more wonder and awe at their similarity, at which point Viola reveals she is really a female and that Sebastian is her lost twin brother. The play ends in a declaration of marriage between the Duke and Viola, and it is learned that Toby has married Maria. An elegiac song from Feste ("heigh-ho, the wind and the rain") brings the entertainment to a close.

Date and text

The full title of the play is *Twelfth Night, or What You Will*. Subtitles for plays were fashionable in the Elizabethan era, and though some editors place *The Merchant of Venice*'s alternate title, *The Jew of Venice*, as a subtitle, this is the single Shakespeare play to bear one when first published. The play was probably finished between 1600 and 1601, but was not printed until its inclusion in the First Folio in 1623. The first recorded performance was on 2 February 1602, at Candlemas, the formal end of Christmastide in the year's calendar.

"Twelfth Night" is a reference to the twelfth night after Christmas Day, called the Eve of the Feast of Epiphany. It was originally a Catholic holiday but, prior to Shakespeare's play, had become a day of revelry. Servants often dressed up as their masters, men as women and so forth. This history of festive ritual and Carnivalesque reversal is the cultural origin of the play's confusion. The source story, "Of Apolonius and Silla" appeared in Barnabe Riche's collection, *Riche His Farwell to the Militarie Profession* (1581), which in turn is derived from a story by Matteo Bandello.

Romeo and Juliet

Romeo and Juliet is a tragedy written early in the career of playwright William Shakespeare about two young "star-cross'd lovers" whose deaths ultimately unite their feuding families. It was among Shakespeare's most popular plays during his lifetime and, along with *Hamlet* and *Macbeth*, is one of his most frequently performed plays. Today, the title characters are regarded as archetypal young lovers.

Romeo and Juliet belongs to a tradition of tragic romances stretching back to antiquity. Its plot is based on an Italian tale, translated into verse as *The Tragical History of Romeus and Juliet* by Arthur Brooke in 1562, and retold in prose in *Palace of Pleasure* by William Painter in 1582. Shakespeare borrowed heavily from both, but developed supporting characters, particularly Mercutio and Paris, in order to expand the plot. Believed to be written between 1591 and 1595, the play was first published in a quarto version in 1597. This text was of poor quality, and later editions corrected it, bringing it more in line with Shakespeare's original text.

Shakespeare's use of dramatic structure, especially effects such as switching between comedy and tragedy to heighten tension, his expansion of minor characters, and his use of sub-plots to embellish the story, has been praised as an early sign of his dramatic skill. The play ascribes different poetic forms to different characters, sometimes changing the form as the character develops. Romeo, for example, grows more adept at the sonnet over the course of the play.

Romeo and Juliet has been adapted numerous times for stage, film, musical and opera. During the Restoration, it was revived and heavily revised by William Davenant. David Garrick's 18th-century version also modified several scenes, removing material then considered indecent, and Georg Benda's operatic adaptation omitted much of the action and added a happy ending. Performances in the 19th century, including Charlotte Cushman's, restored the original text, and focused on greater realism. John Gielgud's 1935 version kept very close to Shakespeare's text, and used Elizabethan costumes and staging to enhance the drama. In the 20th century the play has been adapted in versions as diverse as MGM's comparatively faithful 1936 film, the 1950s stage musical *West Side Story*, and 1996's MTV-inspired *Romeo + Juliet*.

Synopsis

The play, set in Verona, Italy, begins with a street brawl between Montagues and Capulets. The Prince of Verona intervenes and declares that further breach of the peace will be punishable by death. Later, Count Paris talks to Lord Capulet about marrying his daughter, but Capulet is wary of the request because Juliet is only thirteen. Capulet asks Paris to wait another two years and invites him to attend a planned Capulet ball. Lady Capulet and Juliet's nurse try to persuade Juliet to accept Paris' courtship.

Meanwhile, at the house of Montague, Benvolio talks with his cousin Romeo, Lord Montague's son, about Romeo's recent depression. Benvolio discovers that it stems from unrequited infatuation for a girl named Rosaline, one of Lord Capulet's nieces. Persuaded by Benvolio and Mercutio, Romeo attends the ball at the Capulet house in hopes of meeting Rosaline. However, Romeo instead meets and falls in love with Juliet. After the ball, in what is now called the "balcony scene", Romeo sneaks into the Capulet courtyard and overhears Juliet on her balcony vowing her love to him in spite of her family's hatred of the Montagues. Romeo makes himself known to her and they agree to be married. With the help of Friar Laurence, who hopes to reconcile the two families through their children's union, they are secretly married the next day.

Juliet's cousin Tybalt, incensed that Romeo had sneaked into the Capulet ball, challenges him to a duel. Romeo, now considering Tybalt his kinsman, refuses to fight. Mercutio is offended by Tybalt's insolence, as well as Romeo's "vile submission", and accepts the duel on Romeo's behalf. Mercutio is fatally wounded when Romeo attempts to break up the fight. Grief-stricken and racked with guilt, Romeo confronts and slays Tybalt.

Montague argues that Romeo has justly executed Tybalt for the murder of Mercutio. The Prince, now having lost a kinsman in the warring families' feud, exiles Romeo from Verona and declares that if Romeo returns, "that hour is his last". Romeo secretly spends the night in Juliet's chamber, where they consummate their marriage. Lord Capulet, misinterpreting Juliet's grief, agrees to marry her to Count Paris and threatens to disown her when she refuses to become Paris's "joyful bride". When she then pleads for the marriage to be delayed, her mother rejects her.

Juliet visits Friar Laurence for help, and he offers her a drug that will put her into a death-like coma for "two and forty hours". The Friar promises to send a messenger to inform Romeo of the plan, so that he can rejoin her when she awakens. On the night before the wedding, she takes the drug and, when discovered apparently dead, she is laid in the family crypt.

The messenger, however, does not reach Romeo and, instead, he learns of Juliet's apparent death from his servant Balthasar. Heartbroken, Romeo buys poison from an apothecary and goes to the Capulet crypt. He encounters Paris who has come to mourn Juliet privately. Believing Romeo to be a vandal, Paris confronts him and, in the ensuing battle, Romeo kills Paris. Still believing Juliet to be dead, he drinks the poison. Juliet then awakens and, finding Romeo dead, stabs herself with his dagger. The feuding families and the Prince meet at the tomb to find all three dead. Friar Laurence recounts the story of the two "star-cross'd lovers". The families are reconciled by their children's deaths and agree to end their violent feud. The play ends with the Prince's elegy for the lovers: "For never was a story of more woe / Than this of Juliet and her Romeo."

Sources

Romeo and Juliet borrows from a tradition of tragic love stories dating back to antiquity. One of these is Pyramus and Thisbe, from Ovid's Metamorphoses, which contains parallels to Shakespeare's story: the lovers' parents despise each other, and Pyramus falsely believes his lover Thisbe is dead. The *Ephesiaca* of Xenophon of Ephesus, written in the 3rd century, also contains several similarities to the play, including the separation of the lovers, and a potion which induces a deathlike sleep.

The earliest known version of the *Romeo and Juliet* tale is the story of Mariotto and Gianozza by Masuccio Salernitano, in the 33rd novel of his *Il Novellino* published in 1476. Salernitano sets the story in Siena and insists its events took place in his own lifetime. His version of the story includes the secret marriage, the colluding friar, the fray where a prominent citizen is killed, Mariotto's exile, Gianozza's forced marriage, the potion plot, and the crucial message that goes astray. In this version, Mariotto is caught and beheaded and Gianozza dies of grief.

Luigi da Porto adapted the story as *Giulietta e Romeo* and included it in his *Historia novellamente ritrovata di due Nobili Amanti* published in 1530. Da Porto drew on *Pyramus and Thisbe* and Boccacio's Decameron. He gave it much of its modern form, including the names of the lovers, the rival families of Montecchi and Capuleti, and the location in Verona. He also introduces characters corresponding to Shakespeare's Mercutio, Tybalt, and Paris. Da Porto presents his tale as historically true and claims it took place in the days of Bartolomeo II della Scala. Montecchi and Capuleti were actual 13th-century political factions, but the only connection between them is a mention in Dante's Purgatorio as an example of civil dissention. In da Porto's version Romeo takes poison and Giulietta stabs herself with his dagger.

In 1554, Matteo Bandello published the second volume of his *Novelle* which included his version of

Giuletta e Romeo. Bandello emphasises Romeo's initial depression and the feud between the families, and introduces the Nurse and Benvolio. Bandello's story was translated into French by Pierre Boaistuau in 1559 in the first volume of his *Histories Tragiques.* Boaistuau adds much moralising and sentiment, and the characters indulge in rhetorical outbursts.

In his 1562 narrative poem *The Tragical History of Romeus and Juliet,* Arthur Brooke translated Boaistuau faithfully, but adjusted it to reflect parts of Chaucer's *Troilus and Criseyde.* There was a trend among writers and playwrights to publish works based on Italian *novelles*—Italian tales were very popular among theatre-goers—and Shakespeare may well have been familiar with William Painter's 1567 collection of Italian tales titled *Palace of Pleasure.* This collection included a version in prose of the *Romeo and Juliet* story named *"The goodly History of the true and constant love of Rhomeo and Julietta".* Shakespeare took advantage of this popularity: *The Merchant of Venice, Much Ado About Nothing, All's Well That Ends Well, Measure for Measure,* and *Romeo and Juliet* are all from Italian *novelle. Romeo and Juliet* is a dramatisation of Brooke's translation, and Shakespeare follows the poem closely, but adds extra detail to both major and minor characters.

Christopher Marlowe's *Hero and Leander* and *Dido, Queen of Carthage,* both similar stories written in Shakespeare's day, are thought to be less of a direct influence, although they may have helped create an atmosphere in which tragic love stories could thrive.

Date and text

It is unknown when exactly Shakespeare wrote ***Romeo***

and Juliet. Juliet's nurse refers to an earthquake which she says occurred 11 years ago. This may refer to the Dover Straits earthquake of 1580, which would date that particular line to 1591. Other earthquakes—both in England and in Verona—have been proposed in support of different dates. But the play's stylistic similarities with *A Midsummer Night's Dream* and other plays conventionally dated around 1594–95, place its composition sometime between 1591 and 1595. One conjecture is that Shakespeare may have begun a draft in 1591, which he completed in 1595.

Shakespeare's *Romeo and Juliet* was published in two quarto editions prior to the publication of the First Folio of 1623. These are referred to as Q1 and Q2. The first printed edition, Q1, appeared in early 1597, printed by John Danter. Because its text contains numerous differences from the later editions, it is labelled a 'bad quarto'; the 20th-century editor T. J. B. Spencer described it as "a detestable text, probably a reconstruction of the play from the imperfect memories of one or two of the actors", suggesting that it had been pirated for publication. An alternative explanation for Q1's shortcomings is that the play (like many others of the time) may have been heavily edited before performance by the playing company. In any event, its appearance in early 1597 makes 1596 the latest possible date for the play's composition.

The superior Q2 called the play *The Most Excellent and Lamentable Tragedie of Romeo and Juliet*. It was printed in 1599 by Thomas Creede and published by Cuthbert Burby. Q2 is about 800 lines longer than Q1. Its title page describes it as "Newly corrected, augmented and amended". Scholars believe that Q2 was based on Shakespeare's pre-performance draft (called his foul papers), since there are textual oddities such as variable tags for characters and "false starts" for speeches that were presumably struck through by the author but erroneously preserved by the typesetter. It is a much more complete and reliable text, and was reprinted in 1609 (Q3), 1622 (Q4) and 1637 (Q5). In effect, all later Quartos and Folios of *Romeo and Juliet* are based on Q2, as are all modern editions since editors believe that any deviations from Q2 in the later editions (whether good or bad) are likely to arise from editors or compositors, not from Shakespeare.

The First Folio text of 1623 was based primarily on Q3, with clarifications and corrections possibly coming from a theatrical promptbook or Q1. Other Folio editions of the play were printed in 1632 (F2), 1664 (F3), and 1685 (F4). Modern versions—that take into account several of the Folios and Quartos—first appeared with Nicholas Rowe's 1709 edition, followed by Alexander Pope's 1723 version. Pope began a tradition of editing the play to add information such as stage directions missing in Q2 by locating them in Q1. This tradition continued late into the Romantic period. Fully annotated editions first appeared in the Victorian period and continue to be produced today, printing the text of the play with footnotes describing the sources and culture behind the play.

Themes and motifs

Scholars have found it extremely difficult to assign one specific, over-arching theme to the play. Proposals for a main theme include a discovery by the characters that human beings are neither wholly good nor wholly evil, but instead are more or less alike, awaking out of a dream and into reality, the danger of hasty action, or the power of tragic fate. None of these have widespread support. However, even if an overall theme cannot be found it is clear that the play is full of several small, thematic elements which intertwine in complex ways. Several of those which are most often debated by scholars are discussed below.

Love

Romeo and Juliet is sometimes considered to have no unifying theme, save that of young love. Romeo and Juliet have become emblematic of young lovers and doomed love. Since it is such an obvious subject of the play, several scholars have explored the language and historical context behind the romance of the play.

On their first meeting, Romeo and Juliet use a form of communication recommended by many etiquette authors in Shakespeare's day: metaphor. By using metaphors of saints and sins, Romeo was able to test Juliet's feelings for him in a non-threatening way. This method was recommended by Baldassare Castiglione (whose works had been translated into English by this time). He pointed out that if a man used a metaphor as an invitation, the woman could pretend she did not understand him, and he could retreat without losing honour. Juliet, however, participates in the metaphor and expands on it. The religious metaphors of "shrine", "pilgrim" and "saint" were fashionable in the poetry of the time and more likely to be understood as romantic rather than blasphemous, as the concept of sainthood was associated with the Catholicism of an earlier age. Later in the play, Shakespeare removes the more daring allusions to Christ's resurrection in the tomb he found in his source work: Brooke's *Romeus and Juliet*.

In the later balcony scene, Shakespeare has Romeo overhear Juliet's soliloquy, but in Brooke's version of the story her declaration is done alone. By bringing Romeo into the scene to eavesdrop, Shakespeare breaks from the normal sequence of courtship. Usually a woman was required to be modest and shy to make sure that her suitor was sincere, but breaking this rule serves to speed along the plot. The lovers are able to skip a lengthy part of wooing, and move on to plain talk about their relationship—developing into an agreement to be married after knowing each other for only one night. In the final suicide scene, there is a contradiction in the message—in the Catholic religion, suicides were often thought to be condemned to hell, whereas people who die to be with their loves under the "Religion of Love" are joined with their loves in paradise. Romeo and Juliet's love seems to be expressing the "Religion of Love" view rather than the Catholic view. Another point is that although their love is passionate, it is only consummated in marriage, which prevents them from losing the audience's sympathy.

The play arguably equates love and sex with death. Throughout the story, both Romeo and Juliet, along with the other characters, fantasise about it as a dark being, often equating it with a lover. Capulet, for example, when he first discovers Juliet's (faked) death, describes it as having deflowered his daughter. Juliet later erotically compares Romeo and death. Right before her suicide she grabs Romeo's dagger, saying "O happy dagger! This is thy sheath. There rust, and let me die."

Fate and chance

Scholars are divided on the role of fate in the play. No

consensus exists on whether the characters are truly fated to die together or whether the events take place by a series of unlucky chances. Arguments in favour of fate often refer to the description of the lovers as "star-cross'd". This phrase seems to hint that the stars have predetermined the lovers' future. John W. Draper points out the parallels between the Elizabethan belief in the four humours and the main characters of the play (for example, Tybalt as a choleric). Interpreting the text in the light of humours reduces the amount of plot attributed to chance by modern audiences. Still, other scholars see the play as a series of unlucky chances—many to such a degree that they do not see it as a tragedy at all, but an emotional melodrama. Ruth Nevo believes the high degree to which chance is stressed in the narrative makes *Romeo and Juliet* a "lesser tragedy" of happenstance, not of character. For example, Romeo's challenging Tybalt is not impulsive, it is, after Mercutio's death, the expected action to take. In this scene, Nevo reads Romeo as being aware of the dangers of flouting social norms, identity and commitments. He makes the choice to kill, not because of a tragic flaw, but because of circumstance.

Julius Caesar

Julius Caesar is a tragedy by William Shakespeare, believed to have been written in 1599. It portrays the conspiracy against the Roman dictator of the same name, his assassination and its aftermath. It is one of several Roman plays that he wrote, based on true events from Roman history, which also include *Coriolanus* and *Antony and Cleopatra*.

Although the title of the play is *Julius Caesar*, Caesar is not the central character in its action; he appears in only three scenes, and is killed at the beginning of the third act. The protagonist of the play is Marcus Brutus, and the central psychological drama is his struggle between the conflicting demands of honour, patriotism, and friendship.

The play reflected the general anxiety of England over succession of leadership. At the time of its creation and first performance, Queen Elizabeth, a strong ruler, was elderly and had refused to name a successor, leading to worries that a civil war similar to that of Rome might break out after her death.

Synopsis

Marcus Brutus is Caesar's close friend and a Roman praetor (Minister). Brutus allows himself to be cajoled into joining a group of conspiring senators because of a growing suspicion—implanted by Caius Cassius—that Caesar intends to turn republican Rome into a monarchy under his own rule.

Traditional readings of the play maintain that Cassius and the other conspirators are motivated largely by envy and ambition, whereas Brutus is motivated by the demands of honor and patriotism; other commentators, such as Isaac Asimov, suggest that the text shows Brutus is no less moved by envy and flattery. One of the central strengths of the play is that it resists categorizing its characters as either simple heroes or villains. The early scenes deal mainly with Brutus' arguments with Cassius and his struggle with his own conscience. The growing tide of public support soon turns Brutus against Caesar (this public support was actually faked; Cassius wrote letters to Brutus in different handwritings over the next month in order to get Brutus to join the conspiracy). A soothsayer warns Caesar to "beware the Ides of

March", which he ignores, culminating in his assassination at the Capitol by the conspirators that day.

Caesar's assassination is one of the most famous scenes of the play, about halfway through (the other is Marc Antony's oration "Friends, Romans, countrymen".) After ignoring the soothsayer as well as his wife's own premonitions, Caesar comes to the Senate. The conspirators create a superficial motive for the assassination by means of a petition brought by Metellus Cimber, pleading on behalf of his banished brother. As Caesar, predictably, rejects the petition, Casca grazes Caesar in the back of his neck, and the others follow in stabbing him; Brutus is last. At this point, Caesar utters the famous line *"Et tu, Brute?"* ("And you, Brutus?", *i.e.* "You too, Brutus?"). Shakespeare has him add, "Then fall, Caesar," suggesting that Caesar did not want to survive such treachery.

The conspirators make clear that they committed this act for Rome, not for their own purposes and do not attempt to flee the scene. After Caesar's death, Brutus delivers an oration defending his actions, and for the moment, the crowd is on his side. However, Mark Antony, with a subtle and eloquent speech over Caesar's corpse—the much-quoted *Friends, Romans, countrymen, lend me your ears...*—deftly turns public opinion against the assassins by manipulating the emotions of the common people, in contrast to the rational tone of Brutus's speech. Antony rouses the mob to drive the conspirators from Rome. Amid the violence, the innocent poet, Cinna, is confused with the conspirator Lucius Cinna and is murdered by the mob.

The beginning of Act Four is marked by the quarrel scene, where Brutus attacks Cassius for soiling the noble act of regicide by accepting bribes ("Did not great Julius bleed for justice' sake? / What villain touch'd his body, that did stab, / And not for justice?", IV.iii,19–21). The two are reconciled; they prepare for war with Mark Antony and Caesar's adopted son, Octavian (Shakespeare's spelling: Octavius). That night, Caesar's ghost appears to Brutus with a warning of defeat. At the battle, Cassius and Brutus knowing they will probably both die, smile their last smiles to each other and hold hands. During the battle, Cassius commits suicide after seeing the death of his best friend, Titinius. After Titinius, who wasn't really killed, sees Cassius' corpse, he commits suicide. However, Brutus wins the battle. Brutus, with a heavy heart, battles again the next day. He loses and commits suicide. The play ends with a tribute to Brutus by Antony, who proclaims that Brutus has remained "the noblest Roman of them all" (V.v,68) because he was the only conspirator who acted for the good of Rome. There is then a small hint at the friction between Mark Antony and Octavius which will characterise another of Shakespeare's Roman plays, *Antony and Cleopatra.*

Date and text

Julius Caesar was known to be first published in the First Folio in 1623, but a performance was mentioned by Thomas Platter the Younger in his diary in September 1599. The play is not mentioned in the list of Shakespeare's plays published by Francis Meres in 1598. Based on these two points, as well as a number of contemporary allusions, and the belief that the play is similar to *Hamlet* in vocabulary, and to *Henry V* and *As You Like It* in metre, scholars have suggested 1599 as a probable date. The text of *Julius Caesar* in the First Folio is the only authoritative text for the play. The Folio text is notable for its quality and consistency; scholars judge it to have been set into type from a theatrical prompt-book. The source used by Shakespeare was Sir Thomas North's translation of Plutarch's *Life of Brutus* and *Life of Caesar*.

The play contains many anachronistic elements from the Elizabethan period. The characters mention objects such as hats and doublets (large, heavy jackets) – neither of which existed in ancient Rome. Caesar is mentioned to be wearing an Elizabethan doublet instead of a Roman toga. At one point a clock is heard to strike and Brutus notes it with "Count the clock".

Interpretations

Protagonist debate

Critics of Shakespeare's play *Julius Caesar* differ greatly on their views of Caesar and Brutus. Many have debated whether Caesar or Brutus is the protagonist of the play, because of the title character's death in 3.1. But Caesar compares himself to the Northern Star, and perhaps it would be foolish not to consider him as the axial character of the play, around whom the entire story turns. Intertwined in this debate is a smattering of philosophical and psychological ideologies on republicanism and monarchism.

One author, Robert C. Reynolds, devotes attention to the names or epithets given to both Brutus and Caesar in his essay "Ironic Epithet in Julius Caesar". This author points out that Casca praises Brutus at face value, but then inadvertently compares him to a disreputable joke of a man by calling him an alchemist,

"Oh, he sits high in all the people's hearts,/And that which would appear offense in us/ His countenance, like richest alchemy,/ Will change to virtue and to worthiness" (I.iii.158-60). Reynolds also talks about Caesar and his "Colossus" epithet, which he points out has its obvious connotations of power and manliness, but also lesser known connotations of an outward glorious front and inward chaos. In that essay, the conclusion as to who is the hero or protagonist is ambiguous because of the conceit-like poetic quality of the epithets for Caesar and Brutus.

Myron Taylor, in his essay "Shakespeare's Julius Caesar and the Irony of History", compares the logic and philosophies of Caesar and Brutus. Caesar is deemed an intuitive philosopher who is always right when he goes with his gut, for instance when he says he fears Cassius as a threat to him before he is killed, his intuition is correct. Brutus is portrayed as a man similar to Caesar, but whose passions lead him to the wrong reasoning, which he realizes in the end when he says in V.v.50–51, "Caesar, now be still:/ I kill'd not thee with half so good a will". This interpretation is flawed by the fact relies on a very odd reading of "good a will" to mean "incorrect judgments" rather than the more intuitive "good intentions."

Joseph W. Houppert acknowledges that some critics have tried to cast Caesar as the protagonist, but that ultimately Brutus is the driving force in the play and is therefore the tragic hero. Brutus attempts to put the republic over his personal relationship with Caesar and kills him. Brutus makes the political mistakes that bring down the republic that his ancestors created. He acts on his passions, does not gather enough evidence to make reasonable decisions and is manipulated by Cassius and the other conspirators.

Hamlet

The Tragedy of Hamlet, Prince of Denmark, or more simply *Hamlet,* is a tragedy by William Shakespeare, believed to have been written between 1599 and 1601. The play, set in Denmark, recounts how Prince Hamlet exacts revenge on his uncle Claudius, who has murdered Hamlet's father, the King, and then taken the throne and married Gertrude, Hamlet's mother. The play vividly charts the course of real and feigned madness—from overwhelming grief to seething rage—and explores themes of treachery, revenge, incest, and moral corruption.

Despite much literary detective work, the exact year of writing remains in dispute. Three different early versions of the play have survived: these are known as the First Quarto (Q1), the Second Quarto (Q2) and the First Folio (F1). Each has lines, and even scenes, that are missing from the others. Shakespeare probably based *Hamlet* on the legend of Amleth, preserved by 13th-century chronicler Saxo Grammaticus in his Gesta Danorum and subsequently retold by 16th-century scholar François de Belleforest, and a supposedly lost Elizabethan play known today as the *Ur-Hamlet.*

Given the play's dramatic structure and depth of characterization, *Hamlet* can be analyzed, interpreted and argued about from many perspectives. For example, scholars have debated for centuries about Hamlet's hesitation in killing his uncle. Some see it as a plot device to prolong the action, and others see it as the result of pressure exerted by the complex philosophical and ethical issues that surround cold-blooded murder, calculated revenge and thwarted desire. More recently, psychoanalytic critics have examined Hamlet's unconscious desires, and feminist critics have re-evaluated and rehabilitated the often maligned characters of Ophelia and Gertrude.

Hamlet is Shakespeare's longest play and among the most powerful and influential tragedies in the English language. It provides a storyline capable of "seemingly endless retelling and adaptation by others". During Shakespeare's lifetime, the play was one of his most popular works, and it still ranks high among his most-performed, topping, for example, the Royal Shakespeare Company's list since 1879. It has inspired writers from Goethe and Dickens to Joyce and Murdoch and has been described as "the world's most filmed story after *Cinderella*". The title role was almost certainly created for Richard Burbage, the leading tragedian of Shakespeare's time. In the four hundred years since, it has been played by highly acclaimed actors, and sometimes actresses, of each successive age.

Synopsis

The protagonist of *Hamlet* is Prince Hamlet of Denmark, son of the recently deceased King Hamlet and his wife, Queen Gertrude. While the young Hamlet is away at school the recently deceased King's brother, Claudius, is elected king and hastily marries Gertrude. A minor subplot involves Denmark's long-standing feud with neighbouring Norway, and the threat of invasion led by the Norwegian prince Fortinbras.

The play opens on a cold night at Elsinore, the Danish royal castle. Francisco, one of the sentinels, is relieved of his watch by Bernardo, another sentinel, and exits while Bernardo remains. A third sentinel, Marcellus, enters with Horatio, Hamlet's best friend.

The sentinels inform Horatio that they have seen a ghost that looks like the dead King Hamlet. After hearing from Horatio of the Ghost's appearance, Hamlet resolves to see the Ghost himself. That night, the Ghost appears again. It leads Hamlet to seclusion and reveals that it is the actual spirit of his father and discloses that he, the elder Hamlet, was murdered by Claudius pouring poison in his ear. The Ghost demands that Hamlet avenge him; Hamlet agrees, swears his companions to secrecy, and tells them he intends to "put on an antic disposition" (presumably to avert suspicion). Hamlet initially attests to the ghost's reliability, calling him both an "honest ghost" and "truepenny". He later raises doubts about the ghost's nature and intent and claims these as reasons for his inaction.

Polonius is Claudius' trusted chief counsellor; his son, Laertes, is returning to France, and his daughter, Ophelia, is courted by Hamlet. Neither Polonius nor Laertes thinks Hamlet is serious about Ophelia, and they both warn her off. Shortly afterwards, Ophelia is alarmed by Hamlet's strange behaviour and reports to her father that Hamlet rushed into her room, stared at her and said nothing. Polonius assumes that the "ecstasy of love" is responsible for Hamlet's madness, and he informs Claudius and Gertrude.

Busy with affairs of state, Claudius receives the ambassador of Norway who gives assurances of peace between Norway and Denmark. Perturbed by Hamlet's continuing deep mourning for his father and his increasingly erratic behavior, Claudius sends for two of Hamlet's acquaintances —Rosencrantz and Guildenstern—to discover the cause of Hamlet's changed behavior. Hamlet greets his friends warmly but quickly discerns that they have been sent to spy on him.

Together, Claudius and Polonius convince Ophelia to speak with Hamlet while they secretly listen to the conversation. When Hamlet enters, she offers to return his remembrances, upon which Hamlet questions her honesty and furiously rants at her, insisting she go "to a nunnery".

Hamlet remains uncertain if the Ghost has told him the truth, but the arrival of a troupe of actors at Elsinore presents him with a solution. He will stage a play, re-enacting his father's murder, and determine Claudius's guilt or innocence by studying his reaction. The court assembles to watch the play; Hamlet provides an agitated running commentary throughout. When the murder scene is presented, Claudius abruptly rises and leaves the room, which Hamlet sees as proof of his uncle's guilt.

Gertrude summons Hamlet to her closet to demand an explanation. On his way, Hamlet passes Claudius in prayer but hesitates to kill him, reasoning that death in prayer would send him to heaven. However it is revealed that the King is not truly praying, remarking that "words" never made it to heaven without "thoughts." Upon reaching the queen, an argument erupts between Hamlet and Gertrude. Polonius, who is spying on the scene from behind an arras, convinced that the prince's madness is indeed real, panics when it seems as if Hamlet is about to murder the Queen and cries out for help. Hamlet, believing it is Claudius hiding behind the arras, stabs wildly through the cloth, killing Polonius. When he realizes that he has killed Ophelia's father, he is not remorseful, but calls Polonius "Thou wretched, rash, intruding fool". The Ghost appears, urging Hamlet to treat Gertrude gently but reminding him to kill Claudius. Unable to see or hear the Ghost herself, Gertrude takes Hamlet's conversation with it as further evidence of madness.

Claudius, fearing for his life, and finally holding a legitimate excuse to get rid of the prince, makes plans to send Hamlet to England on a diplomatic pretext, closely watched by Rosencrantz and Guildenstern. Alone, Claudius discloses that he is sending Hamlet to his death. Prior to embarking for England, Hamlet hides Polonius's body, ultimately revealing its location to the King. Upon leaving Elsinore, Hamlet encounters the army of Prince Fortinbras en route to do battle in Poland. Upon witnessing so many men going to their death for the brash whim of an impulsive prince, Hamlet decides that he will no longer plot and scheme, but rather finish his plan and kill Claudius.

At Elsinore, further demented by grief at Polonius's death, Ophelia wanders the castle acting erratically and singing bawdy songs. Her brother, Laertes, arrives back from France, enraged by his father's death and his sister's madness. She appears briefly to give out herbs and flowers. Claudius convinces Laertes that Hamlet is solely responsible; then news arrives that Hamlet is still at large— a story is spread that his ship was attacked by pirates on the way to England, and he has returned to Denmark. Claudius swiftly concocts a plot. His plan is to allow Hamlet's death to appear to be an accident, taking all of the blame off of his shoulders. He proposes a fencing match between Laertes and Hamlet, as Hamlet was jealous of Laertes prowess with a sword. Laertes, enraged at the murder of his father informs the king that he will further poison the tip of his sword so as a mere scratch would mean certain death. Claudius, unsure that capable Hamlet could receive even a scratch, plans to offer Hamlet poisoned wine if that fails. Gertrude enters to report that Ophelia has drowned.

In the Elsinore churchyard, two "clowns", typically represented as "gravediggers", enter to prepare Ophelia's grave, and although the coroner has ruled her death accidental, so that she receives Christian burial, they argue over it being a case of suicide. Hamlet arrives with Horatio and banters with one of them, who unearths the skull of a jester whom Hamlet once knew, Yorick. Ophelia's funeral procession approaches, led by her mournful brother Laertes. Upset at the lack of ceremony due to the deemed suicide and overcome by emotion, Laertes leaps into the grave, cursing Hamlet as the cause of her death. Hamlet interrupts and professes his own love and grief for Ophelia. He and Laertes grapple, but the fight is broken up by Claudius and Gertrude. Claudius makes sure to remind Laertes of the planned fencing match.

Later that day, Hamlet tells Horatio how he escaped, and that Rosencrantz and Guildenstern have been sent to their deaths. A courtier, Osric, interrupts to invite Hamlet to fence with Laertes. Despite warnings from Horatio, Hamlet accepts and the match begins. After several rounds, Gertrude toasts Hamlet against the urgent warning of Claudius, accidentally drinking the wine he poisoned. Between bouts, Laertes attacks and pierces Hamlet with his poisoned blade; in the ensuing scuffle, Hamlet is able to use Laertes's own poisoned sword against him, fatally **wounding**

Laertes. Gertrude falls and in her dying breath announces that she has been poisoned. In his dying moments, Laertes is reconciled with Hamlet and reveals Claudius's murderous plot. In his own final moments, Hamlet, at last, forces Claudius to drink from his own poisoned cup, and names Prince Fortinbras of Norway as his heir. Horatio attempts to kill himself with the same poisoned wine, but is stopped by Hamlet, who commands him to tell his story, as he will be the only one left alive that could give a full account. When Fortinbras arrives to greet King Claudius, he encounters the deathly scene: Gertrude, Claudius, Laertes, and Hamlet are all dead. Horatio asks to be allowed to recount the tale to "the yet unknowing world", and Fortinbras orders Hamlet's body borne off in honour.

Sources

Hamlet-like legends are so widely found (for example in Italy, Spain, Scandinavia, Byzantium, and Arabia) that the core "hero-as-fool" theme is possibly Indo-European in origin. Several ancient written precursors to *Hamlet* can be identified. The first is the anonymous Scandinavian *Saga of Hrolf Kraki*. In this, the murdered king has two sons—Hroar and Helgi—who spend most of the story in disguise, under false names, rather than feigning madness, in a sequence of events that differs from Shakespeare's. The second is the Roman legend of Brutus, recorded in two separate Latin works. Its hero, Lucius ("shining, light"), changes his name and persona to Brutus ("dull, stupid"), playing the role of a fool to avoid the fate of his father and brothers, and eventually slaying his family's killer, King Tarquinius. A 17th-century Nordic scholar, Torfaeus, compared the Icelandic hero Amlodi and the

Spanish hero Prince Ambales (from the *Ambales Saga*) to Shakespeare's *Hamlet*. Similarities include the prince's feigned madness, his accidental killing of the king's counsellor in his mother's bedroom, and the eventual slaying of his uncle.

Many of the earlier legendary elements are interwoven in the 13th-century *Vita Amlethi* ("The Life of Amleth") by Saxo Grammaticus, part of *Gesta Danorum*. Written in Latin, it reflects classical Roman concepts of virtue and heroism, and was widely available in Shakespeare's day. Significant parallels include the prince feigning madness, his mother's hasty marriage to the usurper, the prince killing a hidden spy, and the prince substituting the execution of two retainers for his own. A reasonably faithful version of Saxo's story was translated into French in 1570 by François de Belleforest, in his *Histoires tragiques*. Belleforest embellished Saxo's text substantially, almost doubling its length, and introduced the hero's melancholy.

According to a popular theory, Shakespeare's main source is believed to be an earlier play—now lost—known today as the *Ur-Hamlet*. Possibly written by Thomas Kyd or even William Shakespeare himself, the *Ur-Hamlet* would have been in performance by 1589 and the first version of the story known to incorporate a ghost. Shakespeare's company, the Chamberlain's Men, may have purchased that play and performed a version for some time, which Shakespeare reworked. Since no copy of the *Ur-Hamlet* has survived, however, it is impossible to compare its language and style with the known works of any of its putative authors. Consequently, there is no direct evidence that Kyd wrote it, nor any evidence that the play was not an early version of *Hamlet* by Shakespeare himself. This latter idea—placing *Hamlet* far earlier than the generally accepted date, with a much longer period of development—has attracted some support, though others dismiss it as speculation.

The upshot is that scholars cannot assert with any confidence how much material Shakespeare took from the *Ur-Hamlet* (if it even existed), how much from Belleforest or Saxo, and how much from other contemporary sources (such as Kyd's *The Spanish Tragedy*). No clear evidence exists that Shakespeare made any direct references to Saxo's version. However, elements of Belleforest's version which are not in Saxo's story do appear in Shakespeare's play. Whether Shakespeare took these from Belleforest directly or through the *Ur-Hamlet* remains unclear.

Most scholars reject the idea that *Hamlet* is in any way connected with Shakespeare's only son, Hamnet Shakespeare, who died in 1596 at age eleven. Conventional wisdom holds that *Hamlet* is too obviously connected to legend, and the name Hamnet was quite popular at the time. However, Stephen Greenblatt has argued that the coincidence of the names and Shakespeare's grief for the loss of his son may lie at the heart of the tragedy. He notes that the name of Hamnet Sadler, the Stratford neighbor after whom Hamnet was named, was often written as Hamlet Sadler and that, in the loose orthography of the time, the names were virtually interchangeable. Sadler's first name is spelled "Hamlett" in Shakespeare's will.

Date

Any dating of *Hamlet* must be tentative", cautions the

New Cambridge editor, Phillip Edwards. The earliest date estimate relies on *Hamlet*'s frequent allusions to Shakespeare's *Julius Caesar,* itself dated to mid-1599. The latest date estimate is based on an entry, of 26 July 1602, in the Register of the Stationers' Company, indicating that *Hamlet* was "latelie Acted by the Lo: Chamberleyne his servantes".

In 1598, Francis Meres published in his *Palladis Tamia* a survey of English literature from Chaucer to its present day, within which twelve of Shakespeare's plays are named. *Hamlet* is not among them, suggesting that it had not yet been written. As *Hamlet* was very popular, the *New Swan* series editor Bernard Lott believes it "unlikely that he [Meres] would have overlooked... so significant a piece".

The phrase "little eyases" in the First Folio (F1) may allude to the Children of the Chapel, whose popularity in London forced the Globe company into provincial touring. This became known as the War of the Theatres, and supports a 1601 dating.

A contemporary of Shakespere's, Gabriel Harvey, wrote a marginal note in his copy of the 1598 edition of Chaucer's works, which some scholars use as dating evidence. Harvey's note says that "the wiser sort" enjoy *Hamlet,* and implies that the Earl of Essex—executed in February 1601 for rebellion—was still alive. Other scholars consider this inconclusive. Edwards, for example, concludes that the "sense of time is so confused in Harvey's note that it is really of little use in trying to date *Hamlet*". This is because the same note also refers to Spenser and Watson as if they were still alive ("our flourishing metricians"), but also mentions "Owen's new epigrams", published in 1607.

Othello

Othello, the Moor of Venice is a tragedy by William Shakespeare, believed to have been written in approximately 1603, and based on the Italian short story "Un Capitano Moro" ("A Moorish Captain") by Cinthio, a disciple of Boccaccio, first published in 1565. The work revolves around four central characters: Othello, a Moorish general in the Venetian army; his wife Desdemona; his lieutenant, Cassio; and his trusted ensign Iago. Because of its varied themes — racism, love, jealousy, and betrayal — *Othello* is widely felt to remain relevant to the present day and is often performed in professional and community theatres alike. The play has also been the basis for numerous operatic, film, and literary adaptations.

Plot

The play opens with Roderigo, a rich and dissolute gentleman, complaining to Iago, a high-ranking soldier, that Iago has not told him about the secret marriage between Desdemona, the daughter of a Senator named Brabantio, and Othello, a Moorish general in the Venetian army. He is upset by this development because he loves Desdemona and had previously asked her father for her hand in marriage. Iago is upset with Othello for promoting a younger man named Michael Cassio above him, and tells Roderigo that he plans to use Othello for his own advantage. Iago's argument against Cassio is that he is a scholarly tactician with no real battle experience from which he can draw strategy; in contrast, Iago has practical battle skills. By emphasizing Roderigo's failed bid for Desdemona, and his own dissatisfaction with serving under Othello, Iago convinces Roderigo to wake Brabantio, Desdemona's father, and tell him about his daughter's elopement. Next, Iago sneaks away to find Othello and warns him that Brabantio is coming for him.

However, before Brabantio reaches Othello, news arrives in Venice that the Turks are going to attack Cyprus; therefore Othello is summoned to advise the senators. Brabantio arrives and accuses Othello of seducing Desdemona by witchcraft, but Othello defends himself successfully before an assembly that includes the Duke of Venice, Brabantio's kinsman Lodovico and Gratiano, and various senators, explaining that Desdemona became enamored of him for the stories he told of his early life.

By order of the Duke, Othello leaves Venice to command the Venetian armies against invading Turks on the island of Cyprus, accompanied by his new wife, his new lieutenant Cassio, his ensign Iago, and Emilia as Desdemona's attendant.

The party arrives in Cyprus to find that a storm has destroyed the Turkish fleet. Othello orders a general celebration. Iago schemes to use Cassio to ruin Othello and takes the opportunity of Othello's absence at the celebration to persuade Roderigo to engage Cassio in a fight. He achieves this by getting Cassio drunk on wine. The brawl greatly alarms the citizenry, and Othello is forced to quell the disturbance. Othello blames Cassio for the disturbance, and strips him of his rank. Cassio is distraught, but Iago persuades him to importune Desdemona to act as an intermediary between himself and Othello, and persuade her husband to reinstate him.

Iago now persuades Othello to be suspicious of Cassio and Desdemona. As it happens, Cassio is courting a courtesan named Bianca. Desdemona drops a handkerchief that was Othello's first gift to her and which he has stated holds great significance to him in the context of their relationship. Iago asks Emilia to steal it. Emilia, unaware of what Iago plans to do with the handkerchief, steals it. Iago plants it in Cassio's lodgings as evidence of Cassio and Desdemona's affair. After he has planted the handkerchief, Iago tells Othello to stand apart and watch Cassio's reactions while Iago questions him about the handkerchief. Iago goads Cassio on to talk about his affair with Bianca, without mentioning her name; because no name is mentioned, Othello thinks that Cassio is referring to Desdemona. Bianca, on discovering the handkerchief, chastises Cassio, accusing him of giving her a second-hand gift which he received from another lover. Othello sees this, and Iago convinces him that Cassio received the handkerchief from Desdemona. Enraged and hurt, Othello decides he is going to kill his wife and Iago offers to kill Cassio. Othello proceeds to make Desdemona's life a misery, hitting her in front of her family. Desdemona laments her suffering, remembering the fate of her mother's maid, who was forsaken by her lover.

Iago convinces Roderigo to kill Cassio instead, because Cassio has just been appointed in Othello's place, whereas if Cassio lives to take office, Othello and Desdemona will leave Cyprus, thwarting Roderigo's plans to win Desdemona. Roderigo attacks Cassio in the street after Cassio leaves Bianca's lodgings. They fight and both are wounded. Cassio's leg is cut from behind by Iago who manages to hide his identity as perpetrator. Passers-by arrive to help; Iago joins them, pretending to help Cassio. Iago secretly stabs Roderigo to stop him from confessing and accuses Bianca of conspiracy to kill Cassio.In the night, Othello confronts Desdemona, and then kills her by smothering her in bed, before Emilia arrives. At Emilia's distress, Othello tries to explain himself, justifying his actions by accusing Desdemona of adultery. Emilia calls for help. The Governor arrives, with Iago and others, and Emilia begins to explain the situation. When Othello mentions the handkerchief as proof, Emilia realizes what Iago has done; she exposes him, whereupon Iago kills her. Othello, realizing Desdemona's innocence, attacks Iago but does not kill him, saying that he would rather have Iago live the rest of his life in pain. Lodovico, a Venetian nobleman, apprehends both Iago and Othello, but Othello commits suicide with a dagger before they can take him into custody. At the end, it can be assumed, Iago is taken off to be tortured and possibly executed.

Source

Othello is an adaptation of the Italian writer Cinthio's tale, "Un Capitano Moro" from his *Gli Hecatommithi* (1565), a collection of one hundred tales in the style of Boccacio's *Decameron*. No English translation of Cinthio was available in Shakespeare's lifetime, and verbal echoes in *Othello* are closer to the Italian original than to Gabriel Chappuy's 1584 French translation. Cinthio's tale may have been based on an actual incident occurring in Venice about 1508. It also resembles an incident described in the earlier tale of "The Three Apples", one of the stories narrated in the *One Thousand and One Nights* (*Arabian Nights*).

Desdemona is the only named character in Cinthio's tale, with his few other characters identified only as "the Moor", "the squadron leader", "the ensign", and "the ensign's wife". Cinthio drew a moral (which he placed in the mouth of Desdemona) that European women are unwise to marry the temperamental males of other nations.

Cinthio's Moor is the model for Shakespeare's Othello, but some researchers believe the poet also took inspiration from the several Moorish delegations from Morocco to Elizabethan England *circa* 1600.

While Shakespeare closely followed Cinthio's tale in composing *Othello,* he departed from it in some details. Brabantio, Roderigo, and several minor characters are not found in Cinthio, for example, and Shakespeare's Emilia takes part in the handkerchief mischief while her counterpart in Cinthio does not. Unlike Shakespeare's Iago, Cinthio's ensign lusts after Desdemona and is spurred to revenge when she rejects him. Shakespeare's opening scenes are unique to his tragedy as is the tender scene between Emilia and Desdemona as the lady prepares for bed.

Shakespeare's most striking departure from Cinthio is the manner of his heroine's death. In Shakespeare, Othello suffocates Desdemona, but in Cinthio, the Moor commissions his ensign to bludgeon his wife to death with a sand-filled stocking. Cinthio describes each gruesome blow, and, when the lady is dead, the Moor and his ensign place her lifeless body upon her bed, smash her skull, and cause the cracked ceiling above the bed to collapse upon her, giving the impression its falling rafters caused her death.

In Cinthio, the two murderers escape detection. The Moor then misses his wife greatly, and comes to loathe the sight of his ensign. He demotes him, and refuses to have him in his company. The ensign then seeks revenge by disclosing to the "the squadron leader" (the tale's Cassio counterpart), the Moor's involvement in Desdemona's death. The two depart Cyprus for Venice, and denounce the Moor to the Venetian Seignory; the Moor is arrested, taken to Venice, and tortured. He refuses to admit his guilt and is condemned to exile. Desdemona's relatives eventually find and kill him. The ensign, however, continues to escape detection in Desdemona's death, but engages in other crimes while in Venice. He is arrested and dies after being tortured. Cinthio's "ensign's wife" survives her husband's death to tell her story.

Date and text

The earliest mention of the play is found in a 1604 Revels Office account, which records that on "Hallamas Day, being the first of Nouembar... the Kings Maiesties plaiers" performed "A Play in the Banketinghouse att Whit Hall Called The Moor of Venis." The work is attributed to "Shaxberd." The Revels account was first printed by Peter Cunningham in 1842, and, while its authenticity was once challenged, is now regarded as genuine (as authenticated by A. E. Stamp in 1930). Based on its style, the play is usually dated 1603 or 1604, but arguments have been made for dates as early as 1601 or 1602.

The play was entered into the Register of the Stationers Company on October 6, 1621, by Thomas Walkley, and was first published in quarto format by him in 1622:

THE Tragœdy of Othello, The Moore of Venice. *As it hath beene diuerse times acted at the* Globe, and at the Black-Friers, by *his Maiesties Seruants. Written by* VVilliam Shakespeare. *LONDON,* Printed by *N. O.*

[Nicholas Okes] for Thomas Walkley, *and are to be sold at his shop, at the Eagle and Child, in Brittans Bursse, 1622.*

One year later, the play was included among the plays in the First Folio of Shakespeare's collected plays. However, the version in the Folio is rather different in length, and in wording: as the editors of the Folger edition explain,

> ...the Folio play has about 160 lines that do not appear in the Quarto. Some of these cluster together in quite extensive passages. The Folio also lacks a scattering of about a dozen lines or part-lines that are to be found in the Quarto. These two versions also differ from each other in their readings of numerous words.

Scholars differ in their explanation of these differences, and no consensus has emerged. One explanation is that the Quarto may have been cut in the printing house to meet a fixed number of pages. Another is that the Quarto is based on an early version of the play, while the Folio represents Shakespeare's revised version. Most modern editions are based on the longer Folio version, but often incorporate Quarto readings of words when the Folio text appears to be in error.

King Lear

King Lear is a tragedy by William Shakespeare, believed to have been written between 1603 and 1606. It is considered one of his greatest works. The play is based on the legend of Leir of Britain, a mythological pre-Roman Celtic king. It has been widely adapted for stage and screen, with the part of Lear played by many of the world's most accomplished actors.

There are two distinct versions of the play:*The True Chronicle of the History of the Life and Death of King*

Lear and His Three Daughters, which appeared in quarto in 1608, and *The Tragedy of King Lear,* a more theatrical version, which appeared in the First Folio in 1623. The two texts are commonly printed in a conflated version, although many modern editors have argued that each version has its individual integrity.

After the Restoration the play was often modified by theatre practitioners who disliked its dark and depressing tone, but since the 19th century it has been regarded as one of Shakespeare's supreme achievements. The tragedy is particularly noted for its probing observations on the nature of human suffering and kinship.

Synopsis

Lear, who is old, wants to retire from power. He decides to divide his realm among his three daughters, and offers the largest share to the one who loves him best. Goneril and Regan both proclaim in fulsome terms that they love him more than anything in the world, which pleases him. Cordelia speaks temperately and honestly, which annoys him. In his anger he disinherits her, and divides the kingdom between the other two. Kent objects to this unfair treatment. Lear is further enraged by Kent's contradiction, and banishes him from the country. Cordelia's two suitors enter. Learning that she is disinherited, the Duke of Burgundy withdraws his suit, but the King of France is impressed by her honesty and marries her anyway.

Lear announces he will live alternately with Goneril and Regan, and their husbands, the Dukes of Albany and Cornwall. He reserves to himself a retinue of one hundred knights, to be supported by his daughters. Goneril and Regan speak privately, agreeing that Lear is old and foolish. Edmund resents his illegitimate status, and plots to supplant his legitimate older brother Edgar. He tricks their father Gloucester with a forged letter, making him think Edgar plans to usurp the estate. Kent returns from exile in disguise under the name of Caius, and Lear hires him as a servant. Lear discovers that now that Goneril has power, she no longer respects him. She orders him to behave better and reduce his retinue. Enraged, Lear departs for Regan's home. The Fool mocks Lear's misfortune. Edmund fakes an attack by Edgar, and Gloucester is completely taken in. He disinherits Edgar and proclaims him outlaw.

Kent meets Oswald at Gloucester's home, quarrels with him, and is put in the stocks by Regan and her husband Cornwall. When Lear arrives, he objects, but Regan takes the same line as Goneril. Lear is enraged but impotent. Goneril arrives and echoes Regan. Lear yields completely to his rage. He rushes out into a storm to rant against his ungrateful daughters, accompanied by the mocking Fool. Kent later follows to protect him. Gloucester protests Lear's mistreatment. Wandering on the heath after the storm, Lear meets Edgar, in the guise of Tom o' Bedlam, that is, a madman. Edgar babbles madly while Lear denounces his daughters. Gloucester leads them all to shelter.

Edmund betrays Gloucester to Cornwall, Regan, and Goneril. He shows a letter from his father to the King of France asking for help against them; and in fact a French army has landed in Britain. Gloucester is arrested, and Cornwall gouges out his eyes. But one of Cornwall's servants is so outraged by this that he attacks and fatally wounds Cornwall. Regan kills the mutinous servant, and tells Gloucester that Edmund tricked him; then she turns him out to wander the heath too. Edgar, in his madman's guise as Tom, meets blinded Gloucester on the heath. Gloucester begs Tom to lead him to a cliff, so that he may jump to his death.

Goneril meets Edmund and discovers that she finds him more attractive than her honest husband Albany, whom she regards as milk-livered. Albany is disgusted by the sisters' treatment of Lear, and the mutilation of Gloucester, and denounces Goneril. Kent leads Lear to the French army, which is accompanied by Cordelia. But Lear is half-mad and terribly embarrassed by his earlier follies. Albany leads the British army to meet the French. Regan too is attracted to Edmund, and the two sisters become jealous. Goneril sends Oswald with letters to Edmund, and also tells Oswald to kill Gloucester if he sees him. Edgar pretends to lead Gloucester to a cliff, then changes his voice and tells Gloucester he has miraculously survived a great fall. They meet Lear, who is now completely mad. Lear rants that the whole world is corrupt and runs off.

Oswald tries to kill Gloucester, but is slain by Edgar. In Oswald's pocket, Edgar finds a letter from Goneril to Edmund suggesting the murder of Albany. Kent and Cordelia take charge of Lear, whose madness largely passes. Regan, Goneril, Albany, and Edmund meet with their forces. Albany insists that they fight the French invaders, but not harm Lear or Cordelia. The two sisters lust for Edmund, who has made promises to both. He considers the dilemma, and plots the deaths of Albany, Lear, and Cordelia. Edgar gives Goneril's letter to Albany. The armies meet in battle, the British defeat the French, and Lear and Cordelia are captured. Edmund sends them off with secret orders for execution.

The victorious British leaders meet, and Regan now declares she will marry Edmund. But Albany exposes the intrigues of Edmund and Goneril, and proclaims Edmund a traitor. Regan collapses; Goneril has poisoned her. Edmund defies Albany, who calls for a trial by combat. Edgar appears to fight Edmund, and fatally stabs him in a duel. Albany shows Goneril's letter to her; she flees in shame and rage. Edgar reveals himself; Gloucester dies offstage from the overwhelming shock and joy of this revelation.

Offstage, Goneril stabs herself, and confesses to poisoning Regan. Edmund, dying, reveals his order to kill Lear and Cordelia. But it is too late: Cordelia is dead, though Lear slew the killer. Lear recognizes Kent. Albany urges Lear to resume his throne, but Lear is too far gone in grief and hardship. He collapses and dies. Albany offers to share power between Kent and Edgar but Kent, overwhelmed with sadness, refuses. At the end, either Albany or Edgar (depending on whether one reads the Quarto or the Folio version) is crowned King.

Sources

Shakespeare's play is based on various accounts of the semi-legendary Celtic figure Lear/Lir/Llwr. Shakespeare's most important source is probably the second edition of *The Chronicles of England, Scotlande, and Irelande* by Raphael Holinshed, published in 1587. Holinshed himself found the story in the earlier *Historia Regum Britanniae* by Geoffrey of Monmouth, which was written in the 12th century. Edmund Spenser's *The Faerie Queene,* published 1590, also contains a character named Cordelia, who also dies from hanging, as in *King Lear*.

Other possible sources are *A Mirror for Magistrates* (1574), by John Higgins; *The Malcontent* (1604), by John Marston; *The London Prodigal* (1605); *Arcadia* (1580–1590), by Sir Philip Sidney, from which Shakespeare took the main outline of the Gloucester subplot; Montaigne's *Essays,* which were translated into English by John Florio in 1603; *An Historical Description of Iland of Britaine,* by William Harrison; *Remaines Concerning Britaine,* by William Camden (1606); *Albion's England,* by William Warner, (1589); and *A Declaration of egregious Popish Impostures,* by Samuel Harsnett (1603), which provided some of the language used by Edgar while he feigns madness. *King Lear* is also a literary variant of a common fairy tale, in which a father rejects his youngest daughter for a statement of her love that does not please him. The source of the subplot involving Gloucester, Edgar, and Edmund is a tale in Philip Sidney's *Countess of Pembroke's Arcadia,* with a blind Paphlagonian king and his two sons, Leonatus and Plexitrus.

Macbeth

The Tragedy of Macbeth, commonly called *Macbeth,* is a play by William Shakespeare about a regicide and its aftermath. It is Shakespeare's shortest tragedy and is believed to have been written sometime between 1603 and 1607. The earliest account of a performance of what was likely Shakespeare's play is April 1611, when Simon Forman recorded seeing such a play at the Globe Theatre. It was first published in the Folio of 1623, possibly from a prompt book for a specific performance.

Shakespeare's sources for the tragedy are the accounts of Macbeth, Macduff, and Duncan in *Holinshed's Chronicles* (1587), a history of England, Scotland and Ireland familiar to Shakespeare and his contemporaries. In the back-stage world of theatre, some believe the play is cursed and will not mention its name aloud, referring to it instead as *The Scottish play*. Over the centuries, the play has attracted some of the greatest actors in the roles of Macbeth and Lady Macbeth. The play has been adapted to film, television, opera, novels, comic books, and other media.

Synopsis

The first act of the play opens amidst thunder and lightning, with the Three Witches deciding that their next meeting shall be with Macbeth. In the following scene, a wounded captain reports to King Duncan of Scotland that his generals Macbeth, who is the Thane of Glamis, and Banquo have just defeated the allied forces of Norway and Ireland, who were led by the traitor Macdonwald. Macbeth, the King's kinsman, is praised for his bravery and fighting prowess.

The scene changes. Macbeth and Banquo enter, discussing the weather and their victory ("So foul and fair a day I have not seen"). As they wander onto a heath, the three Witches enter, who have been waiting to greet them with prophecies. Even though it is Banquo who first challenges them, they address Macbeth. The first Witch hails Macbeth as *"Thane of Glamis"*, the second as *"Thane of Cawdor"*, and the third proclaims that he shall *"be King hereafter"*. Macbeth appears to be stunned to silence, so again Banquo challenges them. The Witches inform Banquo he shall father a line of kings, though he himself will not be one. While the two men wonder at these pronouncements, the Witches vanish, and another Thane, Ross, a messenger from the King, arrives and informs Macbeth of his newly bestowed title—Thane of Cawdor. The first prophecy is thus fulfilled. Immediately, Macbeth begins to harbour ambitions of becoming king.

Macbeth writes to his wife about the Witches' prophecies. When Duncan decides to stay at the Macbeths' castle at Inverness, Lady Macbeth hatches a plan to murder him and secure the throne for her husband. Although Macbeth raises concerns about the regicide, Lady Macbeth eventually persuades him, by challenging his manhood, to follow her plan.

On the night of the king's visit, Macbeth kills Duncan. The deed is not seen by the audience, but it leaves Macbeth so shaken that Lady Macbeth has to take charge. In accordance with her plan, she frames Duncan's sleeping servants for the murder by planting bloody daggers on them. Early the next morning, Lennox, a Scottish nobleman, and Macduff, the loyal Thane of Fife, arrive.

A porter opens the gate and Macbeth leads them to the king's chamber, where Macduff discovers Duncan's corpse. In a feigned fit of anger, Macbeth murders the guards before they can protest their innocence. Macduff is immediately suspicious of Macbeth, but does not reveal his suspicions publicly. Fearing for their lives, Duncan's sons flee, Malcolm to England and his brother Donalbain to Ireland. The rightful heirs' flight makes them suspects and Macbeth assumes the throne as the new King of Scotland as a kinsman of the dead king.

Despite his success, Macbeth remains uneasy about the prophecy about Banquo. So Macbeth invites him to a royal banquet and discovers that Banquo and his young son, Fleance, will be riding out that night. He hires two men to kill them. A third murderer appears mysteriously in the park before the murder. While the assassins kill Banquo, Fleance escapes. At the banquet, Banquo's ghost enters and sits in Macbeth's place. Only Macbeth can see the spectre; the rest panic at the sight of Macbeth raging at an empty chair, until a desperate Lady Macbeth orders them to leave.

Macbeth, disturbed, goes to the Witches once more. They conjure up three spirits with three further warnings and prophecies, which tell him to *"beware Macduff"*, but also that *"none of woman born shall harm Macbeth"* and he will *"never vanquish'd be until Great Birnam Wood to high Dunsinane Hill shall come against him"*. Since Macduff is in exile in England, Macbeth assumes that he is safe; so he puts to death everyone in Macduff's castle, including Macduff's wife and their young children.

Lady Macbeth becomes wracked with guilt from the crimes she and her husband have committed. She sleepwalks and tries to wash imaginary bloodstains from her hands, all the while speaking of the terrible things she knows.

In England, Malcoim and Macduff are informed by Ross that "your castle is surprised, your wives and babes savagely slaughtered." Macbeth, now viewed as a tyrant, sees many of his thanes defecting. Malcolm leads an army, along with Macduff and Englishmen Siward (the Elder), the Earl of Northumberland, against Dunsinane Castle. While encamped in Birnam

Wood, the soldiers are ordered to cut down and carry tree limbs to camouflage their numbers, thus fulfilling the Witches' third prophecy. Meanwhile, Macbeth delivers a soliloquy (*"Tomorrow, and tomorrow, and tomorrow"*) upon his learning of Lady Macbeth's death (the cause is undisclosed, and it is assumed by some that she committed suicide, as Malcolm's final reference to her reveals "'tis thought, by self and violent hands / took off her life").

A battle culminates in the slaying of the young Siward and Macduff's confrontation with Macbeth. Macbeth boasts that he has no reason to fear Macduff, for he cannot be killed by any man born of woman. Macduff declares that he was *"from his mother's womb untimely ripp'd"* (i.e., born by Caesarean section) and was therefore not *"of woman born"*. Macbeth realizes, too late, he has misinterpreted the Witches' prophecies. Macduff beheads Macbeth off stage and thereby fulfills the last of the prophecies.

Although Malcolm is placed on the throne and not Fleance, the witches' prophecy concerning Banquo, *"Thou shalt [be]get kings"*, was known to the audience of Shakespeare's time to be true, for James I of England (also James VI of Scotland) was supposedly a descendant of Banquo.

Sources

Macbeth has been compared to Shakespeare's *Antony and Cleopatra.* Both Antony and Macbeth as characters seek a new world, even at the cost of the old one. Both are fighting for a throne and have a 'nemesis' to face in order to achieve that throne. For Antony the nemesis is Octavius, whereas for Macbeth it is Banquo. At one point Macbeth even compares himself to

Antony, saying "under Banquo / My Genius is rebuk'd, as it is said / Mark Antony's was by Caesar." Lastly, both plays contain powerful female figures: Cleopatra and Lady Macbeth.

Shakespeare borrowed the story from several tales in *Holinshed's Chronicles,* a popular history of the British Isles known to Shakespeare and his contemporaries. In *Chronicles,* a man named Donwald finds several of his family put to death by his king, King Duff, for dealing with witches. After being pressured by his wife, he and four of his servants kill the King in his own house. In the "Chronicles", Macbeth is portrayed as struggling to maintain the kingdom in the face of King Duncan's ineptitude. He and Banquo meet the three witches, who make exactly the same prophecies as in Shakespeare's version. Macbeth and Banquo then together plot the murder of Duncan, at Lady Macbeth's urging. Macbeth has a long, ten-year reign before eventually being overthrown by Macduff and Malcolm. The parallels between the two versions are clear. However, some scholars think that George Buchanan's *Rerum Scoticarum Historia* matches Shakespeare's version more closely. Buchanan's work was available in Latin in Shakespeare's day.

No other version of the story has Macbeth kill the king in Macbeth's own castle. Scholars have seen this change of Shakespeare's as adding to the darkness of Macbeth's crime as the worst violation of hospitality. Versions of the story that were common at the time had Duncan being killed in an ambush at Inverness, not in a castle. Shakespeare conflated the story of Donwald and King Duff in what was a significant change to the story.

Shakespeare made another revealing change. In the *Chronicles*, Banquo is an accomplice in Macbeth's murder of King Duncan. He also plays an important part in ensuring that Macbeth, not Malcolm, takes the throne in the coup that follows. In Shakespeare's day, Banquo was thought to be a direct ancestor of the Stuart King James I. The Banquo portrayed in historical sources is significantly different from the Banquo created by Shakespeare. Critics have proposed several reasons for this change. First, to portray the king's ancestor as a murderer would have been risky. Second, Shakespeare may have altered Banquo's character simply because there was no dramatic need for another accomplice to the murder; there was, however, a need to provide a dramatic contrast to Macbeth—a role which many scholars argue is filled by Banquo. Other authors of the time who wrote about Banquo, such as Jean de Schelandre in his *Stuartide*, also changed history by portraying Banquo as a noble man rather than a murderer, probably for the same reasons.

Date and text

Macbeth cannot be dated precisely owing to significant evidence of later revisions. Many scholars conjecture the likely date of composition to be between 1603 and 1606. As the play seems to be aimed at celebrating King James's ancestors and the Stuart accession to the throne in 1603 (James believed himself to be descended from Banquo), they argue that the play is unlikely to have been composed earlier than 1603; and suggest that the parade of eight kings—which the witches show Macbeth in a vision in Act IV—is a compliment to King James. Other editors conjecture a more specific date of 1605–6, the principal reasons being possible allusions to the Gunpowder Plot and its ensuing trials. The Porter's speech (Act II, scene III, lines1-21), in particular, may contain allusions to the trial of the Jesuit Henry Garnet in spring, 1606; "equivocator" (line 8) may refer to Garnet's defence of "equivocation", and "farmer" (4) to one of Garnet's aliases. However, "farmer" is a common word, and the concept of "equivocation" was also the subject of a 1583 tract by Queen Elizabeth's chief councillor Lord Burghley, and of the 1584 Doctrine of Equivocation by the Spanish prelate Martin Azpilcueta, which was disseminated across Europe and into England in the 1590s.

Scholars also cite an entertainment seen by King James at Oxford in the summer of 1605 that featured three "sibyls" like the weird sisters; Kermode surmises that Shakespeare could have heard about this and alluded to it with the weird sisters. However, A. R. Braunmuller in the New Cambridge edition finds the 1605-6 arguments inconclusive, and argues only for an earliest date of 1603. The play is not considered to have been written any later than 1607, since, as Kermode notes, there are "fairly clear allusions to the play in 1607." The earliest account of a performance of the play is April 1611, when Simon Forman recorded seeing it at the Globe Theatre.

Macbeth was first printed in the First Folio of 1623 and the Folio is the only source for the text. The text that survives had been plainly altered by later hands. Most notable is the inclusion of two songs from Thomas Middleton's play *The Witch* (1615); Middleton is conjectured to have inserted an extra scene involving the witches and Hecate, for these scenes had proven highly popular with audiences. These revisions, which since the Clarendon edition of 1869 have been assumed to include all of Act III, scene v, and a portion of Act IV, scene I, are often indicated in modern texts. On this basis, many scholars reject all three of the interludes with the goddess Hecate as inauthentic. Even with the Hecate material, the play is conspicuously short, and so the Folio text may derive from a prompt book that had been substantially cut for performance, or an adapter cut the text himself.

6

Classical Works of Mary Shelley

Mary Shelley was a British novelist, short story writer, dramatist, essayist, biographer, and travel writer, best known for her Gothic novel *Frankenstein: or, The Modern Prometheus* (1818). She also edited and promoted the works of her husband, the Romantic poet and philosopher Percy Bysshe Shelley. Her father was the political philosopher William Godwin, and her mother was the philosopher and feminist Mary Wollstonecraft.

Mary Godwin's mother died when she was eleven days old; afterwards, she and her older half-sister, Fanny Imlay, were raised by her father. When Mary was four, Godwin married his neighbour, Mary Jane Clairmont. Godwin provided his daughter with a rich, if informal, education, encouraging her to adhere to his liberal political theories. In 1814, Mary Godwin began a romantic relationship with one of her father's political followers, the married Percy Bysshe Shelley. Together with Mary's stepsister, Claire Clairmont, they left for France and travelled through Europe; upon their return to England, Mary was pregnant with Percy's child. Over the next two years, she and Percy faced ostracism, constant debt, and the death of their prematurely born daughter. They married in late 1816 after the suicide of Percy Shelley's first wife, Harriet.

In 1816, the couple famously spent a summer with Lord Byron, John William Polidori, and Claire Clairmont near Geneva, Switzerland, where Mary conceived the idea for her novel *Frankenstein*. The Shelleys left Britain in 1818 for Italy, where their second and third children died before Mary Shelley gave birth to her last and only surviving child, Percy Florence. In 1822, her husband drowned when his sailing boat sank during a storm in the Bay of La Spezia. A year later, Mary Shelley returned to England and from then on devoted herself to the upbringing of her son and a career as a professional author. The last decade of her life was dogged by illness, probably caused by the brain tumour that was to kill her at the age of 53.

Until the 1970s, Mary Shelley was known mainly for her efforts to publish Percy Shelley's works and for her novel *Frankenstein*, which remains widely read and has inspired many theatrical and film adaptations Recent scholarship has yielded a more comprehensive view of Mary Shelley's achievements. Scholars have shown increasing interest in her literary output, particularly in her novels, which include the historical novels *Valperga* (1823) and *Perkin Warbeck* (1830), the apocalyptic novel *The Last Man* (1826), and her final two novels, *Lodore* (1835) and *Falkner* (1837). Studies of her lesser-known works such as the travel book *Rambles in Germany and Italy* (1844) and the biographical articles for Dionysius Lardner's *Cabinet Cyclopaedia* (1829–46) support the growing view that Mary Shelley remained a political radical throughout her life. Mary Shelley's works often argue that cooperation and sympathy, particularly as practised by women in the family, were the ways to reform civil society. This view was a direct challenge to the individualistic Romantic ethos promoted by Percy Shelley and the Enlightenment political theories articulated by her father, William Godwin.

Literary Themes and Styles

Mary Shelley lived a literary life. Her father encouraged her to learn to write by composing letters, and her favourite occupation as a child was writing stories. Unfortunately, all of Mary's juvenilia were lost when she ran off with Percy in 1814, and none of her surviving manuscripts can be definitively dated before that year. Her first published work is often thought to have been *Mounseer Nongtongpaw,* comic verses written for Godwin's *Juvenile Library* when she was ten and a half; however, the poem is attributed to another writer in the most recent authoritative collection of her works. Percy Shelley enthusiastically encouraged Mary Shelley's writing: "My husband was, from the first, very anxious that I should prove myself worthy of my parentage, and enrol myself on the page of fame. He was forever inciting me to obtain literary reputation."

Novels

Autobiographical Elements

Certain sections of Mary Shelley's novels are often interpreted as masked rewritings of her life. Critics have pointed to the recurrence of the father–daughter motif in particular as evidence of this autobiographical style. For example, commentators frequently read *Mathilda* (1820) autobiographically, identifying the three central characters as versions of Mary Shelley,

William Godwin, and Percy Shelley. Mary Shelley herself confided that she modelled the central characters of *The Last Man* on her Italian circle. Lord Raymond, who leaves England to fight for the Greeks and dies in Constantinople, is based on Lord Byron; and the utopian Adrian, Earl of Windsor, who leads his followers in search of a natural paradise and dies when his boat sinks in a storm, is a fictional portrait of Percy Bysshe Shelley. However, as she wrote in her review of Godwin's novel *Cloudesley* (1830), she did not believe that authors "were merely copying from our own hearts". William Godwin regarded his daughter's characters as types rather than portraits from real life. Some modern critics, such as Patricia Clemit and Jane Blumberg, have taken the same view, resisting autobiographical readings of Mary Shelley's works.

Novelistic Genres

Mary Shelley employed the techniques of many different novelistic genres, most vividly the Godwinian novel, Walter Scott's new historical novel, and the Gothic novel. The Godwinian novel, made popular during the 1790s with works such as Godwin's *Caleb Williams* (1794), "employed a Rousseauvian confessional form to explore the contradictory relations between the self and society", and *Frankenstein* exhibits many of the same themes and literary devices as Godwin's novel. However, Shelley critiques those Enlightenment ideals that Godwin promotes in his works. In *The Last Man,* she uses the philosophical form of the Godwinian novel to demonstrate the ultimate meaninglessness of the world. While earlier Godwinian novels had shown how rational individuals could slowly improve society, *The Last Man* and

Frankenstein demonstrate the individual's lack of control over history.

Shelley uses the historical novel to comment on gender relations; for example, *Valperga* is a feminist version of Scott's masculinist genre. Introducing women into the story who are not part of the historical record, Shelley uses their narratives to question established theological and political institutions. Shelley sets the male protagonist's compulsive greed for conquest in opposition to a female alternative: reason and sensibility. In *Perkin Warbeck*, Shelley's other historical novel, Lady Gordon stands for the values of friendship, domesticity, and equality. Through her, Shelley offers a feminine alternative to the masculine power politics that destroy the male characters. The novel provides a more inclusive historical narrative to challenge the one which usually relates only masculine events.

Gender

With the rise of feminist literary criticism in the 1970s, Mary Shelley's works, particularly *Frankenstein,* began to attract much more attention from scholars. Feminist and psychoanalytic critics were largely responsible for the recovery from neglect of Shelley as a writer. Ellen Moers was one of the first to claim that Shelley's loss of a baby was a crucial influence on the writing of *Frankenstein*. She argues that the novel is a "birth myth" in which Shelley comes to terms with her guilt for causing her mother's death as well as for failing as a parent. In Moers' view, it is a story "about what happens when a man tries to have a baby without a woman... [*Frankenstein*] is profoundly concerned with natural as opposed to unnatural modes of production and reproduction". Victor Frankenstein's failure as a "parent" in the novel has been read as an expression of the anxieties which accompany pregnancy, giving birth, and particularly maternity.

Sandra Gilbert and Susan Gubar argue in their seminal book *The Madwoman in the Attic* (1979) that in *Frankenstein* in particular, Shelley responded to the masculine literary tradition represented by John Milton's *Paradise Lost*. In their interpretation, Shelley reaffirms this masculine tradition, including the misogyny inherent in it, but at the same time "conceal[s] fantasies of equality that occasionally erupt in monstrous images of rage". Mary Poovey reads the first edition of *Frankenstein* as part of a larger pattern in Shelley's writing, which begins with literary self-assertion and ends with conventional femininity. Poovey suggests that *Frankenstein*'s multiple narratives enable Shelley to split her artistic persona: she can "express and efface herself at the same time". Shelley's fear of self-assertion is reflected in the fate of Frankenstein, who is punished for his egotism by losing all his domestic ties.

Feminist critics often focus on how authorship itself, particularly female authorship, is represented in and through Shelley's novels. As Shelley scholar Anne K. Mellor explains, Shelley uses the Gothic style not only to explore repressed female sexual desire but also as way to "censor her own speech in *Frankenstein*". According to Poovey and Mellor, Shelley did not want to promote her own authorial persona and felt deeply inadequate as a writer, and "this shame contributed to the generation of her fictional images of abnormality, perversion, and destruction".

Shelley's writings focus on the role of the family in society and women's role within that family. She celebrates the "feminine affections and compassion" associated with the family and suggests that civil society will fail without them. Shelley was "profoundly committed to an ethic of cooperation, mutual dependence, and self-sacrifice". In *Lodore,* for example, the central story follows the fortunes of the wife and daughter of the title character, Lord Lodore, who is killed in a duel at the end of the first volume, leaving a trail of legal, financial, and familial obstacles for the two "heroines" to negotiate. The novel is engaged with political and ideological issues, particularly the education and social role of women. It dissects a patriarchal culture that separated the sexes and pressured women into dependence on men. In the view of Shelley scholar Betty T. Bennett, "the novel proposes egalitarian educational paradigms for women and men, which would bring social justice as well as the spiritual and intellectual means by which to meet the challenges life invariably brings". However, *Falkner* is the only one of Mary Shelley's novels in which the heroine's agenda triumphs. The novel's resolution proposes that when female values triumph over violent and destructive masculinity, men will be freed to express the "compassion, sympathy, and generosity" of their better natures.

Enlightenment and Romanticism

Frankenstein, like much Gothic fiction of the period, mixes a visceral and alienating subject matter with speculative and thought-provoking themes. Rather than focusing on the twists and turns of the plot, however, the novel foregrounds the mental and moral struggles of the protagonist, Victor Frankenstein, and Shelley imbues the text with her own brand of politicised Romanticism, one that criticised the individualism and egotism of traditional Romanticism. Victor Frankenstein is like Satan in *Paradise Lost,* and Prometheus: he rebels against tradition; he creates life; and he shapes his own destiny. These traits are not portrayed positively; as Blumberg writes, "his relentless ambition is a self-delusion, clothed as quest for truth". He must abandon his family to fulfill his ambition.

Mary Shelley believed in the Enlightenment idea that people could improve society through the responsible exercise of political power, but she feared that the irresponsible exercise of power would lead to chaos. In practice, her works largely criticise the way 18th-century thinkers such as her parents believed such change could be brought about. The creature in *Frankenstein,* for example, reads books associated with radical ideals but the education he gains from them is ultimately useless. Shelley's works reveal her as less optimistic than Godwin and Wollstonecraft; she lacks faith in Godwin's theory that humanity could eventually be perfected.

As literary scholar Kari Lokke writes, *The Last Man,* more so than *Frankenstein,* "in its refusal to place humanity at the center of the universe, its questioning of our privileged position in relation to nature... constitutes a profound and prophetic challenge to Western humanism." Specifically, Mary Shelley's allusions to what radicals believed was a failed revolution in France and the Godwinian, Wollstonecraftian, and Burkean responses to it, challenge "Enlightenment faith in the inevitability of progress through collective efforts". As in *Frankenstein,* Shelley "offers a profoundly disenchanted commentary on the age of revolution, which ends in a total rejection of the progressive ideals of her own generation". Not only does she reject these Enlightenment political ideals, but she also rejects the Romantic notion that the poetic or literary imagination can offer an alternative.

Politics

Critics have until recently cited *Lodore* and *Falkner* as evidence of increasing conservatism in Mary Shelley's later works. In 1984, Mary Poovey influentially identified the retreat of Mary Shelley's reformist politics into the "separate sphere" of the domestic. Poovey suggested that Mary Shelley wrote *Falkner* to resolve her conflicted response to her father's combination of libertarian radicalism and stern insistence on social decorum. Mellor largely agreed, arguing that "Mary Shelley grounded her alternative political ideology on the metaphor of the peaceful, loving, bourgeois family. She thereby implicitly endorsed a conservative vision of gradual evolutionary reform." This vision allowed women to participate in the public sphere but it inherited the inequalities inherent in the bourgeois family.

However, in the last decade or so this view has been challenged. For example, Bennett claims that Mary Shelley's works reveal a consistent commitment to Romantic idealism and political reform and Jane Blumberg's study of Shelley's early novels argues that her career cannot be easily divided into radical and conservative halves. She contends that "Shelley was never a passionate radical like her husband and her later lifestyle was not abruptly assumed nor was it a betrayal. She was in fact challenging the political and literary influences of her circle in her first work." In this reading, Shelley's early works are interpreted as a challenge to Godwin and Percy Bysshe Shelley's radicalism. Victor Frankenstein's "thoughtless rejection of family", for example, is seen as evidence of Shelley's constant concern for the domestic.

Short Stories

In the 1820s and 1830s, Mary Shelley frequently wrote short stories for gift books or annuals, including sixteen for *The Keepsake,* which was aimed at middle-class women and bound in silk, with gilt-edged pages. Mary Shelley's work in this genre has been described as that of a "hack writer" and "wordy and pedestrian". However, critic Charlotte Sussman points out that other leading writers of the day, such as the Romantic poets William Wordsworth and Samuel Taylor Coleridge, also took advantage of this profitable market. She explains that "the annuals were a major mode of literary production in the 1820s and 1830s", with *The Keepsake* the most successful.

Many of Shelley's stories are set in places or times far removed from early 19th-century Britain, such as Greece and the reign of Henry IV of France. Shelley was particularly interested in "the fragility of individual identity" and often depicted "the way a person's role in the world can be cataclysmically altered either by an internal emotional upheaval, or by some supernatural occurrence that mirrors an internal schism". In her stories, female identity is tied to a woman's short-lived value in the marriage market while male identity can be sustained and transformed through the use of money. Although Mary Shelley wrote twenty-one short stories for the annuals between 1823 and 1839, she always saw herself, above all, as a novelist. She wrote to Leigh Hunt, "I write bad articles which help to make me miserable—but I am going to plunge into a novel and hope that its clear water will wash off the mud of the magazines."

Travelogues

When they ran off to France in the summer of 1814, Mary Godwin and Percy Shelley began a joint journal, which they published in 1817 under the title *History of a Six Weeks' Tour,* adding four letters, two by each of them, based on their visit to Geneva in 1816, along with Percy Shelley's poem "Mont Blanc". The work celebrates youthful love and political idealism and consciously follows the example of Mary Wollstonecraft and others who had combined travelling with writing. The perspective of the *History* is philosophical and reformist rather than that of a conventional travelogue; in particular, it addresses the effects of politics and war on France. The letters the couple wrote on the second journey confront the "great and extraordinary events" of the final defeat of Napoleon at Waterloo after his "Hundred Days" return in 1815. They also explore the sublimity of Lake Geneva and Mont Blanc as well as the revolutionary legacy of the philosopher and novelist Jean-Jacques Rousseau.

Mary Shelley's last full-length book, written in the form of letters and published in 1844, was *Rambles in Germany and Italy in 1840, 1842 and 1843,* which recorded her travels with her son Percy Florence and his university friends. In *Rambles,* Shelley follows the tradition of Mary Wollstonecraft's *Letters Written in Sweden, Norway, and Denmark* and her own *A History of a Six Weeks' Tour* in mapping her personal and political landscape through the discourse of sensibility and sympathy. For Shelley, building sympathetic connections between people is the way to build civil society and to increase knowledge: "knowledge, to enlighten and free the mind from clinging deadening prejudices--a wider circle of sympathy with our fellow-creatures;—these are the uses of travel". Between observations on scenery, culture, and "the people, especially in a political point of view", she uses the travelogue form to explore her roles as a widow and mother and to reflect on revolutionary nationalism in Italy. She also records her "pilgrimage" to scenes associated with Percy Shelley. According to critic Clarissa Orr, Mary Shelley's adoption of a persona of philosophical motherhood gives *Rambles* the unity of a prose poem, with "death and memory as central themes". At the same time, Shelley makes an egalitarian case against monarchy, class distinctions, slavery, and war.

Biographies

Between 1832 and 1839, Mary Shelley wrote many biographies of notable Italian, Spanish, Portuguese, and French men and a few women for Dionysius Lardner's *Lives of the Most Eminent Literary and Scientific Men*. These formed part of Lardner's *Cabinet Cyclopaedia*, one of the best of many such series produced in the 1820s and 1830s in response to growing middle-class demand for self-education. Until the republication of these essays in 2002, their significance within her body of work was not appreciated. In the view of literary scholar Greg Kucich, they reveal Mary Shelley's "prodigious research across several centuries and in multiple languages", her gift for biographical narrative, and her interest in the "emerging forms of feminist historiography". Shelley wrote in a biographical style popularized by the 18th-century critic Samuel Johnson in his *Lives of the Poets* (1779–81), combining secondary sources, memoir and anecdote, and authorial evaluation. She records details of each writer's life and character, quotes their writing in the original as well as in translation, and ends with a critical assessment of their achievement.

For Shelley, biographical writing was supposed to, in her words, "form as it were a school in which to study the philosophy of history", and to teach "lessons". Most frequently and importantly, these lessons consisted of criticisms of male-dominated institutions such as primogeniture. Shelley emphasises domesticity, romance, family, sympathy, and compassion in the lives of her subjects. Her conviction that such forces could improve society connects her biographical approach with that of other early feminist historians such as Mary Hays and Anna Jameson. Unlike her novels, most of which had an original print run of several hundred copies, the *Lives* had a print run of about 4,000 for each volume: thus, according to Kucich, Mary Shelley's "use of biography to forward the social agenda of women's historiography became one of her most influential political interventions".

Frankenstein

Frankenstein; or, The Modern Prometheus, generally known as *"Frankenstein"*, is a novel written by Mary Shelley. Shelley started writing when she was 18 and the novel was published when she was 20. The first edition was published anonymously in London in 1818. Shelley's name appears on the second edition, published in 1831. The title of the novel refers to a scientist, Victor Frankenstein, who learns how to create life and creates a being in the likeness of man, but larger than average and more powerful. In popular culture, people have tended incorrectly to refer to the monster as "Frankenstein". *Frankenstein* is infused with some elements of the Gothic novel and the Romantic movement. It was also a warning against the expansion of modern man in the Industrial Revolution, alluded to in the novel's subtitle, *The Modern Prometheus*. The story has had an influence across literature and popular culture and spawned a complete genre of horror stories and films.

Plot

Frankenstein begins in epistolary form, documenting the correspondence between Captain Robert Walton and his sister, Margaret Walton Saville. These letters form the framework of the story in which Walton tells his sister the story of Victor Frankenstein and his creature as Frankenstein tells it to him. Walton sets out to explore the North Pole and expand his scientific knowledge in hopes of achieving fame and friendship. Unfortunately, the ship becomes trapped in ice. One day, the crew observes a being in the stature of a giant man in the distance on a dogsled. Frankenstein was in pursuit of his monster, when all but one of his dogs from his dogsled died. He broke apart his dogsled to make oars to row an ice-raft toward the vessel. Hours later they find Frankenstein, weak and in need of sustenance, near the ship. Saved by the kind occupants of the ship, Frankenstein starts to recover from his exertion and recounts to Walton his story, warning Walton of the wretched effects of allowing one's ambition to push one to aim beyond what one is capable of achieving.

Victor's narrative

Victor Frankenstein begins by telling Walton of his

childhood. Frankenstein was raised by a wealthy family, and was always encouraged to seek a greater understanding of the world around him (in science), whilst remaining in a safe environment surrounded by loving family and friends.

Frankenstein grew up with close ties to Elizabeth Lavenza, an orphan brought to his family who is raised with Frankenstein like a sister. As a young boy, Frankenstein becomes obsessed with studying outdated theories of science that focus on achieving natural wonders. He plans to attend university at Ingolstadt, Germany when a week before departure his mother and sister, Elizabeth, become very ill with scarlet fever. Elizabeth recovers, but Victor's mother dies from the disease. The whole family is in grief, and Frankenstein views it as his first misfortune. At university, he excels at chemistry and other sciences and discovers the secret to imbuing the inanimate with life, in part by studying how life decays. He also becomes interested in galvanism, a technique discovered in the 1790s.

In contrast with later film adaptations the monster in the original novel was not created from dead body parts. In fact Frankenstein himself concedes that he later found that reversing death was impossible. While the exact details of the monster's construction are left ambiguous Shelley's depiction of the monster is akin to that of a golem. Frankenstein explains that he has been forced to make the monster much larger than a normal man, in part because of the difficulty in replicating the minute parts of the human body. After giving the monster life, Frankenstein, disgusted by and fearful of the monster's appearance, flees

After his exhausting and secretive efforts to create a human life, Frankenstein is nursed by Henry Clerval and recovers from his illness in four months. He determines to come home, for his five-year-old brother William has been found murdered.

After several harsh encounters with humans, the monster becomes afraid of them and spends a year living near a cottage and observing the family who lived there. Through these observations he becomes educated and self-aware and realises that he is very different in physical appearance from the humans he watches. In loneliness, the monster seeks the friendship of the family of cottagers (the De Laceys). The family was previously wealthy, but is forced into exile when Felix De Lacey rescues the father of his love, Safie. The father, a Turkish merchant, was wrongfully accused of a crime and sentenced to death. When the man is rescued, he promises Felix that he may marry Safie. But, he loathes the idea of his beloved daughter marrying a Christian and flees. Safie comes back, though, eager for the freedom of European women. Eventually, the monster tries to befriend the family, but they are afraid of him, and this rejection makes him seek vengeance against his creator. He travels to Geneva and meets a little boy in the woods. In the vain hope that because the boy is still young and potentially unaffected by older humans' perception of his hideousness, the monster hopes to kidnap him and keep him as a companion, but the boy reveals himself as a relation of Frankenstein, so the monster kills him in his first act of vengeance against his creator. The monster plants a necklace he removes from the child's body on a sleeping girl, Justine Moritz, the Frankensteins' trusted servant who is like a member of the family. She is found with the necklace and, under pressure of threats of excommunication, confesses to the murder. She then is put on trial and executed.

When Frankenstein learns of his brother's death, he returns to Geneva to be with his family. In the woods where his young brother is murdered, Frankenstein sees the monster and becomes sure that he is William's murderer. Frankenstein, ravaged by his grief and guilt for creating the monster who wreaked so much destruction, retreats into the mountains alone to find peace. After a time in solitude, the monster approaches Frankenstein. Initially furious and intending to kill it, Frankenstein composes himself upon the monster's pleading. The monster delves into a lengthy narrative of his short life, beginning with his creation, which fashions an impression of him as an initially harmless innocent whom humans abused into wretchedness. He concludes his story with a demand that Frankenstein create for him a female counterpart, reasoning that no human will accept his existence and character due to his hideous outer appearance. He argues that as a living thing, he has a right to happiness and that Frankenstein, as his creator, has the duty to facilitate it. He promises to never reappear in his life if Frankenstein does so.

Frankenstein, fearing for his family, reluctantly agrees and travels to England to do his work. Clerval accompanies Frankenstein, but they separate in Scotland. In the process of creating a second being on the Orkney Islands, Frankenstein becomes plagued by the notion of the carnage another monster could wreak and destroys the unfinished project. The monster vows revenge on Frankenstein's upcoming wedding night. Before Frankenstein returns to Ireland, the monster murders Clerval. Once arriving in Ireland, Frankenstein is imprisoned for the crime, and falls violently ill. After being acquitted and back to health, Frankenstein returns home.

Once home, Frankenstein marries his cousin Elizabeth and, in full knowledge of and belief in the monster's threat, prepares for a fight to the death with the monster. He doesn't want Elizabeth to be frightened at the sight of the monster, so he asks her to stay in her room for the night. Instead, the monster kills Elizabeth; the grief of his wife's, William's, Justine's, Clerval's, and Elizabeth's deaths kills Frankenstein's father. After that, Frankenstein vows to pursue the monster until one destroys the other. Over months of pursuit, the two end up in the Arctic Circle near the North Pole.

Walton's later writings

Here, Frankenstein's narrative ends and Captain Walton reassumes the telling of the story. A few days after Frankenstein finishes his story, Walton and his crew decide to turn back and go home, since they cannot break through the ice. As Frankenstein dies, the monster appears in his room. Walton hears the monster's adamant justification for his vengeance as well as expressions of remorse before he leaves the ship and travels toward the Pole to destroy himself on his own funeral pyre so that no others will ever know of his existence.

Composition

During the rainy summer of 1816, the "Year Without a Summer," the world was locked in a long cold volcanic winter caused by the eruption of Mount Tambora in 1815. Mary Wollstonecraft Godwin, aged 18, and her lover (and later husband) Percy Bysshe

Shelley, visited Lord Byron at the Villa Diodati by Lake Geneva in Switzerland. The weather was consistently too cold and dreary that summer to enjoy the outdoor holiday activities they had planned, so the group retired indoors until dawn.

Amongst other subjects, the conversation turned to galvanism and the feasibility of returning a corpse or assembled body parts to life, and to the experiments of the 18th-century natural philosopher and poet Erasmus Darwin, who was said to have animated dead matter. Sitting around a log fire at Byron's villa, the company also amused themselves by reading German ghost stories, prompting Byron to suggest they each write their own supernatural tale. Shortly afterwards, in a waking dream, Mary Godwin conceived the idea for *Frankenstein*:

> I saw the pale student of unhallowed arts kneeling beside the thing he had put together. I saw the hideous phantasm of a man stretched out, and then, on the working of some powerful engine, show signs of life, and stir with an uneasy, half vital motion. Frightful *must* it be; for *SUPREMELY* frightful would be the effect of any human endeavour to mock the stupendous mechanism of the Creator of the world.

She began writing what she assumed would be a short story. With Percy Shelley's encouragement, she expanded this tale into a full-fledged novel. She later described that summer in Switzerland as the moment "when I first stepped out from childhood into life". Byron managed to write just a fragment based on the vampire legends he heard while travelling the Balkans, and from this John Polidori created *The Vampyre* (1819), the progenitor of the romantic vampire literary genre. Thus, two legendary horror tales originated from this one circumstance.

Mary's and Percy Bysshe Shelley's manuscripts for the first three-volume edition in 1818 (written 1816–1817), as well as Mary Shelley's fair copy for her publisher, are now housed in the Bodleian Library in Oxford. The Bodleian acquired the papers in 2004, and they belong now to the Abinger Collection. On 1 October 2008, the Bodleian published a new edition of Frankenstein which contains comparisons of Mary Shelley's original text with Percy Shelley's additions and interventions alongside. The new edition is edited by Charles E. Robinson: *The Original Frankenstein.*

Valperga

Valperga, or the Life and Adventures of Castruccio, Prince of Lucca is an 1823 historical novel by the Romantic novelist Mary Shelley. Mary Shelley's original title is now the subtitle; "Valperga" was selected by her father, William Godwin, who edited the work for publication between 1821 and February 1823. His edits emphasized the female protagonist and shortened the novel.

Plot summary

Valperga is a historical novel which relates the adventures of the early fourteenth-century despot Castruccio Castracani, a real historical figure who became the lord of Lucca and conquered Florence. In the novel, his armies threaten the fictional fortress of Valperga, governed by Countess Euthanasia, the woman he loves. He forces her to choose between her feelings for him and political liberty. She chooses the latter and sails off to her death.

Themes

Through the perspective of medieval history, Mary

Shelley addresses a live issue in post-Napoleonic Europe, the right of autonomously governed communities to political liberty in the face of imperialistic encroachment. She opposes Castruccio's compulsive greed for conquest with a female alternative, Euthanasia's government of Valperga on the principles of reason and sensibility. In the view of *Valperga*'s recent editor Stuart Curran, the work represents a feminist version of Walter Scott's new and often masculine genre, historical novel. Modern critics draw attention to Mary Shelley's republicanism, and her interest in questions of political power and moral principles.

The Last Man

The Last Man is an apocalyptic science fiction novel by Mary Shelley, which was first published in 1826. The book tells of a future world that has been ravaged by a plague. The novel was harshly reviewed at the time, and was virtually unknown until a scholarly revival beginning in the 1960s. It is notable in part for its semi-biographical portraits of Romantic figures in Shelley's circle, particularly Shelley's late husband Percy Bysshe Shelley and Lord Byron.

Mary Shelley claims that in 1818 she discovered, in the Sibyl's cave near Naples, a collection of prophetic writings painted on leaves by the Cumaean Sibyl. She has edited these writings into the current narrative, the first-person narrative of a man living at the end of the 21st century, which proves to be the end of humanity.

Lionel's father was a friend of the king before he was cast away because of his gambling. Lionel's father left to take his life but before he did, he left a letter for the king to take care of his family after his death. After Lionel's father died the letter was never delivered. Lionel and his sister grew up with no support and because of it grew to be uncivilized. Lionel grew to hate the royal family and Perdita grew to enjoy her isolation from society. When the king left the throne the monarchy came to an end and a republic is created. When the king dies the Countess attempts to raise their son, Adrian, to reclaim the throne, but Adrian opposes his mother and refuses to take the throne. Adrian moves to Cumberland where Lionel, who bears a grudge against Adrian and his family for the neglect of the Verney family, intends to terrorize and confront Adrian. He is mollified by Adrian's good nature and his explanation that he only recently discovered the letter. Lionel and Adrian become close friends, and Lionel becomes civilised and philosophical under Adrian's influence.

Lionel returns to England to face the personal turmoil amongst his acquaintances. Lord Raymond, who came to renown for his exploits in the war between Greece and Turkey, has returned to England in search of political position, and soon Perdita and Evadne both fall in love with him. On discovering that his beloved, Evadne, is in love with Raymond, Adrian goes into exile, presumably mad. Raymond intends to marry Idris (with whom Lionel is in love) as a first step towards becoming king, with the help of the Countess. However, he ultimately chooses his love for Perdita over his ambition, and the two marry. Under Lionel's care Adrian recovers, although he remains physically weak. On learning of the love between Idris and Lionel, the Countess schemes to drug Idris, bring her to Austria, and force her to make a politically motivated marriage. Idris discovers the plot and flees to Lionel, who marries her soon after. The Countess leaves for Austria, resentful of her children and of Lionel.

Adrian and the others live happily together until Raymond runs for Lord Protector and wins. Perdita soon adjusts to her newfound social position, while Raymond becomes well-beloved as a benevolent administrator. He discovers, however, that Evadne; after the political and financial ruin of her husband (on account of her own political schemes) is living in poverty and obscurity in London, unwilling to plead for assistance. Raymond attempts to support Evadne by employing her artistic skills in secrecy, and later nursing her in illness, but Perdita learns of the relationship and suspects infidelity. Her suspicions arouse Raymond's proud and passionate nature, and the two separate. Raymond resigns his position and leaves to rejoin the war in Greece, accompanied for a time by Adrian. Shortly after the wounded Adrian returns to England, rumors arise that Raymond has been killed. Perdita, loyal in spite of everything, convinces Lionel to bring her and Clara to Greece to find him.

Lionel finds Raymond and brings him back to Greece. Lionel and Raymond then go back to fighting and go to Constantinople. Lionel discovers Evadne, dying of wounds received fighting in the war. Before she dies, Evadne prophesies Raymond's death, a prophecy which confirms Raymond's own suspicions. Raymond's intention to enter Constantinople causes dissension and desertion amongst the army because of reports of the plague. Raymond enters the city alone, and soon dies in a fire. He is taken to Athens for burial.

In 2092, while Lionel and Adrian attempt to return their lives to normality, the plague continues to spread across Europe and the Americas, and reports of a black sun cause panic throughout the world. At first England is thought to be safe, but soon the plague reaches even there. Ryland, recently elected Lord Protector, is unprepared for the plague, and flees northward, later dying alone amidst a stockpile of provisions. Adrian takes command and is largely effective at maintaining order and humanity in England, although the plague rages on summer after summer. Ships arrive in Ireland carrying survivors from America, who lawlessly plunder Ireland and Scotland before invading England. Adrian raises a military force against them, but ultimately is able to resolve the situation peacefully.

The few remaining survivors decide to abandon England in search of an easier climate. On the eve of their departure Alfred before reaching Dover Lionel receives a letter from Lucy Martin, who was unable to join the exiles because of her mother's illness. Lionel and Idris travel through a snowstorm to assist Lucy, but Idris, weak from years of stress and maternal fears, dies along the way. Lionel and the Countess, who had shunned Idris and her family out of resentment towards Lionel, are reconciled at Idris' tomb. Lionel recovers Lucy (whose mother has died), and the party reaches Dover en route to France.

In France, Adrian discovers that the earlier emigrants have divided into factions, amongst them a fanatical religious sect led by a false messiah who claims that his followers will be saved from disease. Adrian unites most of the factions, but this latter group declares violent opposition to Adrian. Lionel sneaks into Paris, where the cult has settled, to try to rescue Juliet. She refuses to leave because the imposter has her baby, but she helps Lionel to escape. Later, when Juliet's baby sickens, Juliet discovers that the imposter has been hiding the effects of the plague from his followers. She is killed warning the other followers, after which the imposter commits suicide, and his followers return to the main body of exiles at Versailles.

The exiles travel towards Switzerland, hoping to spend the summer in a colder climate less favorable to the plague. By the time they reach Switzerland, however, all but four (Lionel, Adrian, Clara, and Evelyn) have died. The four spend a few relatively happy seasons at Switzerland, Milan, and Como before Evelyn dies of typhus. The survivors attempt to sail across the Adriatic Sea to Greece, but a sudden storm drowns Clara and Adrian. Lionel, the last man, swims to shore. The story ends in the year 3000.

Themes

Biographical elements

Many of the central characters are wholly or partially based upon Shelley's acquaintances (Peck, 1923). Shelley had been forbidden by her father-in-law, Sir Timothy Shelley, from publishing a biography of her husband, so she memorialized him, amongst others, in *The Last Man.* The utopian Adrian, Earl of Windsor, who leads his followers in search of a natural paradise and dies when his boat sinks in a storm, is a fictional portrait of Percy Bysshe Shelley, although other minor characters such as Merrival bear traces of Percy as well. Lord Raymond, who leaves England to fight for the Greeks and dies in Constantinople, is based on

Lord Byron. The novel expresses Mary Shelley's pain at the loss of her community of the "Elect", as she called them, and Lionel Verney has been seen as an outlet for her feelings of loss and boredom following their deaths and the deaths of her children.

It appears that Shelley found inspiration for the novel in Jean-Baptiste Cousin de Grainville's *Le Dernier Homme* (1805), translated into English in 1806 as *Omegarus and Syderia.*

Failure of romantic political ideals

The Last Man not only laments the loss of Shelley's friends, but also questions the Romantic political ideals they stood for. In a sense, the plague is metaphorical, since the revolutionary idyll of the élite group is corroded from within by flaws of human nature. As literary scholar Kari Lokke writes, "in its refusal to place humanity at the center of the universe, its questioning of our privileged position in relation to nature, then, *The Last Man* constitutes a profound and prophetic challenge to Western humanism." Specifically, Mary Shelley, in making references to the failure of the French Revolution and the Godwinian, Wollstonecraftian, and Burkean responses to it, "attacks Enlightenment faith in the inevitability of progress through collective efforts".

Isolation

Hugh Luke argues that "By ending her story with the picture of the Earth's solitary inhabitant, she has brought nearly the whole weight of the novel to bear upon the idea that the condition of the individual being is essentially isolated and therefore ultimately tragic" (xvii). Shelley shares this theme of tragic isolation with the poetry of Lord Byron and William Wordsworth.

The Fortunes of Perkin Warbeck: A Romance

The Fortunes of Perkin Warbeck: A Romance is an 1830 historical novel by Mary Shelley about the life of Perkin Warbeck. In this novel, Mary Shelley returned to *The Last Man's* message that an idealistic political system is impossible without an improvement in human nature. This historical novel, influenced by those of Sir Walter Scott, fictionalises the exploits of Perkin Warbeck, a pretender to the throne of King Henry VII who claimed to be Richard, Duke of York, the second son of King Edward IV. Mary Shelley believed that Warbeck really was Richard and had escaped from the Tower of London. She endows his character with elements of Percy Shelley, portraying him sympathetically as "an angelic essence, incapable of wound", who is led by his sensibility onto the political stage. She seems to have identified herself with Richard's wife, Lady Katherine Gordon, who survives after her husband's death by compromising with his political enemies. Lady Gordon stands for the values of friendship, domesticity and equality; through her, Mary Shelley offers a female alternative to the masculine power politics that destroy Richard as well as the typical historical narrative which only relates those events. *Perkin Warbeck* was generally well received; the *Edinburgh Literary Journal*'s critic, for example, said it bore "the stamp of a powerful mind". The novel is not now, however, regarded as one of Mary Shelley's most important.

Lodore

Lodore, also published under the title *The Beautiful*

Widow, is the penultimate novel by Romantic novelist Mary Shelley, completed in 1833 and published in 1835. In *Lodore*, Shelley focused her theme of power and responsibility on the microcosm of the family. The central story follows the fortunes of the wife and daughter of the title character, Lord Lodore, who is killed in a duel at the end of the first volume, leaving a trail of legal, financial, and familial obstacles for the two "heroines" to negotiate. Mary Shelley places female characters at the centre of the ensuing narratives: Lodore's daughter, Ethel, raised to be over-dependent on paternal control; his estranged wife, Cornelia, preoccupied with the norms and appearances of aristocratic society; and the intellectual and independent Fanny Derham, with whom both are contrasted.

The novel's modern editor, Lisa Vargo, has noted the text's engagement with political and ideological issues, particularly the education and social role of women. She suggests that *Lodore* dissects a patriarchal culture that separated the sexes and pressured women into dependence on men. In the view of critic Betty T. Bennett, "the novel proposes egalitarian educational paradigms for women and men, which would bring social justice as well as the spiritual and intellectual means by which to meet the challenges life invariably brings".

Reception

Lodore was a success with the reviewers: *Fraser's Magazine* praised its "depth and sweep of thought", for example; and it prompted *The Literary Gazette* to call Mary Shelley "one of the most original of our modern writers". Later nineteenth-century critics were more dubious: in 1886, Edward Dowden called *Lodore* "biography transmuted for the purposes of fiction"; in 1889, Florence Marshall remarked that *Lodore* was "written in a style that is now out of date". It was believed for instance that Ethel's encounter with Clorinda Saville was based upon Emilia Viviani.

Falkner

Falkner (1837) is the last novel published by the Romantic writer Mary Shelley. Like Shelley's novel *Lodore* (1835), *Falkner* charts a young woman's education under a tyrannical father figure. As a six-year-old orphan, Elizabeth Raby prevents Rupert Falkner from committing suicide; Falkner then adopts her and brings her up to be a model of virtue. However, she falls in love with Gerald Neville, whose mother Falkner had unintentionally driven to her death years before. When Falkner is finally acquitted of murdering Neville's mother, Elizabeth's female values subdue the destructive impulses of the two men she loves, who are reconciled and unite with Elizabeth in domestic harmony. *Falkner* is the only one of Mary Shelley's novels in which the heroine's agenda triumphs. In critic Kate Ferguson Ellis's view, the novel's resolution proposes that when female values triumph over violent and destructive masculinity, men will be freed to express the "compassion, sympathy, and generosity" of their better natures.

Critics have until recently cited *Lodore* and *Falkner* as evidence of a conservative retrenchment by Shelley. In 1984, Mary Poovey identified the retreat of Mary Shelley's reformist politics into the "separate sphere" of the domestic. As with *Lodore,* contemporary critics reviewed the novel as a romance, overlooking its political subtext and noting its moral issues as purely familial. Betty Bennett argues, however, that *Falkner* is as much concerned with power and political responsibility as Shelley's previous novels. Poovey suggested that Mary Shelley wrote *Falkner* to resolve her conflicted response to her father's combination of libertarian radicalism and stern insistence on social decorum. Critics view *Falkner* neither as notably feminist, nor as one of Mary Shelley's strongest novels, though she herself believed it could be her best. The novel has been criticised for its two-dimensional characterisation. In Bennett's view, "*Lodore* and *Falkner* represent fusions of the psychological social novel with the educational novel, resulting not in romances but instead in narratives of destabilization: the heroic protagonists are educated women who strive to create a world of justice and universal love".

7

Milton's *Paradise Lost*

John Milton (9 December 1608 – 8 November 1674) was an English poet, author, polemicist and civil servant for the Commonwealth of England. He is best known for his epic poem *Paradise Lost.* He was a scholarly man of letters, a polemical writer, and an official serving under Oliver Cromwell. Milton is believed to have been a Calvinist and the question of predestination and freedom was crucial to his intellectual orientation. He wrote at a time of religious and political flux in England, and his poetry and prose reflect deep convictions, often reacting to contemporary circumstances such as his treatise condemning censorship, *Areopagitica.* As well as English, he wrote in Latin and Italian, and had an international reputation during his lifetime.

After his death, Milton's personal reputation oscillated, a state of affairs that continued through the centuries. At an early stage he became the subject of partisan biographies, such as that of John Toland from the nonconformist perspective, and a hostile account by Anthony à Wood. Samuel Johnson described him as "an acrimonious and surly republican"; but William Hayley's 1796 biography called him the "greatest

English author". He remains generally regarded "as one of the preeminent writers in the English language and as a thinker of world importance."

Biography

One can situate both Milton's poetry and his politics historically. The phases of his life parallel major historical divisions of Stuart Britain. Under the increasingly personal rule of Charles I and its breakdown in constitutional confusion and war, Milton studied, travelled, wrote poetry mostly for private circulation, and launched a career as pamphleteer and publicist. A more detailed treatment can be found at John Milton's early life. Under the Commonwealth of England, from being thought dangerously radical and even heretical, the shift in accepted attitudes in government placed him in public office, and he even acted as an official spokesman in certain of his publications.

The Restoration of 1660 deprived Milton, now completely blind, of his public platform, but this period saw him complete most of his major works of poetry. Milton had a great impact on the Romantic movement in England, as shown in fellow poet William Wordsworth's sonnet London, 1802. Wordsworth calls upon him to rise from the dead and aid in returning England to its former glory.

Milton's views developed from his very extensive reading, as well as travel and experience, from his student days of the 1620s to the English Revolution. By the time of his death in 1674, Milton was impoverished and on the margins of English intellectual life, yet unrepentant for his political choices, and of Europe-wide fame.

Early Life

John Milton's father, also named John Milton (1562-1647), moved to London around 1583 after being disinherited by his devout Catholic father, Richard Milton, for embracing Protestantism. In London, the senior John Milton married Sarah Jeffrey (1572-1637), the poet's mother, and found lasting financial success as a scrivener. He lived and worked out of a house on Bread Street, where the Mermaid Tavern was located in Cheapside. The elder Milton was noted for his skill as a musical composer, and this talent left Milton with a lifetime appreciation for music and friendship with musicians like Henry Lawes.

After Milton was born, on 9 December 1608 his father's prosperity provided his eldest son with a private tutor, Thomas Young, and then a place at St Paul's School in London. There he began the study of Latin and Greek, and the classical languages left an imprint on his poetry in English (he wrote also in Italian and Latin). His first datable compositions are two psalms done at age 15 at Long Bennington. One contemporary source is the *Brief Lives* of John Aubrey, an uneven compilation including first-hand reports. In the work, Aubrey quotes Christopher, Milton's younger brother: "When he was young, he studied very hard and sat up very late, commonly till twelve or one o'clock at night".

Milton matriculated at Christ's College, Cambridge, in 1625 and graduated with a B.A. in 1629, ranking fourth of 24 honours graduates that year in the University of Cambridge. Preparing to become an Anglican priest, he stayed on to obtain his Master of Arts degree on 3 July 1632.

Milton was probably rusticated for quarrelling in his first year with his tutor, William Chappell. He was certainly at home in the Lent Term 1626; there he wrote his *Elegia Prima*, a first Latin elegy, to Charles Diodati, a friend from St Paul's. Based on remarks of John Aubrey, Chappell "whipt" Milton. This story is now disputed. Certainly Milton disliked Chappell. Christopher Hill cautiously notes that Milton was "apparently" rusticated, and that the differences between Chappell and Milton may have been either religious or personal, as far as we can know. Another factor, possibly, was the plague, by which Cambridge was badly affected in 1625. Later in 1626 Milton's tutor was Nathaniel Tovey.

At Cambridge Milton was on good terms with Edward King, for whom he later wrote *Lycidas*. He also befriended Anglo-American dissident and theologian, Roger Williams. Milton tutored Williams in Hebrew in exchange for lessons in Dutch. Otherwise at Cambridge he developed a reputation for poetic skill and general erudition, but experienced alienation from his peers and university life as a whole. Watching his fellow students attempting comedy upon the college stage, he later observed 'they thought themselves gallant men, and I thought them fools'. Milton, due to his hair, which he wore long, and his general delicacy of manner, was known as the "Lady of Christ's".

The university curriculum was dour, and he worked towards formal debates on topics, conducted in Latin. Yet his corpus is not devoid of humour, notably his sixth prolusion and his epitaphs on the death of Thomas Hobson. While at Cambridge he wrote a number of his well-known shorter English poems, among them *On the Morning of Christ's Nativity,* his *Epitaph on the admirable Dramatick Poet, W. Shakespeare,* his first poem to appear in print, *L'Allegro* and *Il Penseroso.*

Study, Poetry and Travel

Upon receiving his M.A. in 1632, Milton retired to Hammersmith, his father's new home since the previous year. He also lived at Horton, Berkshire, from 1635 and undertook six years of self-directed private study. Christopher Hill points out that this was not retreat into a rural or pastoral idyll at all: Hammersmith was then a "suburban village" falling into the orbit of London, and even Horton was becoming deforested, and suffered from the plague. He read both ancient and modern works of theology, philosophy, history, politics, literature and science, in preparation for a prospective poetical career. Milton's intellectual development can be charted via entries in his commonplace book (like a scrapbook), now in the British Library. As a result of such intensive study, Milton is considered to be among the most learned of all English poets; in addition to his years of private study, Milton had command of Latin, Greek, Hebrew, French, Spanish, and Italian from his school and undergraduate days; he also added Old English to his linguistic repertoire in the 1650s while researching his *History of Britain,* and probably acquired proficiency in Dutch soon after.

Milton continued to write poetry during this period of study: his *Arcades* and *Comus* were both commissioned for masques composed for noble patrons, connections of the Egerton family, and performed in 1632 amd 1634 respectively. *Comus* argues for the virtuousness of temperance and chastity.

He contributed his pastoral elegy *Lycidas* to a memorial collection for one of his Cambridge classmates. Drafts of these poems are preserved in Milton's poetry notebook, known as the Trinity Manuscript because it is now kept at Trinity College, Cambridge.

In May 1638, Milton embarked upon a tour of France and Italy that lasted up to July or August 1639. His travels supplemented his study with new and direct experience of artistic and religious traditions, especially Roman Catholicism. He met famous theorists and intellectuals of the time, and was able to display his poetic skills. For specific details to what happened within Milton's "grand tour", there appears to be just one primary source: Milton's own *Defensio Secunda.* Although there are other records, some letters and some references in his other prose tracts, the bulk of the information about the tour comes therefore from a work that, according to Barbara Lewalski, "was not intended as autobiography but as rhetoric, designed to emphasize his sterling reputation with the learned of Europe."

He travelled a route common to other Englishmen touring Europe at the time. He first went to Calais, and then on to Paris, riding horseback. While in Paris, he brought a letter from diplomat Henry Wotton which allowed him to be introduced at the British embassy. From ambassador John Scudamore, Milton received other letters of introduction and met Hugo Grotius, a Dutch law philosopher, playwright and poet. Milton left France after this meeting and visiting various landmarks. He traveled south, from Nice to Genoa and then onto Livorno and Pisa. He reached Florence in July 1638. While there, Milton enjoyed many of the sites and structures of the city. His candor of manner and erudite neo-Latin poetry made him friends in Florentine intellectual circles, and he met a number of famous and influential people through these connections including the astronomer Galileo who was under virtual house arrest at Arcetri, as well as others. He also spent time at the Florentine academies. In particular, Milton probably visited the Florentine Academy and the Academia della Crusca along with smaller academies in the area including the Apatisti (those free from the *pathos*, hence free from emotions and passions) and the Svogliati.

He left Florence in September to continue to Rome. With the connections from Florence, Milton was able to have easy access into Rome's intellectual society. His poetic abilities impressed those like Giovanni Salzilli, who praised Milton within an epigram. In late October, Milton, despite his dislike for the Society of Jesus attended a dinner given by the English College, Rome, meeting English Catholics who were also guests, theologian Henry Holden and the poet Patrick Cary. There is little else known about this time beyond that he met David Codner, an English Benedictine with court connections, who also praised Milton's poetry, and that he attended various musical events, including oratorios, operas, and melodramas. Milton left for Naples near the end of November, where he stayed only for a month because of the Spanish control.

During that time, he was introduced to Giovanni Battista Manso, patron to both Torquato Tasso and to Giovanni Battista Marino. Manso became Milton's guide through Naples. He gave Milton books, and a teasing distich based on Gregory the Great's pun on

"Angle" and "angel" when describing the English. Milton responded in his *Mansus* that he was grateful for the gesture of goodwill and claims Manso as his patron.

Originally, Milton wanted to leave Naples in order to travel to Sicily, and then on to Greece, but he returned to England during the summer of 1639 because of what he claimed, in *Defensio Secunda,* were "sad tidings of civil war in England." To further complicate matters, Milton received word that his childhood friend, Diodati, had died. Milton in fact stayed another seven months on the continent, and spent time at Geneva with Diodati's uncle after he returned to Rome.

In *Defensio Secunda,* Milton proclaimed he was warned against a return to Rome because of his frankness about religion, but he stayed in the city for two months and was able to experience Carnival and meet Lukas Holste, a Vatican librarian who guided Milton through its collection. He was introduced to Cardinal Francesco Barberini, who invited Milton to an opera hosted by the Cardinal. Around March, Milton traveled once again to Florence and stayed there for two months, he attended further meetings of the academies and spent time with friends.

After leaving Florence, he traveled through Lucca, Bologna, and Ferrara before coming to Venice. In Venice, Milton was exposed to a model of Republicanism, but he soon found another model when he traveled to Geneva. From Switzerland, Milton traveled to Paris and then to Calais before finally arriving back in England in either July or August 1639.

Civil wàr, Prose Tracts and Marriage

On returning to England, where the Bishops' Wars presaged further armed conflict, Milton began to write prose tracts against episcopacy, in the service of the Puritan and Parliamentary cause. Milton's first foray into polemics was *Of Reformation touching Church Discipline in England* (1641), followed by *Of Prelatical Episcopacy,* the two defences of Smectymnuus (a group of presbyterian divines named from their initials: the "TY" belonged to Milton's old tutor Thomas Young), and *The Reason of Church-Government Urged against Prelaty*. With frequent passages of real eloquence lighting up the rough controversial style of the period, and deploying a wide knowledge of church history, he vigorously attacked the High-church party of the Church of England and their leader, William Laud, Archbishop of Canterbury.

Though supported by his father's investments, at this time Milton became a private schoolmaster, educating his nephews and other children of the well-to-do. This experience, and discussions with educational reformer Samuel Hartlib, led him to write in 1644 his short tract, *Of Education,* urging a reform of the national universities.

In June 1643 Milton paid a visit to the manor house at Forest Hill, Oxfordshire and returned with a 16-year-old bride, Mary Powell. A month later, finding life difficult with the severe 35-year-old schoolmaster and pamphleteer, Mary returned to her family. Because of the outbreak of the Civil War, she did not return until 1645; in the meantime her desertion prompted Milton, over the next three years, to publish a series of pamphlets arguing for the legality and morality of divorce. In 1643 Milton had a brush with the authorities over these writings, in parallel with Hezekiah Woodward who had more trouble. It was the hostile response accorded the divorce tracts that spurred Milton to write *Areopagitica,* his celebrated attack on censorship.

Secretary for Foreign Tongues

With the parliamentary victory in the Civil War, Milton used his pen in defence of the republican principles represented by the Commonwealth. *The Tenure of Kings and Magistrates* (1649) defended popular government and implicitly sanctioned the regicide; Milton's political reputation got him appointed Secretary for Foreign Tongues by the Council of State in March 1649. Though Milton's main job description was to compose the English Republic's foreign correspondence in Latin, he also was called upon to produce propaganda for the regime and to serve as a censor. In October 1649 he published *Eikonoklastes,* an explicit defence of the regicide, in response to the *Eikon Basilike,* a phenomenal best-seller popularly attributed to Charles I that portrayed the King as an innocent Christian martyr. A month after Milton had tried to break this powerful image of Charles I (the literal translation of Eikonoklastes is 'the image breaker'), the exiled Charles II and his party published a defence of monarchy, *Defensio Regia Pro Carolo Primo,* written by the leading humanist Claudius Salmasius. By January of the following year, Milton was ordered to write a defence of the English people by the Council of State. Given the European audience and the English Republic's desire to establish diplomatic and cultural legitimacy, Milton worked more slowly than usual, as he drew on the learning marshalled by his years of study to compose a riposte. On 24 February 1652

Milton published his Latin defence of the English People, *Defensio Pro Populo Anglicano,* also known as the *First Defence.* Milton's pure Latin prose and evident learning, exemplified in the *First Defence,* quickly made him a European reputation, and the work ran to numerous editions.

In 1654, in response to an anonymous Royalist tract *Regii sanguinis clamor,* a work that made many personal attacks on Milton, he completed a second defence of the English nation, *Defensio secunda,* which praised Oliver Cromwell, now Lord Protector, while exhorting him to remain true to the principles of the Revolution. Alexander Morus, to whom Milton wrongly attributed the *Clamor* (in fact by Peter du Moulin), published an attack on Milton, in response to which Milton published the autobiographical *Defensio pro se* in 1655. In addition to these literary defences of the Commonwealth and his character, Milton continued to translate official correspondence into Latin. The probable onset of glaucoma finally resulted in total blindness by 1654, forcing him to dictate his verse and prose to amanuenses (helpers), one of whom was the poet Andrew Marvell. One of his best-known sonnets, *On His Blindness,* is presumed to date from this period.

Published Poetry

Milton's poetry was slow to see the light of day, at least under his name. His first published poem was *On Shakespear* (1630), anonymously included in the Second Folio edition of Shakespeare. In the midst of the excitement attending the possibility of establishing a new English government, Milton collected his work in *1645 Poems.* The anonymous edition of *Comus* was published in 1637, and the publication of *Lycidas* in 1638 in *Justa Edouardo King Naufrago* was signed J. M. Otherwise the 1645 collection was the only poetry of his to see print, until *Paradise Lost* appeared in 1667.

Paradise Lost

Paradise Lost is an epic poem in blank verse by the 17th-century English poet John Milton. It was originally published in 1667 in ten books. A second edition followed in 1674, redivided into twelve books (in the manner of the division of Virgil's *Aeneid*) with minor revisions throughout and a note on the versification. The poem concerns the Christian story of the Fall of Man: the temptation of Adam and Eve by the fallen angel Satan and their expulsion from the Garden of Eden. Milton's purpose, stated in Book I, is to "justify the ways of God to men" and elucidate the conflict between God's eternal foresight and free will.

Milton incorporates Paganism, classical Greek references, and Christianity within the poem. It deals with diverse topics from marriage, politics (Milton was politically active during the time of the English Civil War), and monarchy, and grapples with many difficult theological issues, including fate, predestination, the Trinity, and the introduction of sin and death into the world, as well as angels, fallen angels, Satan, and the war in heaven. Milton draws on his knowledge of languages, and diverse sources — primarily Genesis, much of the New Testament, the deuterocanonical Book of Enoch, and other parts of the Old Testament.

Synopsis

The story was revised into twelve books after initial publication, following the model of the *Aeneid* of

Virgil. The book lengths vary — the longest being Book IX, with 1,189 lines and the shortest, Book VII, having 640. In the second edition, each book was preceded by a summary titled "The Argument". The poem follows the epic tradition of starting *in medias res* (Latin for *in the midst of things*), the background story being told in Books V-VI.

Milton's story contains two arcs: one of Satan (Lucifer) and another of Adam and Eve. The story of Satan follows the epic convention of large-scale warfare. It begins after Satan and the other rebel angels have been defeated and cast by God into Hell, or as it is also called in the poem, Tartarus. In Pandæmonium, Satan employs his rhetorical skill to organize his followers; he is aided by his lieutenants Mammon and Beelzebub. Belial and Moloch are also present. At the end of the debate, Satan nominates himself to poison the newly-created Earth. He braves the dangers of the Abyss alone in a manner reminiscent of Odysseus or Aeneas.

The story of Adam and Eve's temptation and fall is a fundamentally different, new kind of epic: a domestic one. Adam and Eve are presented for the first time in Christian literature as having a full relationship while still without sin. They have passions and distinct personalities. Satan successfully tempts Eve by preying on her vanity and tricking her with rhetoric, and Adam, seeing Eve has sinned, knowingly commits the same sin. He declares to Eve that since she was made from his flesh, they are bound to one another so that if she dies, he must also die. In this manner Milton portrays Adam as a heroic figure but also as a deeper sinner than Eve since he is smarter than Eve and knows that what he's doing is wrong.

After eating the fruit, Adam and Eve have lustful sex, and at first, Adam is convinced that Eve was right in thinking that eating the fruit would be beneficial. However, they soon fall asleep, having terrible nightmares, and after they awake, they experience guilt and shame for the first time. Realizing that they have committed a terrible act against God, they engage in mutual recrimination.

However, Eve's pleas to Adam reconcile them somewhat. Her encouragement enables Adam and Eve both to approach God, to "bow and sue for grace with suppliant knee," and to receive grace from God. Adam goes on a vision journey with an angel where he witnesses the errors of man and the Great Flood, and is saddened by the sin that they have released through consumption of the fruit. However, he is also shown hope — the possibility of redemption — through a vision of Jesus Christ. They are then cast out of Eden and the archangel Michael says that Adam may find "A paradise within thee, happier far." They now have a more distant relationship with God, who is omnipresent but invisible (unlike the previous, tangible, Father in the Garden of Eden).

The contents of the 12 books are:

Book I: In a long, twisting opening sentence mirroring the epic poetry of the Ancient Greeks, the poet invokes the "Heavenly Muse" (the Holy Spirit) and states his theme, the Fall of Man, and his aim, to "justify the ways of God to men." Satan, Beelzebub, and the other rebel angels are described as lying on a lake of fire, from which Satan rises up to claim Hell as his own domain and delivers a rousing speech to his followers ("Better to reign in Hell than serve in Heaven."). The logic of Satan (Satanic Logic) is introduced by: "The mind is its own place, and in itself/ Can make a Heaven of Hell, a Hell of Heaven."

Book II: Satan and the rebel angels debate whether to wage another war on Heaven, and Beelzebub tells them of a new world being built which is to be the home of Man. Satan decides to visit this new world, passes through the Gates of Hell, past the sentries Sin and Death, and journeys through the realm of Chaos. Here, Satan is described as having given birth to Sin with a burst of flame from his forehead, before he began open warfare with God — as Athena was born from the head of Zeus.

Book III: God observes Satan's journey and foretells how Satan will bring about Man's Fall. God emphasises, that the Fall will come about as a result of Man's own free will, and excuses himself of responsibility. The Son of God offers himself as a ransom for Man's disobedience, an offer which God accepts, ordaining the Son's future incarnation and punishment. Satan arrives at the rim of the universe, disguises himself as an angel, and is directed to Earth by Uriel, Guardian of the Sun.

Book IV: Satan journeys to the Garden of Eden, where he observes Adam and Eve discussing the forbidden Tree of Knowledge of Good and Evil. Satan, observing their innocence and beauty hesitates in his task, but concludes that "reason just,/ Honour and empire" compel him to do this deed which he "should abhor." Satan tries to tempt Eve while she sleeps, but is discovered by the angels. The angel Gabriel expels Satan from the Garden.

Book V: Eve awakes and relates her dream to Adam. God sends Raphael to warn and encourage Adam: they talk of free will and predestination;

Raphael tells Adam the story of how Satan inspired his angels to revolt against God.

Book VI: Raphael goes on to describe further the war in Heaven and explains how the Son of God drove Satan and his minions down to Hell.

Book VII: Raphael explains to Adam that God then decided to create another world (the Earth); he again warns Adam not to eat the fruit of the Tree of Knowledge, for "in the day thou eat'st, thou diest;/ Death is the penalty imposed, beware,/ And govern well thy appetite, lest Sin/ Surprise thee, and her black attendant Death".

Book VIII: Adam tells the story of his creation from his own perspective, providing a counterpoint to Raphael's instruction in Book VI. Adam asks Raphael for knowledge concerning the stars and the angelic nature; Raphael warns "heaven is for thee too high/ To know what passes there; be lowly wise", and advises modesty and patience.

Book IX: Satan returns to Eden and enters into the body of a sleeping serpent. The serpent tempts Eve to eat the fruit of the Tree of Knowledge. She eats and takes some fruit for Adam. Adam, realising Eve has been tricked, decides he would rather die with Eve than live without her; he eats of the fruit. At first the two become intoxicated by the fruit; they become lustful, engaging in sexual intercourse; afterwards, in their loss of innocence Adam and Eve cover their nakedness and fall into despair: "They sat them down to weep, nor only tears/ Rained at their eyes, but high winds worse within/ Began to rise, high passions, anger, hate,/ Mistrust, suspicion, discord, and shook greatly/ Their inward state of mind."

Book X: God sends his Son to Eden to deliver judgment on Adam and Eve. Satan returns in triumph to Hell.

Book XI: The Son of God pleads with his Father on behalf of Adam and Eve. God decrees the couple must be expelled from the Garden, and the angel Michael descends to deliver God's judgment. Michael begins to unfold the future history of the world to Adam.

Book XII: Michael tells Adam of the eventual coming of the Messiah, before leading Adam and Eve from the Garden. They have lost the physical Paradise, but now have the opportunity to enjoy a "Paradise within... happier farr." The poem ends: "The World was all before them/ where to choose Their place of rest/ and Providence Their guide: They hand in hand with wandering steps and slow/ Through Eden took, Their solitaire way." Milton has connected the condition of Adam and Eve with the condition of the reader of the epic.

Characters

Satan: Satan is the first major character introduced in the poem. He is introduced to Hell after a failed rebellion to wrestle control of Heaven from God. Satan's desire to rebel against his creator stems from his unwillingness to accept the fact he is a created being, and that he is not self-sufficient, which is rooted in his extreme Pride. One of the ways he tries to justify his rebellion against God is by claiming that he and the angels are self-created, declaring the angels "self-begot, self-raised", thereby eliminating God's authority over them as their creator.

Satan is narcissistic, self-pitying, and persuasive although his logic is almost always flawed, disingenuous, misguiding, or all three. Satan's persuasive powers are first evident when he makes arguments to his angel-followers as to why they should try to overthrow God. He argues that they ought to have equal rights to God and that Heaven is an unfair monarchy, stating, "Who can in reason then or right assume/ Monarchy over such as live by right/ His equals, if in power and splendor less / In freedom equal? or can introduce/ Law and edict on us, who without law/ Err not, much less for this to be our Lord,/ And look for adoration to th' abuse/ Of those imperial titles which assert/ Our being ordained to govern, not to serve?."

Satan's persuasive powers are also evident during the scene in which he assumes the body of a snake in order to convince Eve to eat from the Tree of Knowledge of Good and Evil. First, he wins Eve's trust by giving her endless compliments. And when she is perplexed (and impressed) by a "serpent" that is able to talk, Satan tells her that he gained the ability to talk by eating from the Tree of Knowledge and argues that if she were to also eat from the Tree, she would become god-like. He convinces her that the fruit will not kill her and that God will not be upset with her if she eats from the tree. Like his argument to his followers, Satan also argues against God's omnipotence, stating "Why then was [eating from the Tree of Knowledge of Good and Evil] forbid? Why but to awe,/ Why but to keep ye low and ignorant, / [God's] worshippers; he knows that in the day/ Ye eat thereof, your eyes that seem so clear,/ Yet are but dim, shall perfectly be then/ Opened and cleared, and ye shall be as gods./ So ye shall die perhaps, by putting off/ Human, to put on gods."

Unlike the Biblical Satan, Milton's Satan feels guilt and doubt before he tricks Eve, knowing the results of his actions will curse innocents. Similarly, Satan has feelings of guilt when he first enters Paradise. But his feelings always turn to hate once he reflects on his own exile from Heaven.

The role of Satan as a driving force in the poem has been the subject of much scholarly debate. Positions range from views of William Blake who stated Milton "wrote in fetters when wrote of Angels and God, and at liberty when of Devils and Hell, [because] he was a true Poet and of the Devil's party without knowing it" to critic William H. Marshall's interpretation of the poem as a Christian morality tale.

Adam: Adam is the first human in Eden created by God. He is more intelligent than Eve and is also stronger, not only physically but morally. From the questions he asks the angel Raphael, it is clear that Adam has a deep, intellectual curiosity about his existence, God, Heaven, and the nature of the world. This is a kind of curiosity that Eve does not have.

As in the Bible, Eve is subservient to Adam, but in Milton's version of the story, Adam is rather easily manipulated by Eve's charms and good looks. Adam, in Milton's version of the character, is worshipful of Eve, partially because of her great beauty, and at times, is subservient to her wishes. His fall will result from this excessive and almost submissive love to his wife, namely his "uxoriousness". Hence, the power dynamic between Adam and Eve is more complicated than the one that is established in the Bible.

Adam also feels a noble sense of responsibility towards Eve (since she was, after all, created from his rib), and he fears for her safety, especially after hearing from the angel Raphael of Satan's infiltration of Paradise.

As opposed to the Biblical Adam, this version of Adam is given a glimpse of the future of mankind (this includes a synopsis of stories from The Old and New Testaments), by the angel Michael, before he has to leave Paradise.

Eve: Eve is the second human created, taken from one of Adam's ribs and shaped into a female form of Adam. In a positive sense (depending on your point of view), she is the model of a good subject and wife. She consents to Adam leading her away from her reflection when they first meet, trusting Adam's authority in their relationship until she is influenced by Satan.

She is extremely beautiful, and her beauty not only obsesses Adam but also herself. After she is born, she gazes at her reflection in a pool of water, transfixed by her image. Even after Adam calls out to her, she returns to her image. It is not until God tells her to go to Adam that she consents to being led from the pool.

Eve first comes into contact with satanic influence in her dreams. After this incident she starts to develop the independent streak that perplexes Adam, particularly when she insists on going off by herself to work in the garden, even though Adam warns her against it.

Once she is alone, Satan tempts her to eat from the Tree of Knowledge of Good and Evil. He approaches her in the body of a snake and manipulates her by appealing to her pride and vanity.

Likewise, she soon gets Adam to eat from the tree as well, though he does this because he doesn't want to lose Eve. This creates a complexity that is not in the Biblical version of the story. In this version, Adam reasons that Eve will probably die soon from eating the fruit, so he eats the fruit because he would rather die with her than live alone.

Later, when they don't die and Adam realizes that their actions in the garden have cursed all of mankind, he is harsh on Eve, blaming her for their transgression. At this point, Eve gets on her knees and begs Adam for forgiveness. And since Adam still loves Eve, he forgives her, sharing some of the blame with her.

The Son of God: The Son of God in Paradise Lost is Jesus Christ, though he is never named explicitly, since he has not yet entered human form. The Son is very heroic and powerful, singlehandedly defeating Satan and his followers when they violently rebel against God and driving them into Hell. Also, after the Father explains to him how Adam and Eve shall fall, and how the rest of humanity will be doomed to follow them in their cursed footsteps, the Son selflessly and heroically proclaims that he will take the punishment for humanity. The Son endows hope to the poem, because although Satan conquers humanity by successfully tempting Adam and Eve, the victory is temporary because the Son will save the human race.

God the Father: God the Father is the creator of Eden, Heaven, Hell, and of each of the main characters. He is an all-powerful and all-knowing being who cannot be overthrown by even the one-third of the angels Satan incites against him. The poem portrays God's process of creation in the way that Milton believed it was done, that God created Heaven, Earth, Hell, and all the creatures that inhabit these separate planes from part of himself, not out of nothing. Thus, according to Milton, the ultimate authority of God derives from his being the "author" of creation. Satan tries to justify his rebellion by denying this aspect of God and claiming self-creation, but he admits to himself this is not the case, and that God "deserved no such return/ From me, whom he created what I was."

Raphael: Raphael is an angel who is sent by God to warn Adam about Satan's infiltration of Eden and to warn him that Satan is going to try to curse Adam and Eve. Raphael initially meets with both Adam and Eve but has a private discussion about Satan with Adam only. During this discussion, Raphael tells Adam the story of Satan's rebellion and subsequent exile into Hell. After this, because of Adam's curiosity, Raphael also explains to Adam how God created the Earth and the universe.

Michael: After Adam and Eve disobey God by eating from the Tree of Knowledge, God sends the angel Michael to visit Adam and Eve. His duty is to escort Adam and Eve out of Paradise. But before this happens, Michael shows Adam visions of the future which cover an outline of the Bible, from the story of Cain and Abel in Genesis, up through the story of Jesus in the New Testament. This vision is meant to show Adam what happens to mankind and to show Adam how Jesus will redeem humanity and eventually drive out Satan, Sin, and Death from the Earth.

Composition

Milton began writing the epic in 1658 at the age of fifty, during the last years of the English Republic. Infighting among different military and political factions that doomed the Republic may show up in the

Council of Hell scenes in Book II. Although he probably finished the work by 1664, Milton did not publish until 1667, because of Great Plague and the Great Fire. Milton composed the entire work while completely blind. It is presumed he had glaucoma, necessitating the use of paid amanuenses and his daughters. The poet claimed that a divine spirit inspired him during the night, leaving him with verses that he would recite in the morning.

Context

The work is influenced by the Bible, Milton's own Puritan upbringing and religious perspective (including elements of Arminianism, Phineas Fletcher, Edmund Spenser, the Roman poets Virgil and Ovid, Greek poets Theocritus and Homer, Italian poet Dante Alighieri, and the traditions of epic poetry). It may also have been influenced by Lucifer, a play by Joost van den Vondel.Later in life, Milton wrote the much shorter sequel to Paradise Lost entitled *Paradise Regained,* charting the temptation of Christ by Satan, and the return of the possibility of paradise. The reputation of the sequel never equaled its antecedent.

Themes

Marriage

Milton first presents Adam and Eve in Book IV with impartiality. The relationship between Adam and Eve is one of "mutual dependence, not a relation of domination or hierarchy." While the author does place Adam above Eve in regard to his intellectual knowledge, and in turn his relation to God, he also grants Eve the benefit of knowledge through experience. Hermine Van Nuis clarifies that although there is a sense of stringency associated with the specified roles of the male and the female, each unreservedly accepts the designated role because it is viewed as an asset. Instead of believing that these roles are forced upon them, each uses the obligatory requirement as a strength in their relationship with each other. These minor discrepancies reveal the author's view on the importance of mutuality between a husband and a wife.

When examining the relationship between Adam and Eve, critics tend to accept an either Adam-or Eve—centered view in terms of hierarchy and importance to God. David Mikics argues, by contrast, these positions "overstate the independence of the characters' stances, and therefore miss the way in which Adam and Eve are entwined with each other". Milton's true vision reflects one where the husband and wife (in this instance, Adam and Eve) depend on each other and only through each other's differences are able to thrive. While most readers believe that Adam and Eve fail because of their fall from paradise, Milton would argue that the resulting strengthening of their love for one another is true victory.

Although Milton does not directly mention divorce, critics posit theories on Milton's view of divorce based on inferences found within the poem. Other works by Milton suggest he viewed marriage as an entity separate from the church. Discussing *Paradise Lost*, Biberman entertains the idea that "marriage is a contract made by both the man and the woman". Based on this inference, Milton would believe that both man and woman would have equal access to divorce, as they do to marriage.

Feminist critics of *Paradise Lost* suggest that Eve is forbidden the knowledge of her own identity. Moments after her creation, before Eve is led to Adam, she becomes enraptured by an image reflected in the water (her own, unbeknownst to Eve). God urges Eve to look away from her own image, her beauty, which is also the object of Adam's desire. Adam delights in both her beauty and submissive charms, yet Eve may never be permitted to gaze upon her individual form. Critic Julia M. Walker argues that because Eve "neither recognizes nor names herself...she can know herself only in relation to Adam." "Eve's sense of self becomes important in its absence...[she] is never allowed to know what she is supposed to see." Eve therefore knows not what she is, only what she is not: male. Starting in Book IV, Eve learns that Adam, the male form, is superior and "How beauty is excelled by manly grace/ And wisdom which alone is truly fair." Led by his gentle hand, she yields, a woman without individual purpose, destined to fall by "free will."

Idolatry

Milton's 17th century contemporaries by and large criticized Milton's ideas and considered him as a radical, mostly because of his well-known Protestant views on politics and religion. One of Milton's greatest and most controversial arguments centers on his concept of what is idolatrous; this topic is deeply embedded in *Paradise Lost.*

Milton's first criticism of idolatry focuses on the practice of constructing temples and other buildings to serve as places of worship. In Book XI of Paradise Lost, Adam tries to atone for his sins by offering to build altars to worship God. In response, the angel Michael explains Adam does not need to build physical objects to experience the presence of God. Joseph Lyle points to this example, explaining "When Milton objects to architecture, it is not a quality inherent in buildings themselves he finds offensive, but rather their tendency to act as convenient loci to which idolatry, over time, will inevitably adhere." Even if the idea is pure in nature, Milton still believes that it will unavoidably lead to idolatry simply because of the nature of humans. Instead of placing their thoughts and beliefs into God, as they should, humans tend to turn to erected objects and falsely invest their faith. While Adam attempts to build an altar to God, critics note Eve is similarly guilty of idolatry, but in a different manner. Harding believes Eve's narcissism and obsession with herself constitutes idolatry. Specifically, Harding claims that "... under the serpent's influence, Eve's idolatry and self-deification foreshadow the errors into which her 'Sons' will stray." Much like Adam, Eve falsely places her faith into herself, the Tree of Knowledge, and to some extent, the Serpent, all of which do not compare to the ideal nature of God.

Furthermore, Milton makes his views on idolatry more explicit with the creation of Pandemonium and the exemplary allusion to Solomon's temple. In the beginning of Paradise Lost, as well as throughout the poem, there are several references to the rise and eventual fall of Solomon's temple. Critics elucidate that "Solomon's temple provides an explicit demonstration of how an artifact moves from its genesis in devotional practice to an idolatrous end." This example, out of the many presented, conveys Milton's views on the dangers of idolatry distinctly. Even if one builds a structure in the name of God, even the best of intentions can become immoral. In addition, critics have drawn parallels between both Pandemonium and Saint Peter's Basilica, and the Pantheon. The majority of these similarities revolve around a structural likeness, but as Lyle explains, they play a greater role. By linking Saint Peter's Basilica and the Pantheon to Pandemonium—an ideally false structure, the two famous buildings take on a false meaning. This comparison best represents Milton's Protestant views, as it rejects both the purely Catholic perspective and the Pagan perspective.

In addition to rejecting Catholicism, Milton revolted against the idea of a monarch ruling by divine right. He saw the practice as idolatrous. Barbara Lewalski concludes that the theme of idolatry in Paradise Lost "... is an exaggerated version of the idolatry Milton had long associated with the Stuart ideology of divine kingship". In the opinion of Milton, any object, human or non-human, that receives special attention befitting of God, is considered idolatrous.

Response and criticism

This epic is generally considered one of the greatest works in the English language. In the verses below the portrait in the fourth edition, John Dryden linked Milton with Homer and Virgil, suggesting Milton encompassed and surpassed both:

> "Three Poets, in three distant Ages born,
> Greece, Italy, and England did adorn.
> The First in loftiness of thought surpass'd;
> The Next in Majesty; in both the Last.
> The force of Nature cou'd no farther goe:
> To make a third she joynd the former two."

Since Paradise Lost is based upon scripture, its significance in the Western canon has been thought by some to have lessened due to increasing secularism. This is not the general consensus, and even academics labelled as secular realize the merits of the work. In William Blake's *The Marriage of Heaven and Hell,* the "voice of the devil" argues:

> The reason Milton wrote in fetters when he wrote of Angels & God, and at liberty when of Devils & Hell, is because he was a true Poet and of the Devil's party without knowing it.

This statement summarizes what would become the most common interpretation of the work in the twentieth century. Some critics, including C. S. Lewis, and later Stanley Fish, reject this interpretation. Rather, such critics hold that the theology of *Paradise Lost* conforms to the passages of Scripture on which it is based.

The latter half of the twentieth century saw critical understanding of Milton's epic shift to a more political and philosophical focus. Rather than the Romantic conception of the Devil as hero, it is generally accepted that Satan is presented in terms that begin classically heroic, then diminish him until he is finally reduced to a dust-eating serpent unable even to control his own body. The political angle enters into consideration in the underlying friction between Satan's conservative, hierarchical view of the universe, and the contrasting "new way" of God and the Son of God as illustrated in Book III. In other words, in contemporary criticism the main thrust of the work becomes not the perfidy or heroism of Satan, but rather the tension between classical conservative "Old Testament" hierarchs (evidenced in Satan's worldview and even in that of the archangels Raphael and Gabriel), and "New Testament" revolutionaries (embodied in the Son of

God, Adam, and Eve) who represent a new system of universal organization. This new order is based not in tradition, precedence, and unthinking habit, but on sincere and conscious acceptance of faith and on station chosen by ability and responsibility. Naturally, this interpretation makes much use of Milton's other works and his biography, grounding itself in his personal history as an English revolutionary and social critic.

Samuel Johnson praised the poem lavishly, but conceded that "None ever wished it longer than it is." In Paul Stevens of University of Toronto's *Milton's Satan,* he claimed the Satan figure was one of the earliest examples of an anti-hero who does not submit to authority, but the actions are greatly based on his own arrogance and delusion. Stevens also claimed Paradise Lost was a story about Milton himself, who wrote in support of events that eventually led to English Civil War. That analysis was debuted in 2009 season of TVO's Best Lecturer series.

Iconography

The first illustrations were to the fourth edition of 1688, with one engraving prefacing each book, of which up to eight of the twelve were by Sir John Baptist Medina, one by Bernard Lens II, and perhaps up to four (including Books I and XII, perhaps the most memorable) by another hand. The most notable illustrators of *Paradise Lost* are William Blake, Gustave Doré and Henry Fuseli (1799); however, the epic's illustrators also include, among others, John Martin, Edward Burney, Richard Westall, Francis Hayman. Salvador Dalí executed a set of ten colour engravings in 1974. As of June 2009, examples from this series can be viewed at the William Bennett Gallery in

Manhattan. Strikingly, two *capriccios* by Gian Battista Tiepolo were used to illustrate an Italian 18th century edition. Surreal-visionary artist Terrance Lindall's rendition was published in 1982.

8

Classical Works of Leo Tolstoy

Leo Tolstoy was a Russian writer widely regarded as among the greatest of novelists. His masterpieces *War and Peace* and *Anna Karenina* represent in their scope, breadth and vivid depiction of 19th-century Russian life and attitudes, the peak of realist fiction. Tolstoy's further talents as essayist, dramatist, and educational reformer made him the most influential member of the aristocratic Tolstoy family. His literal interpretation of the ethical teachings of Jesus, centering on the Sermon on the Mount, caused him in later life to become a fervent Christian anarchist and pacifist. His ideas on nonviolent resistance, expressed in such works as *The Kingdom of God Is Within You*, were to have a profound impact on such pivotal twentieth-century figures as Gandhi and Martin Luther King, Jr.

Biography

Tolstoy was born in Yasnaya Polyana, the family estate in the Tula region of Russia. The Tolstoys were a well-known family of old Russian nobility; he was connected to the grandest of Russian aristocracy. Pushkin was his fourth cousin. He was the fourth of five children of Countess Mariya Tolstaya

(Volkonskaya). Tolstoy's parents died when he was young, so he and his siblings were brought up by relatives. In 1844, he began studying law and oriental languages at Kazan University. His teachers described him as "both unable and unwilling to learn." Tolstoy left university in the middle of his studies, returned to Yasnaya Polyana and then spent much of his time in Moscow and Saint Petersburg. In 1851, after running up heavy gambling debts, he went with his elder brother to the Caucasus and joined the army. Around this time, he started writing.

His conversion from a dissolute and privileged society author to the non-violent and spiritual anarchist of his latter days was brought about by two trips around Europe in 1857 and 1860-61, a period when many liberal-leaning Russian aristocrats escaped the stifling political repression in Russia; others who followed the same path were Alexander Herzen, Mikhail Bakunin, and Peter Kropotkin. During his 1857 visit, Tolstoy witnessed a public execution in Paris, a traumatic experience that would mark the rest of his life. Writing in a letter to his friend V. P. Botkin:

The truth is that the State is a conspiracy designed not only to exploit, but above all to corrupt its citizens... Henceforth, I shall never serve any government anywhere. His European trip in 1860-61 shaped both his political and literary transformation when he met Victor Hugo, whose literary talents Tolstoy praised after reading Hugo's newly finished *Les Miserables*. A comparison of Hugo's novel and Tolstoy's *War and Peace* shows the influence of the evocation of its battle scenes. Tolstoy's political philosophy was also influenced by a March 1861 visit to French anarchist Pierre-Joseph Proudhon, then living in exile under an assumed name in Brussels. Apart from reviewing Proudhon's forthcoming publication, *La Guerre et la Paix,* whose title Tolstoy would borrow for his masterpiece, the two men discussed education, as Tolstoy wrote in his educational notebooks:

> If I recount this conversation with Proudhon, it is to show that, in my personal experience, he was the only man who understood the significance of education and of the printing press in our time.

Fired by enthusiasm, Tolstoy returned to Yasnaya Polyana and founded thirteen schools for his serfs' children, based on ground-breaking libertarian principles Tolstoy described in his 1862 essay "The School at Yasnaya Polyana". Tolstoy's educational experiments were short-lived due to harassment by the Tsarist secret police, but as a direct forerunner to A. S. Neill's Summerhill School, the school at Yasnaya Polyana can justifiably be claimed to be the first example of a coherent theory of libertarian education.

On 23 September 1862, Tolstoy married Sophia Andreevna Bers, the daughter of a court physician, who was 16 years his junior. (Sonya, the Russian dimunitive of Sofya, is the name that was used by her family and friends) They had thirteen children, five of whom died during childhood. The marriage was marked from the outset by sexual passion and emotional insensitivity when Tolstoy, on the eve of their marriage, gave her his diaries detailing his extensive sexual past and the fact that one of the serfs on his estate had borne him a son. Even so, their early married life was ostensibly happy and allowed Tolstoy much freedom to compose the literary masterpieces *War and Peace* and *Anna Karenina* with Sonya acting as his secretary, proof-reader and financial manager. However, their later life together has been described by A. N. Wilson as one of the unhappiest in literary history. His relationship with his wife deteriorated as his beliefs became increasingly radical and he sought to reject his inherited and earned wealth, including the renunciation of the copyrights on his earlier works.

Novels and Fictional Works

Tolstoy is one of the giants of Russian literature. His most famous works include the novels *War and Peace* and *Anna Karenina* and novellas such as *Hadji Murad* and *The Death of Ivan Ilyich*. His contemporaries paid him lofty tributes. Dostoevsky thought him the greatest of all living novelists. Flaubert exclaimed, "What an artist and what a psychologist!". Chekhov, who often visited Tolstoy at his country estate, wrote, "When literature possesses a Tolstoy, it is easy and pleasant to be a writer; even when you know you have achieved nothing yourself and are still achieving nothing, this is not as terrible as it might otherwise be, because Tolstoy achieves for everyone. What he does serves to justify all the hopes and aspirations invested in literature."

Later critics and novelists continue to bear testament to Tolstoy's art. Virginia Woolf declared him the greatest of all novelists. James Joyce noted that, "He is never dull, never stupid, never tired, never pedantic, never theatrical!". Thomas Mann wrote of Tolstoy's seemingly guileless artistry: "Seldom did art work so much like nature". Such sentiments were shared by the likes of Proust, Faulkner and Nabokov. The latter heaped superlatives upon *The Death of Ivan Ilyich* and *Anna Karenina*; he questioned, however, the reputation of *War and Peace,* and sharply criticized *Resurrection* and *The Kreutzer Sonata.*

Tolstoy's earliest works, the autobiographical novels *Childhood, Boyhood,* and *Youth* (1852–1856), tell of a rich landowner's son and his slow realization of the chasm between himself and his peasants. Though he later rejected them as sentimental, a great deal of Tolstoy's own life is revealed. They retain their relevance as accounts of the universal story of growing up.

Tolstoy served as a second lieutenant in an artillery regiment during the Crimean War, recounted in his *Sevastapol Sketches.* His experiences in battle helped stir his subsequent pacifism and gave him material for realistic depiction of war's horrors in his later work..

His fiction consistently attempts to convey realistically the Russian society in which he lived.. *The Cossacks* (1863) describes the Cossack life and people through a story of a Russian aristocrat in love with a Cossack girl. *Anna Karenina* (1877) tells parallel stories of an adulterous woman trapped by the conventions and falsities of society and of a philosophical landowner (much like Tolstoy), who works alongside the peasants in the fields and seeks to reform their lives.

Tolstoy not only drew from his experience of life but created characters in his own image, such as Pierre Bezukhov and Prince Andrei in *War and Peace,* Levin in *Anna Karenina* and to some extent, Prince Nekhlyudov in *Resurrection.*

War and Peace is generally thought to be one of the greatest novels ever written, remarkable for its breadth and unity. Its vast canvas includes 580 characters, many historical, others fictional. The story moves from family life to the headquarters of Napoleon, from the court of Alexander I of Russia to the battlefields of Austerlitz and Borodino. Tolstoy's original idea for the novel was to investigate the causes of the Decembrist revolt, to which it refers only in the last chapters, from which can be deduced that Andrei Bolkonski's son will become one of the Decembrists. The novel explores Tolstoy's theory of history, and in particular the insignificance of individuals such as Napoleon and Alexander. Somewhat surprisingly, Tolstoy did not consider *War and Peace* to be a novel. This view becomes less surprising if one considers that Tolstoy was a novelist of the realist school who considered the novel to be a framework for the examination of social and political issues in nineteenth-century life.. *War and Peace* (which is to Tolstoy really an epic in prose) therefore did not qualify. Tolstoy thought that *Anna Karenina* was his first true novel..

After *Anna Karenina,* Tolstoy concentrated on Christian themes, and his later novels such as *The Death of Ivan Ilyich* (1886) and *What Is to Be Done?* develop a radical anarcho-pacifist Christian philosophy which led to his excommunication from the Russian Orthodox Church in 1901.

For all the praise showered on *Anna Karenina* and *War and Peace,* Tolstoy rejected the two works later in his life as something not as true of reality.. Such an argument is supported in *The Death of Ivan Ilyich,* whose main character continually battles with his family and servants, demanding honesty above the water and food needed to sustain him.

Religious and Political Beliefs

Tolstoy's Christian beliefs centered on the Sermon on the Mount, particularly the injunction to turn the other cheek, which he saw as a justification for pacifism, nonviolence and nonresistance. Various versions of "Tolstoy's Bible" have been published, indicating the passages Tolstoy most relied on, specifically, the reported words of Jesus himself. Tolstoy believed being a Christian required him to be a pacifist; the consequences of being a pacifist, and the apparently inevitable waging of war by government, made him a philosophical anarchist.

Tolstoy believed that a true Christian could find lasting happiness by striving for inner self-perfection through following the Great Commandment of loving one's neighbor and God rather than looking outward to the Church or state for guidance and meaning. His belief in nonresistance (nonviolence) when faced by conflict is another distinct attribute of his philosophy based on Christ's teachings. By directly influencing Mahatma Gandhi with this idea through his work *The Kingdom of God is Within You*, Tolstoy has had a huge influence on the nonviolent resistance movement to this day.

He believed that the aristocracy were a burden on the poor, and that the only solution to how we live together is through anarchism. He also opposed private property and the institution of marriage and valued the ideals of chastity and sexual abstinence (discussed in *Father Sergius* and his preface to *The Kreutzer Sonata*), ideals also held by the young Gandhi. Tolstoy's later work is often criticised as being overly didactic and patchily written, but derives a passion and verve from the depth of his austere moral views.

The sequence of the temptation of Sergius in *Father Sergius,* for example, is among his later triumphs. Gorky relates how Tolstoy once read this passage before himself and Chekhov and that Tolstoy was moved to tears by the end of the reading. Other later passages of rare power include the crises of self faced by the protagonists of *The Death of Ivan Ilyich* and *Master and Man,* where the main character in the former or the reader in the latter is made aware of the foolishness of the protagonists' lives.

Tolstoy had a profound influence on the development of anarchist thought. The Tolstoyans were a small Christian anarchist group formed by Tolstoy's companion, Vladimir Chertkov (1854 - 1936), in order to spread Tolstoy's religious teachings. Prince Peter Kropotkin wrote of Tolstoy in the article on anarchism in the 1911 Encyclopædia Britannica:

Without naming himself an anarchist, Leo Tolstoy, like his predecessors in the popular religious movements of the fifteenth and sixteenth centuries, Chojecki, Denk and many others, took the anarchist position as regards the state and property rights, deducing his conclusions from the general spirit of the teachings of Jesus and from the necessary dictates of reason. With all the might of his talent he made (especially in *The Kingdom of God is Within You*) a powerful criticism of the church, the state and law altogether, and especially of the present property laws. He describes the state as the domination of the wicked ones, supported by brutal force. Robbers, he says, are far less dangerous than a well-organized government. He makes a searching criticism of the prejudices which are current now concerning the benefits conferred upon men by the church, the state and the existing distribution of property, and from the teachings of Jesus he deduces the rule of non-resistance and the absolute condemnation of all wars. His religious arguments are, however, so well combined with arguments borrowed from a dispassionate observation of the present evils, that the anarchist portions of his works appeal to the religious and the non-religious reader alike.

In hundreds of essays over the last twenty years of his life, Tolstoy reiterated the anarchist critique of the State and recommended books by Kropotkin and Proudhon to his readers, whilst rejecting anarchism's espousal of violent revolutionary means, writing in the 1900 essay, "On Anarchy":

The Anarchists are right in everything; in the negation of the existing order, and in the assertion that, without Authority, there could not be worse violence than that of Authority under existing conditions. They are mistaken only in thinking that Anarchy can be instituted by a revolution. But it will be instituted only by there being more and more people who do not require the protection of governmental power... There can be only one permanent revolution - a moral one: the regeneration of the inner man.

Despite his misgivings about anarchist violence, Tolstoy took risks to circulate the prohibited publications of anarchist thinkers in Russia, and corrected the proofs of Kropotkin's "Words of a Rebel", illegally published in St Petersburg in 1906.

A letter Tolstoy wrote in 1908 to an Indian newspaper entitled "A Letter to a Hindu" resulted in intense correspondence with Mohandas Gandhi, who was in South Africa at the time and was beginning to become an activist. Reading *The Kingdom of God is Within You* had convinced Gandhi to abandon violence and espouse nonviolent resistance, a debt Gandhi acknowledged in his autobiography, calling Tolstoy "the greatest apostle of non-violence that the present age has produced". The correspondence between Tolstoy and Gandhi would only last a year, from October 1909 until Tolstoy's death in November 1910, but led Gandhi to give the name the Tolstoy Colony to his second ashram in South Africa. Besides non-violent resistance, the two men shared a common belief in the merits of vegetarianism, the subject of several of Tolstoy's essays. Along with his growing idealism, Tolstoy also became a major supporter of the Esperanto movement. Tolstoy was impressed by the pacifist beliefs of the Doukhobors and brought their persecution to the attention of the international community, after they burned their weapons in peaceful protest in 1895. He aided the Doukhobors in migrating to Canada.

In 1904, during the Russo-Japanese War, Tolstoy condemned the war and wrote to the Japanese Buddhist priest Soyen Shaku in a failed attempt to make a joint pacifist statement.

Tolstoy was a wealthy member of the Russian nobility. He came to believe that he was undeserving of his inherited wealth, and was renowned among the peasantry for his generosity. He would frequently return to his country estate with vagrants whom he felt needed a helping hand, and would often dispense large sums of money to street beggars while on trips to the city, much to his wife's chagrin.

He died of pneumonia at Astapovo station in 1910 after leaving home in the middle of winter at the age of 82. His death came only days after gathering the nerve to abandon his family and wealth and take up the path of a wandering ascetic; a path that he had agonized over pursuing for decades. He had not been at the peak of health before leaving home, his wife and daughters were all actively engaged in caring for him daily. He had been speaking and writing of his own death in the days preceding his departure from home, but fell ill at the train station not far from home. The station master took Tolstoy to his apartment, where his personal doctors were called to the scene. He was given injections of morphine and camphor. The police tried to limit access to his funeral procession, but thousands of peasants lined the streets at his funeral. Still, some peasants were heard to say that, other than knowing that "some nobleman had died," they knew little else about Tolstoy.

War and Peace

War and Peace, is considered one of the world's greatest works of fiction. It is regarded, along with *Anna Karenina* (1873–7), as his finest literary achievement. Epic in scale, *War and Peace* delineates in graphic detail events leading up to Napoleon's invasion of Russia, and the impact of the Napoleonic era on Tsarist society, as seen through the eyes of five Russian aristocratic families. Portions of an earlier version having been serialized in the magazine *The Russian Messenger* between 1865 and 1867, the novel was first published in its entirety in 1869. *Newsweek* in 2009 ranked it top of its list of *Top 100 Books*. Tolstoy himself, somewhat enigmatically, said of *War and Peace* that it was "not a novel, even less is it a poem, and still less an historical chronicle."

Crafting the novel

War and Peace is famously long for a novel (though not the longest by any means). It is subdivided into four books or volumes, each with subparts containing many chapters. Nathaniel Leonardo Huszell gave the chapters brief descriptions, which do not appear in many of the earliest English translations.

Tolstoy got the title, and some of his themes, from an 1861 work of Proudhon: *La Guerre et la Paix*. Tolstoy had served in the Crimean War and written a series of short stories and novellas featuring scenes of war. He began writing *War and Peace* in the year that he finally married and settled down at his country estate. During the writing of the second half of the book, after the first half had already been written under the name "1805", he read widely, acknowledging Schopenhauer as one of his main inspirations, although he developed his own views of history and the role of the individual within it.

The novel can be generally classified as historical fiction. It contains elements present in many types of popular 18th and 19th century literature, especially the romance novel. *War and Peace* attains its literary status by transcending genres. Tolstoy was instrumental in bringing a new kind of consciousness to the novel. His narrative structure is noted for its "god-like" ability to hover over and within events, but also swiftly and seamlessly to take a particular character's point of view. His use of visual detail is often cinematic in its scope, using the literary equivalents of panning, wide shots and close-ups, to give dramatic interest to battles and ballrooms alike. These devices, while not exclusive to Tolstoy, are part of the new novel that is arising in the mid-19th century and of which Tolstoy proves himself a master.

Realism

Tolstoy incorporated extensive historical research, and he was influenced by many other novels as well. He was quite critical of standard history, especially the standard military history, in *War and Peace*. Tolstoy read all the standard histories available in Russian and French about the Napoleonic Wars and combined more traditional historical writing with the novel form - he explains at the start of the novel's third volume his views on how history ought to be written. His aim was to blur the line between fiction and history, in order to get closer to the truth, as he states in Volume II.

The novel is set 60 years earlier than the time at which Tolstoy wrote it, "in the days of our grandfathers," as he puts it. He had spoken with people who had lived through the war of 1812 (In Russia), so the book is also, in part, accurate ethnography fictionalized. He read letters, journals, autobiographical and biographical materials pertaining to Napoleon and the dozens of other historical characters in the novel. There are approximately 160 real persons named or referred to in *War and Peace*.

Reception

The first draft of *War and Peace* was completed in 1863. In 1865, the periodical *Russkiy Vestnik* published the first part of this early version under the title *1805* and the following year published more of the same early version. Tolstoy was increasingly dissatisfied with this version, although he allowed several parts of it to be published (with a different ending) in 1867 still under the title "1805" He heavily rewrote the entire novel between 1866 and 1869. Tolstoy's wife Sophia Tolstoy handwrote as many as 8 or 9 separate complete manuscripts before Tolstoy considered it again ready for publication. The version that was published in *Russkiy Vestnik* had a very different ending than the version eventually published under the title *War and Peace* in 1869.

The completed novel was then called *Voyna i mir* (new style orthography; in English *War and Peace*). Tolstoy did not destroy the *1805* manuscript (sometimes referred to as "the original War and Peace"), which was re-edited and annotated in Russia in 1983 and since has been translated separately from the "known" version, to English, German, French, Spanish, Dutch, Swedish, Finnish and Korean. The fact that so many extant versions of *War and Peace* survive make it one of the best revelations into the mental processes of a great novelist.

Russians who had read the serialized version, were anxious to acquire the complete first edition, which included epilogues, and it sold out almost immediately. The novel was translated almost immediately after publication into many other languages.

Language

Although Tolstoy wrote most of the book, including all the narration, in Russian, significant portions of dialogue (including its opening paragraph) are written in French and characters often switch between the languages. This reflected 19th century reality since Russian aristocracy in the early nineteenth century were conversant in French, which was often considered more refined than Russian—many were much less competent in Russian. An example in the novel is Julie Karagina, Princess Marya's friend, who has to take Russian lessons in order to master her native language.

It has been suggested that it is a deliberate strategy of Tolstoy to use French to portray artifice and insincerity, as the language of the theater and deceit while Russian emerges as a language of sincerity, honesty and seriousness. When Pierre proposes to Helene he speaks to her in French—*Je vous aime*—and as the marriage emerges as a sham he blames those words.

As the book progresses, and the wars with the French intensify, culminating in the capture and eventual burning of Moscow, the use of French diminishes. The progressive elimination of French from the text is a means of demonstrating that Russia has freed itself from foreign cultural domination. It is also, at the level of plot development, a way of showing that a once-admired and friendly nation, France, has turned into an enemy. By midway through the book, several of the Russian aristocracy, whose command of French is far better than their command of Russian, are anxious to find Russian tutors for themselves.

Background and Historical Context

The novel begins in the year 1805 and leads up to the war of 1812. The era of Catherine the Great is still fresh in the minds of older people. It was Catherine who ordered the Russian court to change to speaking French, a custom that was stronger in Petersburg than in Moscow. Catherine's son and successor, Paul I, is the father of the current Czar, Alexander I. Alexander I came to the throne in 1801 at the age of 24. His mother, Marya Feodorovna, is the most powerful woman in the court.

The novel tells the story of five aristocratic families – the Bezukhovs, the Bolkonskys, the Rostovs, the Kuragins and the Drubetskoys—and the entanglements of their personal lives with the history of 1805–1813, principally Napoleon's invasion of Russia in 1812. The Bezukhovs, while very rich, are a fragmented family as the old Count, Kirill Vladimirovich, has fathered dozens of illegitimate sons. The Bolkonskys are an old established and wealthy family based at Bald Hills. Old Prince Bolkonsky, Nikolai Andreevich, served as a general under Catherine the Great, in earlier wars. The Moscow Rostovs have many estates, but never enough cash. They are a closely knit, loving family who live for the moment regardless of their financial situation. The Kuragin family has three children, who are all of questionable character. The Drubetskoy family is of impoverished nobility, and consists of an elderly mother and her only son, Boris, whom she wishes to push up the career ladder.

Tolstoy spent years researching and rewriting the book. He worked from primary source materials (interviews and other documents), as well as from history books, philosophy texts and other historical novels. Tolstoy also used a great deal of his own experience in the Crimean War to bring vivid detail and first-hand accounts of how the Russian army was structured.

The standard Russian text of 'War and Peace' is divided into four books (fifteen parts) and two epilogues – one mainly narrative, the other thematic. While roughly the first half of the novel is concerned strictly with the fictional characters, the later parts, as well as one of the work's two epilogues, increasingly consist of essays about the nature of war, power, history, and historiography. Tolstoy interspersed these essays into the story in a way that defies previous fictional convention. Certain abridged versions remove these essays entirely, while others, published even during Tolstoy's life, simply moved these essays into an appendix.

Plot Summary

War and Peace has a huge cast of characters, some historically real, like Napoleon and Alexander I, the majority of whom are introduced in the first book. The scope of the novel is vast, but the focus is primarily on five aristocratic families and their experiences in life. The interactions of these characters are set in the era leading up to, around and following the French invasion of Russia during the Napoleonic wars.

Book/Volume One

The novel begins in Saint Petersburg, at a soirée given in July 1805 by Anna Pavlovna Scherer — the maid of honour and confidante to the queen mother Maria Feodorovna. Many of the main players and aristocratic families of the novel are introduced as they enter Anna Pavlovna's salon. Pierre (Pyotr Kirilovich) Bezukhov is the illegitimate son of a wealthy count, an elderly man who is dying after a series of strokes. He is about to become embroiled in a struggle for his inheritance. Educated abroad after his mother's death and at his father's expense, Pierre is essentially kindhearted, but socially awkward owing in part to his open, benevolent nature, and finds it difficult to integrate into Petersburg society. He is his father's favorite of all the old count's illegitimate children, and this is known to everyone at Anna Pavlovna's.

Pierre's friend, the intelligent and sardonic Prince Andrei Nikolayevich Bolkonsky, husband of the charming society favourite Lise, also attends the soireé. Finding Petersburg society unctuous and disillusioned with married life after discovering his wife is empty and superficial, Prince Andrei makes the fateful choice to be an aide-de-camp to Prince Mikhail Ilarionovich Kutuzov in the coming war against Napoleon.

The plot then moves to Moscow, Russia's ancient city and former capital, contrasting its provincial, more Russian ways to the highly mannered society of Petersburg. The Rostov family are introduced. Count Ilya Andreyevich Rostov has four adolescent children. Thirteen-year-old Natasha (Natalia Ilyinichna) believes herself in love with Boris Drubetskoy, a disciplined young man who is about to join the army as an officer. Twenty-year-old Nikolai Ilyich pledges his teenage love to Sonya (Sofia Alexandrovna), his fifteen-year-old cousin, an orphan who has been brought up by the Rostovs. The eldest child of the Rostov family, Vera Ilyinichna, is cold and somewhat haughty but has a good prospective marriage in a Russian-German officer, Adolf Karlovich Berg. Petya (Pyotr Ilyich) is nine and the youngest of the Rostov family; like his brother, he is impetuous and eager to join the army when of age. The heads of the family, Count Ilya Rostov and Countess Natalya Rostova, are an affectionate couple but forever worried about their disordered finances.

At Bald Hills, the Bolkonskys' country estate, Prince Andrei leaves his terrified, pregnant wife Lise with his eccentric father Prince Nikolai Andreyevich Bolkonsky and his devoutly religious sister Maria Nikolayevna Bolkonskaya, and departs for the war.

The second part opens with descriptions of the impending Russian-French war preparations. At the Schöngrabern engagement, Nikolai Rostov, who is now conscripted as ensign in a squadron of hussars, has his first taste of battle. He meets Prince Andrei, whom he insults in a fit of impetuousness. Even more than most young soldiers, he is deeply attracted by Tsar Alexander's charisma. Nikolai gambles and socializes with his officer, Vasily Dmitrich Denisov, and befriends the ruthless and perhaps psychopathic Fyodor Ivanovich Dolokhov.

Book/Volume Two

Book Two begins with Nikolai Rostov briefly returning home to Moscow on home leave in early 1806. Nikolai finds the Rostov family facing financial ruin due to poor estate management. He spends an eventful winter at home, accompanied by his friend Denisov, his officer from the Pavlograd Regiment in which he serves. Natasha has blossomed into a beautiful young girl. Denisov falls in love with her, proposes marriage but is rejected. Although his mother pleads with Nikolai to find himself a good financial prospect in marriage, Nikolai refuses to accede to his mother's request. He promises to marry his childhood sweetheart, the dowry-less Sonya.

Pierre Bezukhov, upon finally receiving his massive inheritance, is suddenly transformed from a bumbling young man into the richest and most eligible bachelor in the Russian Empire. Despite rationally knowing that it is wrong, he proposes marriage with Prince Kuragin's beautiful and immoral daughter Hélène (Elena Vasilyevna Kuragina), to whom he is sexually attracted. Hélène, who is rumoured to be involved in an incestuous affair with her brother, the equally charming and immoral Anatol, tells Pierre that she will never have children with him. Hélène has an affair with Dolokhov, who mocks Pierre in public. Pierre loses his temper and challenges Dolokhov, a seasoned dueller and a ruthless killer, to a duel. Unexpectedly, Pierre wounds Dolokhov. Hélène denies her affair, but Pierre is convinced of her guilt and, after almost being violent to her, leaves her. In his moral and spiritual confusion, he joins the Freemasons, and becomes embroiled in Masonic internal politics. Much of Book Two concerns his struggles with his passions and his spiritual conflicts to be a better man. Now a rich aristocrat, he abandons his former carefree behavior and enters upon a philosophical quest particular to Tolstoy: how should one live a moral life in an ethically imperfect world? The question continually baffles and confuses Pierre. He attempts to liberate his serfs, but ultimately achieves nothing of note.

Pierre is vividly contrasted with the intelligent and ambitious Prince Andrei Bolkonsky. At the Battle of Austerlitz, Andrei is inspired by a vision of glory to lead a charge of a straggling army. He suffers a near fatal artillery wound. In the face of death, Andrei realizes all his former ambitions are pointless and his former hero, Napoleon (who rescues him in a horseback excursion to the battlefield), is apparently as vain as himself.

Prince Andrei recovers from his injuries in a military hospital and returns home, only to find his wife Lise dying in childbirth. He is stricken by his guilty conscience for not treating Lise better when she was alive and is haunted by the pitiful expression on his dead wife's face. His child, Nikolenka, survives.

Burdened with nihilistic disillusionment, Prince Andrei does not return to the army but chooses to remain on his estate, working on a project that would codify military behavior and help solve some of the problems of Russian disorganization that he believes were responsible for the loss of life in battle on the Russian side. Pierre comes to visit him and brings new questions: where is God in this amoral world? Pierre is interested in panentheism and the possibility of an afterlife.

Pierre's estranged wife, Hélène, begs him to take her back, and against his better judgment he does. Despite her vapid shallowness, Hélène establishes herself as an influential hostess in Petersburg society.

Prince Andrei feels impelled to take his newly written military notions to Petersburg, naively expecting to influence either the Emperor himself or those close to him. Young Natasha, also in Petersburg, is caught up in the excitement of dressing for her first grand ball, where she meets Prince Andrei and briefly reinvigorates him with her vivacious charm. Andrei believes he has found purpose in life again and, after paying the Rostovs several visits, proposes marriage to Natasha. However, old Prince Bolkonsky, Andrei's father, dislikes the Rostovs, opposes the marriage, and insists on a year's delay. Prince Andrei leaves to recuperate from his wounds abroad, leaving Natasha initially distraught. She soon recovers her spirits, however, and Count Rostov takes her and Sonya to spend some time with a friend in Moscow.

Natasha visits the Moscow opera, where she meets Hélène and her brother Anatol. Anatol has since married a Polish woman whom he has abandoned in Poland. He is very attracted to Natasha and is determined to seduce her. Hélène and Anatol conspire together to accomplish this plan. Anatol kisses Natasha and writes her passionate letters, eventually establishing plans to elope. Natasha is convinced that she loves Anatol and writes to Princess Maria, Andrei's sister, breaking off her engagement. At the last moment, Sonya discovers her plans to elope and foils them. Pierre is initially shocked and horrified at Natasha's behavior, but comes to realize he has fallen in love with her himself. During the time when the Great Comet of 1811–2 streaks the sky, life appears to begin anew for Pierre.

Prince Andrei accepts coldly Natasha's breaking of the engagement. He tells Pierre that his pride will not allow him to renew his proposal of marriage. Shamed by her near-seduction and at the realisation that Andrei will not forgive her, Natasha makes a suicide attempt and is left seriously ill.

Book/Volume Three

With the help of her family, especially Sonya, and the stirrings of religious faith, Natasha manages to persevere in Moscow through this dark period. Meanwhile, the whole of Russia is affected by the coming showdown between Napoleon's troops and the Russian army. Pierre convinces himself through numerology that Napoleon is the Antichrist of the *Book of Revelation*. Old prince Bolkonsky dies of a stroke while trying to protect his estate from French marauders. No organized help from any Russian army seems available to the Bolkonskys, but Nikolai Rostov turns up at their estate in time to help put down an incipient peasant revolt. He finds himself attracted to Princess Maria, but remembers his promise to Sonya.

Back in Moscow, the war-obsessed Petya manages to snatch a loose piece of the Tsar's biscuit outside the Cathedral of the Assumption; he finally convinces his parents to allow him to enlist.

Napoleon himself is a main character in this section of the novel and is presented in vivid detail, as both thinker and would-be strategist. His *toilette* and his customary attitudes and traits of mind are depicted in detail. Also described are the well-organized force of over 400,000 French Army (only 140,000 of them actually French-speaking) which marches quickly through the Russian countryside in the late summer and reaches the outskirts of the city of Smolensk. Pierre decides to leave Moscow and go watch the Battle of Borodino from a vantage point next to a Russian artillery crew. After watching for a time, he begins to join in carrying ammunition. In the midst of the turmoil he experiences firsthand the death and destruction of war. The battle becomes a hideous slaughter for both armies and ends in a standoff. The Russians, however, have won a moral victory by standing up to Napoleon's reputedly invincible army. For strategic reasons and having suffered grievous losses, the Russian army withdraws the next day, allowing Napoleon to march on to Moscow. Among the casualties are Anatol Kuragin and Prince Andrei. Anatol loses a leg, and Andrei suffers a cannon wound in the abdomen. Both are reported dead, but their families are in such disarray that no one can be notified.

Book/Volume Four

The Rostovs have waited until the last minute to abandon Moscow, even after it is clear that Kutuzov has retreated past Moscow and Muscovites are being given contradictory, often propagandistic, instructions on how to either flee or fight. Count Rostopchin is publishing posters, rousing the citizens to put their faith in religious icons, while at the same time urging them to fight with pitchforks if necessary. Before fleeing himself, he gives orders to burn the city. The Rostovs have a difficult time deciding what to take with them, and in the end load their carts with the wounded and dying from the Battle of Borodino. Unknown to Natasha, Prince Andrei is amongst the wounded.

When Napoleon's Grand Army finally occupies an abandoned and burning Moscow, Pierre takes off on a quixotic mission to assassinate Napoleon. He becomes an anonymous man in all the chaos, shedding his responsibilities by wearing peasant clothes and shunning his duties and lifestyle. The only people he sees while in this garb are Natasha and some of her family, as they depart Moscow. Natasha recognizes and smiles at him, and he in turn realizes the full scope of his love for her.

Pierre saves the life of a French officer who fought at Borodino, yet is taken prisoner by the retreating French after his attempted assassination of Napoleon. He becomes friends with a fellow prisoner, Platon Karataev, a peasant with a saintly demeanor, who is incapable of malice. In Karataev, Pierre finally finds what he has been seeking: an honest person of integrity (unlike the aristocrats of Petersburg society) who is utterly without pretense. Pierre discovers meaning in life simply by living and interacting with him. After witnessing French soldiers sacking Moscow and shooting Russian civilians arbitrarily, Pierre is forced to march with the Grand Army during its disastrous retreat from Moscow in the harsh Russian winter. After months of trial and tribulation—during which the fever-plagued Karataev is shot by the French—Pierre is finally freed by a Russian raiding party, after a small skirmish with the French that sees the young Petya Rostov killed in action.

Meanwhile, Andrei, wounded during Napoleon's invasion, has been taken in as a casualty and cared for by the fleeing Rostovs. He is reunited with Natasha and his sister Maria before the end of the war. Having lost all will to live, he forgives Natasha in a last act before dying.

As the novel draws to a close, Pierre's wife Hélène dies in a botched operation (implied to be an abortion). Pierre is reunited with Natasha, while the victorious Russians rebuild Moscow. Natasha speaks of Prince Andrei's death and Pierre of Karataev's. Both are aware of a growing bond between them in their bereavement. With the help of Princess Maria, Pierre finds love at last and, revealing his love after being released by his former wife's death, marries Natasha.

Epilogues

The first epilogue begins with the wedding of Pierre and Natasha in 1813. It is the last happy event for the Rostov family, which is undergoing a transition. Count Rostov dies soon after, leaving his eldest son Nikolai to take charge of the debt-ridden estate.

Nikolai finds himself with the task of maintaining the family on the verge of bankruptcy. His pride almost gets in his way, but finally he accedes to his mother's wishes and marries the now-rich Maria Bolkonskaya, from both genuine feeling and the necessity to save his family from financial ruin.Nikolai and Maria then move to Bald Hills with his mother and Sonya, whom he supports for the rest of their life. Buoyed by his wife's fortune, Nikolai pays off all his family's debts. They also raise Prince Andrei's orphaned son, Nikolai Andreyevich (Nikolenka) Bolkonsky. As in all good marriages, there are misunderstandings, but the couples–Pierre and Natasha, Nikolai and Maria–remain devoted to their spouses. Pierre and Natasha visit Bald Hills in 1820, much to the jubilation of everyone concerned. There is a hint in the closing chapters that the idealistic, boyish Nikolenka and Pierre would both become part of the Decembrist Uprising. The first epilogue concludes with Nikolenka promising he would do something with which even his late father "would be satisfied...".

The second epilogue contains Tolstoy's critique of all existing forms of mainstream history. He attempts to show that there is a great force behind history, which he first terms divine. He offers the entire book as evidence of this force, and critiques his own work. God, therefore, becomes the word Tolstoy uses to refer to all the forces that produce history, taken together and operating behind the scenes.

Anna Karenina

Anna Karenina is a novel by Leo Tolstoy, published in serial installments from 1873 to 1877 in the periodical *The Russian Messenger*. Tolstoy clashed with its editor Mikhail Katkov over issues that arose in the final installment; therefore, the novel's first complete appearance was in book form. Widely regarded as a pinnacle in realist fiction, Tolstoy considered *Anna Karenina* his first true novel, when he came to consider

War and Peace to be more than a novel. The character of Anna was likely inspired, in part, by Maria Hartung (Russian spelling Maria Gartung, 1832–1919), the elder daughter of the Russian poet Alexander Pushkin. Soon after meeting her at dinner, Tolstoy began reading Pushkin's prose and once had a fleeting daydream of "a bare exquisite aristocratic elbow", which proved to be the first intimation of Anna's character.

Although Russian critics dismissed the novel on its publication as a "trifling romance of high life", Fyodor Dostoevsky declared it to be "flawless as a work of art". His opinion was shared by Vladimir Nabokov, who especially admired "the flawless magic of Tolstoy's style" and the motif of the moving train, subtly introduced in the first chapters (the children playing with a toy train) and inexorably developed in subsequent chapters (Anna's nightmare), heralding the novel's majestic finale. The novel is currently enjoying popularity as demonstrated by a recent poll of 125 contemporary authors by J. Peder Zane, published in 2007 in *The Top Ten,* which declared that *Anna Karenina* is the "greatest novel ever written".

The title: *Anna Karenin* vs *Anna Karenina*

The title has been translated as both *Anna Karenin* and *Anna Karenina*. The first instance naturalizes the Russian name into English, whereas the second is a direct transliteration of the actual Russian name.

Vladimir Nabokov explains: "In Russian, a surname ending in a consonant acquires a final 'a' (except for the cases of such names that cannot be declined) when designating a woman; but only when the reference is to a female stage performer should English feminise a Russian surname (following a

French custom: *la Pavlova,* 'the Pavlova'). Ivanov's and Karenin's wives are Mrs Ivanov and Mrs Karenin in England and America—not 'Mrs Ivanova' or 'Mrs Karenina'."

As seen from the above quotation, Nabokov favours the first convention, but subsequent translators mostly allow the actual Russian name to stand. Larissa Volokhonsky, herself a Russian, prefers the second option, while other translators like Constance Garnett and Rosemary Edmonds prefer the first solution.

Plot summary

The novel is divided into eight parts. The novel begins with one of its most quoted lines:

"Happy families are all alike; every unhappy family is unhappy in its own way."

Part 1

The novel opens with a scene introducing Prince Stepan Arkadyevitch Oblonsky, "Stiva", a Moscow aristocrat and civil servant who has been unfaithful to his wife Darya Alexandrovna, nicknamed "Dolly". Dolly has discovered his affair - with the family's governess - and the house and family are in turmoil. Stiva's affair and his reaction to his wife's distress shows an amorous personality that he cannot seem to suppress.

In the midst of the turmoil, Stiva reminds the household that his married sister, Anna Arkadyevna Karenina is coming to visit from Saint Petersburg. Meanwhile, Stiva's childhood friend Konstantin Dmitrievich Levin ("Kostya") arrives in Moscow with the aim of proposing to Dolly's youngest sister Princess Katerina Alexandrovna Shcherbatskaya,

"Kitty". Levin is a passionate, restless but shy aristocratic landowner who, unlike his Moscow friends, chooses to live in the country on his large estate. He discovers that Kitty is also being pursued by Count Alexei Kirillovich Vronsky, an army officer.

At the railway station to meet Anna, Stiva bumps into Vronsky. Vronsky is there to meet his mother. Anna and the Countess Vronskaya have travelled together in the same carriage and talked together. As the family members are reunited, and Vronsky sees Anna for the first time, a railway worker accidentally falls in front of a train and is killed. Anna interprets this as an "evil omen." Vronsky is infatuated with Anna. Anna, who is uneasy about leaving her young son, Seryozha, alone for the first time, talks openly and emotionally to Dolly about Stiva's affair and convinces Dolly that her husband still loves her, despite his infidelity. Dolly is moved by Anna's speeches and decides to forgive Stiva.

Dolly's youngest sister, Kitty, comes to visit her sister and Anna. Kitty, just 18, is in her first season as a debutante and is expected to make an excellent match with a man of her social standing. Vronsky has been paying her considerable attention, and she expects to dance with him at a ball that evening. Kitty is very struck by Anna's beauty and personality and is infatuated with her. When Levin proposes to Kitty at her home, she clumsily turns him down, because she believes she is in love with Vronsky and that he will propose to her.

At the ball, Vronsky pays Anna considerable attention, and dances with her, choosing her as a partner instead of Kitty, who is shocked and heartbroken. Kitty realises that Vronsky has fallen in love with Anna, and that despite his overt flirtations with her he has no intention of marrying her and in fact views his attentions to her as mere amusement, believing that she does the same.

Anna, shaken by her emotional and physical response to Vronsky, returns at once to Saint Petersburg. Vronsky travels on the same train. During the overnight journey, the two meet and Vronsky confesses his love. Anna refuses him, although she is deeply affected by his attentions to her.

Levin, crushed by Kitty's refusal, returns to his estate farm, abandoning any hope of marriage, and Anna returns to her husband Alexei Alexandrovich Karenin, a senior government official, and their son Sergei ("Seryozha") in Petersburg.

On seeing her husband for the first time since her encounter with Vronsky, Anna realises that she finds him repulsive, noting the odd way that his ears press against his hat.

Part 2

The Shcherbatskys consult doctors over Kitty's health which has been failing since she realizes that Vronsky did not love her and that he did not intend to propose marriage to her, and that she refused and hurt Levin, whom she cares for, in vain. A specialist doctor advises that Kitty should go abroad to a health spa to recover. Dolly speaks to Kitty and understands that she is suffering because of Vronsky and Levin. Kitty, humiliated by Vronsky and tormented by her rejection of Levin, upsets her sister by referring to Stiva's infidelity and says she could never love a man who betrayed her.

Stiva stays with Levin on his country estate when he makes a sale of a plot of land, to provide funds for his expensive city lifestyle. Levin is upset at the poor deal he makes with the buyer and his lack of understanding of the rural lifestyle.

In St. Petersburg, Anna begins to spend more time with the fashionable socialite and gossip Princess Betsy and her circle, in order to meet Vronsky, Betsy's cousin. Vronsky continues to pursue Anna. Although Anna initially tries to reject him, she eventually succumbs to his attentions.

Karenin warns Anna of the impropriety of paying too much attention to Vronsky in public, which is becoming a subject of society gossip. He is concerned about his and his wife's public image, although he believes that Anna is above suspicion.

Vronsky, a keen horseman, takes part in a steeplechase event, during which he rides his mare Frou-Frou too hard and she falls and breaks her back. Vronsky escapes with minimal injuries but is devastated that his mare must be shot. Anna tells him that she is pregnant with his child, and is unable to hide her distress when Vronsky falls from the racehorse. Karenin is also present at the races and remarks to her that her behaviour is improper. Anna, in a state of extreme distress and emotion, confesses her affair to her husband. Karenin asks her to break off the affair to avoid society gossip and believes that their relationship can then continue as previously.

Kitty goes with her mother to a resort at a German spa to recover from her ill health. There they meet the Pietist Madame Stahl and the saintly Varenka, her adopted daughter. Influenced by Varenka, Kitty becomes extremely pious, but is disillusioned by her father's criticism. She then returns to Moscow.

Part 3

Levin continues his work on his large country estate, a setting closely tied to his spiritual thoughts and struggles. Levin wrestles with the idea of falseness, wondering how he should go about ridding himself of it, and criticising what he feels is falseness in others. He develops ideas relating to agriculture and the unique relationship between the agricultural labourer and his native land and culture. He believes that the agricultural reforms of Europe will not work in Russia because of the unique culture and personality of the Russian peasant.

Levin pays Dolly a visit, and she attempts to understand what happened between him and Kitty and to explain Kitty's behaviour to him. Levin is very agitated by Dolly's talk about Kitty, and he begins to feel distant from her as he perceives her behaviour towards her children as false. Levin resolves to forget Kitty and contemplates the possibility of marriage to a peasant woman. However, a chance sighting of Kitty in her carriage as she travels to Dolly's house makes Levin realise he still loves her.

In St. Petersburg, Karenin exasperates Anna by refusing to separate from her. He insists that their relationship remain as it was and threatens to take away their son Seryozhra if she continues to pursue her affair with Vronsky.

Part 4

Anna continues to pursue her affair with Vronsky. Karenin begins to find the situation intolerable. He talks with a lawyer about obtaining a divorce. In Russia at that time, divorce could only be requested by the innocent party in an affair, and required either that the guilty party confessed (which would ruin Anna's position in society) or that the guilty party was discovered in the act. Karenin forces Anna to give him some letters written to her by Vronsky as proof of the affair. However, Anna's brother Stiva argues against it and persuades Karenin to speak with Dolly first.

Dolly broaches the subject with Karenin and asks him to reconsider his plans to divorce Anna. She seems to be unsuccessful, but Karenin changes his plans after hearing that Anna is dying after a difficult childbirth. At her bedside, Karenin forgives Vronsky. Vronsky, embarrassed by Karenin's magnanimity, attempts suicide by shooting himself. He fails in his attempt but wounds himself badly.

Anna recovers, having given birth to a daughter, Anna ("Annie"). Although her husband has forgiven her, and has become attached to the new baby, Anna cannot bear living with him. She hears that Vronsky is about to leave for a military posting in Tashkent and becomes desperate. Stiva finds himself pleading to Karenin on her behalf to free her by giving her a divorce. Vronsky is intent on leaving for Tashkent, but changes his mind after seeing Anna.

The couple leave for Europe - leaving behind Anna's son Seryozha - without obtaining a divorce.

Much more straightforward is Stiva's matchmaking with Levin: a meeting he arranges between Levin and Kitty results in their reconciliation and betrothal.

Part 5

Levin and Kitty marry and immediately go to start their new life together on Levin's country estate. The couple are happy but do not have a very smooth start to their married life and take some time to get used to each other. Levin feels some dissatisfaction at the amount of time Kitty wants to spend with him and is slightly scornful of her preoccupation with domestic matters, which he feels are too prosaic and not compatible with his romantic ideas of love.

A few months later, Levin learns that his brother Nikolai is dying of consumption. Levin wants to go to him, and is initially angry and put out that Kitty wishes to accompany him. Levin feels that Kitty, whom he has placed on a pedestal, should not come down to earth and should not mix with people from a lower class. Levin assumes her instance on coming must relate to a fear of boredom from being left alone, despite her true desire to support her husband in a difficult time. Kitty persuades him to take her with him after much discussion, where she proves a great help nursing Nikolai for weeks over his slow death. She also discovers she is pregnant.

In Europe, Vronsky and Anna struggle to find friends who will accept their situation. Whilst Anna is happy to be finally alone with Vronsky, he feels suffocated. They cannot socialize with Russians of their own social set and find it difficult to amuse themselves. Vronsky, who believed that being with Anna in freedom was the key to his happiness, finds himself increasingly bored and unsatisfied. He takes up painting, and makes an attempt to patronize an émigré Russian artist of genius. Vronsky cannot see that his own art lacks talent and passion, and that his clever conversation about art is an empty shell. Bored and restless, Anna and Vronsky decide to return to Russia.

In Petersburg, Anna and Vronsky stay in one of the best hotels but take separate suites. It becomes clear that whilst Vronsky is able to move in Society, Anna is barred from it. Even her old friend, Princess Betsy - who has had affairs herself - evades her company. Anna starts to become very jealous and anxious that Vronsky no longer loves her. Karenin is comforted – and influenced – by the strong-willed Countess Lidia Ivanovna, an enthusiast of religious and mystic ideas fashionable with the upper classes. She counsels him to keep Seryozha away from Anna and to make him believe that his mother is dead. However, Seryozha refuses to believe that this is true. Anna manages to visit Seryozha unannounced and uninvited on his ninth birthday, but is discovered by Karenin.

Anna, desperate to resume at least in part her former position in Society, attends a show at the theatre at which all of Petersburg's high society are present. Vronsky begs her not to go, but is unable to bring himself to explain to her why she cannot go. At the theatre, Anna is openly snubbed by her former friends, one of whom makes a deliberate scene and leaves the theatre. Anna is devastated. Unable to find a place for themselves in Petersburg, Anna and Vronsky leave for Vronsky's country estate.

Part 6

Dolly, her mother the Princess Scherbatskaya, and Dolly's children spend the summer with Levin and Kitty on the Levins' country estate. The Levins' life is simple and unaffected, although Levin is uneasy at the "invasion" of so many Scherbatskys. He is able to cope until he is consumed with an intense jealousy when one of the visitors, Veslovsky, flirts openly with the pregnant Kitty. Levin tries to overcome his jealousy but eventually succumbs to it and in an embarrassing scene evicts Veslovsky from his house. Veslovsky immediately goes to stay with Anna and Vronsky, whose estate is close by.

Dolly also pays a short visit to Anna at Vronsky's estate. The difference between the Levins' aristocratic but simple home life and Vronsky's overtly luxurious and lavish country home strikes Dolly, who is unable to keep pace with Anna's fashionable dresses or Vronsky's extravagant spending on the hospital he is building. However, all is not quite well with Anna and Vronsky. Dolly is also struck by Anna's anxious behaviour and new habit of half closing her eyes when she alludes to her difficult position. When Veslovsky flirts openly with Anna, she plays along with him even though she clearly feels uncomfortable. Vronsky makes an emotional request to Dolly, asking her to convince Anna to divorce her husband so that the two might marry and live normally. Dolly broaches the subject with Anna, who appears not to be convinced. However, Anna is becoming intensely jealous of Vronsky, and cannot bear it when he leaves her for short excursions. The two have started to quarrel about this and when Vronsky leaves for several days of provincial elections, a combination of boredom and suspicion convinces Anna she must marry him in order to prevent him from leaving her. She writes to Karenin, and she and Vronsky leave the countryside for Moscow.

***Part** 7*

The Levins are in Moscow for Kitty's confinement. Despite initial reservations, Levin quickly gets used to the fast-paced, expensive and frivolous Moscow society life. He starts to accompany Stiva to his Moscow gentleman's club, where drinking and gambling are popular pastimes. At the club, Levin meets Vronsky and Stiva introduces them. Levin and Stiva pay a visit to Anna, who is occupying her empty days by being a patroness to an orphaned English girl. Levin is uneasy about the visit and not sure it is the proper thing to do, and Anna easily makes Levin fall in love with her. When he confesses to Kitty where he has been, she accuses him of falling in love with Anna. The couple are reconciled, realising that Moscow life has had a negative, corrupting effect on Levin.

Anna, who has made a habit of inducing the young men who visit her to fall in love with her, cannot understand why she can attract a man like Levin, who has a young and beautiful new wife, but cannot attract Vronsky in the way she wants to. Anna's relationship with Vronsky is under increasing strain, as whilst he can move freely in Society - and continues to spend considerable time doing so to stress to Anna his independence as a man - she is excluded from all her previous social connections. She is estranged from baby Annie, her child with Vronsky. and her increasing bitterness, boredom, jealousy and emotional strain cause the couple to argue. Anna uses morphine to help her sleep, a habit we learned she had begun during her time living with Vronsky at his country estate. Now she has become dependent on it.

After a long and difficult labour, Kitty gives birth to a son, Mitya. Levin is both extremely moved and horrified by the sight of the tiny, helpless baby. Stiva visits Karenin to encourage his commendation for a new post he is seeking. During the visit he asks him to grant Anna a divorce, but Karenin's decisions are now governed by a French "clairvoyant" – recommended by Lidia Ivanovna – who apparently has a vision in his sleep during Stiva's visit, and gives Karenin a cryptic message that is interpreted as meaning that he must decline the request for divorce.

Anna becomes increasingly jealous and irrational towards Vronsky, whom she suspects of having love affairs with other women, and of giving in to his mother's plans to marry him off to a rich Society woman. There is a bitter row, and Anna believes that the relationship is over. She starts to think of suicide as an escape from her torments. In her mental and emotional confusion, she sends a telegram to Vronsky asking him to come home to her, and pays a visit to Dolly and Kitty. Anna's confusion overcomes her, and in a parallel to the railway worker's accidental death in part 1, she commits suicide by throwing herself in the path of a train.

Part 8

Stiva gets the job he desired so much, and Karenin takes custody of baby Annie. A group of Russian volunteers, including Vronsky, who does not plan to return alive, depart from Russia to fight in the Orthodox Serbian revolt that has broken out against the Turks. Meanwhile, amid the joys and fears of fatherhood, Levin no longer feels he lacks Christian faith; he decides to give his life its own meaning through acts of goodness.

Style

Tolstoy's style in *Anna Karenina* is considered by many critics to be transitional, forming a bridge between the realist and modernist novel. The novel is narrated from a third-person-omniscient perspective, shifting between the perspectives of several major characters, though most frequently focusing on the opposing lifestyles and attitudes of its central protagonists of Anna and Levin. As such, each of the novel's eight sections contains internal variations in tone: it assumes a relaxed voice when following Stepan Oblonsky's thoughts and actions and a much more tense voice when describing Levin's social encounters. Much of the novel's seventh section depicts Anna's thoughts fluidly, following each one of her ruminations and free associations with its immediate successor. This groundbreaking use of stream-of-consciousness would be utilised by such later authors as James Joyce, Virginia Woolf, and William Faulkner.

Also of significance is Tolstoy's use of real events in his narrative, to lend greater verisimilitude to the fictional events of his narrative. Characters debate significant sociopolitical issues affecting Russia in the latter half of the nineteenth century, such as the place and role of the Russian peasant in society, education reform, and women's rights. Tolstoy's depiction of the characters in these debates, and of their arguments, allows him to communicate his own political beliefs. Characters often attend similar social functions to those which Tolstoy attended, and he includes in these passages his own observations of the ideologies, behaviors, and ideas running through contemporary Russia through the thoughts of Levin. The broad array of situations and ideas depicted in *Anna Karenina* allows Tolstoy to present a treatise on his era's Russia, and, by virtue of its very breadth and depth, all of human society. This stylistic technique, as well as the novel's use of perspective, greatly contributes to the thematic structure of *Anna Karenina*.

Anna Karenina is commonly thought to explore the themes of hypocrisy, jealousy, faith, fidelity, family, marriage, society, progress, carnal desire and passion, and the agrarian connection to land in contrast to the lifestyles of the city. Translator Rosemary Edmonds wrote that Tolstoy doesn't explicitly moralise in the book, he allows his themes to emerge naturally from the "vast panorama of Russian life." She also writes that a key message is that "no one may build their happiness on another's pain," which is why things don't work out for Anna.

Levin is often considered as a semi-autobiographical portrayal of Tolstoy's own beliefs, struggles and life events. Tolstoy's first name is "Lev", and the Russian surname "Levin" means "of Lev". According to footnotes in the Pevear/Volokhonsky translation, the viewpoints Levin supports throughout the novel in his arguments match Tolstoy's outspoken views on the same issues. Moreover, according to W. Gareth Jones, Levin proposed to Kitty in the same way as Tolstoy to Sophie Behrs. Additionally, Levin's request that his fiancée read his diary as a way of disclosing his faults and previous sexual encounters, parallels Tolstoy's own requests to his fiancée Sophie Behrs.

Bibliography

Beard, Mary; Henderson, John. *Classics: A very short introduction*. Oxford: Oxford University Press, 1995.

Briggs, Ward W.; Calder, III, William M. *Classical scholarship: A biographical encyclopedia (Garland reference library of the humanities)*. London: Taylor & Francis, 1990.

Bryce, Jackson. "Teaching the Classics", *The Classical Journal*, Vol. 96, No. 3. (2001), pp. 323–334.

Eccles, Sir John Carew (1989). *Evolution of the Brain: Creation of the Self*. Routledge. p. 118.

Geraldine McCaughrean, Rosamund Fowler (1999), *One Thousand and One Arabian Nights*, Oxford University Press, pp. 247–51.

Grimbly, Shona (2000). *Encyclopedia of the Ancient World*. Taylor & Francis. p. 216.

Hamori, Andras (1971), "An Allegory from the Arabian Nights: The City of Brass", *Bulletin of the School of Oriental and African Studies*. Cambridge University Press. 34 (1): 9–19.

Harrington Becker, Trudy. "Broadening Access to a Classical Education: State Universities in Virginia in the Nineteenth Century", *The Classical Journal*, Vol. 96, No. 3. (2001), pp. 309–322.

Irwin, Robert (2003), *The Arabian Nights: A Companion*, Tauris Parke Paperbacks, p. 209.

James Thurber, "The Wizard of Chitenango", p 64 *Fantasists on Fantasy* edited by Robert H. Boyer and Kenneth J. Zahorski.

Jones, Mark (2006). *Criminals of the Bible: Twenty-Five Case Studies of Biblical Crimes and Outlaws*. FaithWalk Publishing. p. 6.

Knox, Bernard. *The Oldest Dead White European Males, And Other Reflections on the Classics*. New York; London: W.W. Norton & Co., 1993.

Krevans, Nita. "Class and Classics: A Historical Perspective," *The Classical Journal*, Vol. 96, No. 3. (2001), p. 293.

Macrone, Michael. *Brush Up Your Classics*. New York: Gramercy Books, 1991.

Moroney, Siobhan. "Latin, Greek and the American Schoolboy: Ancient Languages and Class Determinism in the Early Republic", *The Classical Journal*, Vol. 96, No. 3. (2001), pp. 295–307.

Nagy, Péter Tibor. "The meanings and functions of classical studies in Hungary in the 18th–20th century", in *The social and political history of Hungarian education*.

Nahyan A. G. Fancy (2006), "Pulmonary Transit and Bodily Resurrection: The Interaction of Medicine, Philosophy and Religion in the Works of Ibn al-Naf+s (d. 1288)", p. 95-101, *Electronic Theses and Dissertations*, University of Notre Dame.

Pinault, David (1992), *Story-Telling Techniques in the Arabian Nights*, Brill Publishers, pp. 148–9 & 217-9.

Richardson, Matthew (2001), *The Halstead Treasury of Ancient Science Fiction*, Rushcutters Bay, New South Wales: Halstead Press, September 2002,

Toomer G. J. (1996), *Eastern Wisedome and Learning: The Study of Arabic in Seventeenth-Century England*, p. 222, Oxford University Press.

Wellek, René. "Classicism in Literature", in *Dictionary of the History of Ideas, Studies of Selected Pivotal Ideas*, ed. by Philip P. Wiener. New York: Charles Scribner's Sons, 1968.

Winterer, Caroline. *The Mirror of Antiquity: American Women and the Classical Tradition, 1750–1900*. Ithaca, NY; London: Cornell University Press, 2007.

Index

A Declaration of egregious Popish Impostures 94
Actaeon 28
Adonis 28
Aeneas 6, 28
Aesacus 28
Aesculapius 28
Agamemnon 6
Agenor 7
Ages of Man 28
Anna Karenina 257
Authorial evaluation 211
Beware Macduff 96

Cadmus 28
Caesar 28
Callisto 28
Cassandra 7
Catholicism 260
Centaurs 28
Cephalus and Procris 28
Classical era 1
Classical Greek literature 1
Classical period 1
Cosmogony 28
Cultural domination 271
Cyparissus 28

Deiphobus 6
Diomedes, 5

Echo and Pentheus 28
Edward Gibbon 28
Epic poems 3
Ethnography 269
Eurydice 28

Feminist historiography 211
Feminist literary criticism 201
Frankenstein 200

Gibbon 28
Greek commander 6
Greek literature 2

He Rape of Proserpina 28
Hector 5, 6
Hecuba 7
Hephaestus 7
Heracles 28
Hilomela and Procne 28
Hippolytus 28
Holinshed's Chronicles 95
Hyacinth 28

Iconography 262
Iliad and Odyssey 28
Iphigeneia 28

Jean-Jacques Rousseau 207
Jupiter and Europa 28

King of Ithaca 6
King of Mycenae 6

Leader of the Myrmidons 6
Les Miserables 258
Lyrical poets 1

Mary Shelley 200
Medea 28
Menelaus 6
Midas 28
Military behavior 277
Montesquieu 28
Moscow opera 277
Music historians 24

New Testament 261

Odysseus 5, 6
Old Testament 238
Orpheus 28
Ovid works 28

Paganism 238
Paradise Lost 251
Patroclus 6
Perseus and Andromeda 28
Phaëton 28
Phineas 28
Princess Scherbatskaya 146
Psychoanalytic critics 201
Pygmalion 28
Pyramus and Thisbe 28
Pythagoras 28

Realism 269
Reflections on the Causes of the Grandeur and Deci 28
Remaines Concerning Britaine 94
Roman poet 28
Romantic movement 212
Romulus 28
Russian Empire 275

Scamander 7
Scylla, 28

Thane of Cawdor 95
Thane of Glamis 95
The Roman History 28
The Scottish play 95
The Tragedy of Macbeth 94
Thetis 7
Thought-provoking themes 203
Thracian allies 5
Trojan Dolon 5
Trojan men 6
Trojan priest 4
Trojan war 3
Trojan warrior 7

Valperga 216

War and Peace 257
Western literature 1
William Shakespeare 94